North by North-East

The Region's Contemporary Poetry

Editors

Andy Croft
Cynthia Fuller

IRON
PRESS

First published 2006 by IRON Press
5 Marden Terrace, Cullercoats
Northumberland, NE30 4PD
tel/fax: +44 (0)191 253 1901
ironpress@blueyonder.co.uk
www.ironpress.co.uk

ISBN 0 906228 93 X
Printed by Aeroprinting
Jarrow, Tyneside

Typeset in Garamond 10pt

Cover painting by Barrie Ormsby

IRON Press books
are distributed by Central Books
and represented by Inpress Limited,
Northumberland House,
11 The Pavement, Pope's Lane,
Ealing, London W5 4NG
Tel: +44 (0)20 8832 7464
Fax: +44 (0)20 8832 7465
www.inpressbooks.co.uk

IRON Press is a member of Independent Northern Publishers

Introduction

'We despise the deformed, uncandid class-conscious compass points. North, for instance, does not mean good.' (James Fenton)

Well, sometimes it does, sometimes it doesn't. It depends where you are standing. 'The North' has many meanings; it depends on your point of view. From the perspective of James Fenton's Oxfordshire rose-garden the North may seem alien, other, class-conscious, inauthentic. For the poets in this book it is a place in which to live and work, to write and to write about. A sense of place, a feeling of belonging, an understanding of shared loyalties - these can be useful moral and cultural compass points. Knowing your place can mean deferring to those who would claim to know better ; or it can mean that you know your place - geographical, sexual, intellectual, social, economic, cultural - better than anyone else.

According to opinion polls, no region of the UK defines itself so surely in terms of a distinctive and common identity as the North East. It is an identity based on a shared heavy-industrial past and an uncertain economic future, on participation in the same broken political narrative, and on an historic distance from the metropolitan centres of authority, whether they are to be found in Rome or in the Anglo-Saxon kingdoms to the south, in Westminster governments or the London media.

The North East - like other English regions - suffers from an acute crisis of representation. It is poorly represented by a regional One Party State characterised by low electoral turnouts, intellectual inertia and cynicism. All but one of the region's twenty-one MPs, three of the four MEPs and nineteen out of twenty-one local authorities in the region are New Labour. And yet the region overwhelmingly rejected government proposals for a directly-elected regional assembly in the 2004 referendum. The currency of trust saved over a century of Labour activism in the North East is now overdrawn, even - especially - in its heartland. The home-grown institutions of civil society - political parties, trade unions, adult education and chapel - have been replaced by commercial interests.

The North East is under-represented on the national political stage, despite - or perhaps because of - the concentration of current and ex-cabinet ministers in the region (including of course the Prime Minister). Average earnings in the North East are just £396 per week (compared to £551 in London). Only 15% of the workforce has a degree (less than half the proportion of graduates in the South East). 9% of the workforce is out of work due to ill health (over twice the number in the South East). The rate of unemployment in the region is currently 5.3% (compared to 3.9% in the South East).

The North East is mis-represented culturally in the national imagination. On Saturday afternoons visiting fans from the South still celebrate the economic gap between North and South by waving their wallets at the home terraces, taunting them with, 'you're just a small town in Scotland' (to which crowds at the Riverside and St James's Park reply, 'we're just a small town in Europe'). The period covered by this book may be characterised as one of economic, industrial and political decline. But at the same time, the North East has acquired a distinctive reputation as an example of the role of the Arts in urban regeneration. This is especially true of Newcastle-Gateshead, where the Baltic, the Sage, the Blinking Eye and the Angel of the North have entered the national imagination, even if only on the level of visual cliché for the London media.

This contradiction of course contains its tensions. In Julia Darling's novel *The Taxi Driver's Daughter* two teenagers throw some shoes up into the branches of a tree. Soon other people are adding their own shoes to the tree until it becomes an emblem of beauty, defiance and magic in the middle of the city, like a tree in a fairy-tale. Eventually the council decides to clean up the area ; as one of the council workers removes the shoes from the tree he observes, 'They wouldn't take it down if someone from fucking London had done it'.

It is fair to say that writers - especially poets - have a less problematic relationship with the region, indeed with the rest of the country. The North East arguably enjoys the single greatest concentration of published poets and poetry presses anywhere in the UK. Among the writers in this book are several of international reputation, notably Tony Harrison, Anne Stevenson, Sean O'Brien, Julia Darling, Bill Herbert and Gillian Allnutt. The region is currently home to Bloodaxe Books, the most important publisher of poetry in the UK.

The Morden Tower has been an internationally-known centre for readings and workshops since Tom and Connie Pickard leased the building in 1964, setting in motion what has been called 'the Newcastle poetry revival of the late 1960s'. Colpitts Poetry in Durham was started in 1975 by Richard Caddel and David Burnett. Durham also has the Basil Bunting Poetry Centre housing the poet's archive. There are currently several other regular poetry reading venues in Newcastle (The Blue Room, The Lit and Phil, the Cluny, City Library), Stockton (The Arc), Darlington (The Hydrogen Jukebox), Middlesbrough (Crossing The Tees) and Bishop Auckland (Town Hall). In addition to Bloodaxe, there are twelve other poetry-publishers in the region - Arrowhead, Biscuit, Diamond Twig, Dogeater, Ek Zuban, Flambard, IRON, Morning Star, Mudfog, Sand, Smokestack, Vane Women. The Northern Poetry Library in Morpeth houses the largest collection of poetry outside London and Edinburgh. All this activity has been supported by a number of key institutions - New Writing North, Northern Arts (now the Arts Council England North East), Independent Northern Publishers, the North Eastern Literary Fellowship and the Northern Rock Foundation. As Claire Malcolm of New Writing North has said, the North East really is 'a better place to be a better writer'.

It seems to us therefore to be a good time to take stock of the region's poetry. This book is, we hope, a representative selection of poetry written in the North East since the death of Basil Bunting in 1985. Bunting was a major twentieth-century poet, a crucial link between European and US Modernism and the North East of England. His autobiographical epic *Briggflatts* alludes to the defeat in 954AD of Eric Bloodaxe ('king of York, / King of Dublin, king of Orkney'), the last king of an independent North. Although Bunting's poetry was barely known in this country during his life-time, his influence is evident in the work of many of the poets in this book. One of Neil Astley's first publishing projects at Bloodaxe (the name of which is of course a nod to Bunting) was an LP record of Bunting reading *Brigflatts* to the accompaniment of Scarlatti sonatas (1980).

This is not, of course, the first attempt to take a snap-shot of poetry in the region. Howard Sergeant's *An Anthology of Contemporary Northern Poetry* (1947) contained fifty-two poets (including Elizabeth Daryush, Roy Fuller, Wilfred Gibson, Norman Nicholson, Kathleen Raine and Herbert Read) born North of the Trent. But only one of these - James Kirkup - was identifiably from the North East. Anyway, Sergeant was less interested in 'poems with a North Country accent' than in inserting a version of the provincial into metropolitan literature - and thus into the imperial triumphs of Anglophone literary culture. As Thomas Moult (then the editor of *Poetry Review*) argued in an introduction to the book, its purpose was to demonstrate that poets 'of the North' could write 'with as much truth, beauty and strength' as writers from the South :

> 'North Country people will find plenty to be proud about in the pages of this anthology. For the first time in the present generation they are made aware of how many local boys - and girls - have made good in one of the great arts of the world. Moreover, they may even discover that their next-door neighbour has written poetry. And not only written it, but become known as a poet to the rest of the country, probably to more than one country, and possibly - either already or with certain sureness in good time - to all the civilised earth.'

Two other anthologies are worth noting. One of Bloodaxe's first anthologies was Neil Astley (ed) *Ten North-East Poets* (Bloodaxe, 1980), an introduction to the work of ten young poets (three of whom - Peter Armstrong, George Charlton and Desmond Graham - are represented in this book) by a new publisher. Unfortunately this is no longer available. And a selection of North East poets appeared in Moscow in 1988 as *Modern Poets of Northern England*, (a complenentry publication to IRON Press' *The Poetry of Perestroika*) but it was only published in Russian and is long out of print ; of the twenty-two poets chosen by Ekaterina Shevelyova, eight are represented here.

In other words, this book is long over-due. But this is not intended as a comprehensive or canonical selection. These are not necessarily the 'best' poems by the 'best' poets writing in the North East. Another day, another selection. Different editors, a different book. Some of those whose work is included here are probably better known these days as novelists (Julia Darling, Neil Astley) or playwrights (Tony Harrison, Peter Mortimer). Some no longer consider themselves poets at all (George Charlton, Graeme Rigby). We also wanted the book to represent the work of several distinguished North East poets who have died in recent years – Richard Caddel, Julia Darling, Barry MacSweeney, John Longden, Evangeline Paterson, Fred Reed, Jon Silkin, Andrew Waterhouse - but without whose generous energies (not to mention their poems) the region's literary life would be a much poorer place. We have not included the work of those who, like Rodney Pybus, Maria Makepeace, James Kirkup and Michael Blackburn, left the region some time ago. Tom Pickard - a shaping force in Newcastle poetry in the 1960s and 1970s - ruled himself out on the basis that he has not lived in the region since 1974. Bill Griffiths did not want to be included.

For reasons of space, we have only included the work of poets who have published at least two books, one of which is a full-length collection. We are acutely conscious that there are many fine poets - for example, Ellen Phethean, Alan Brown, Joanna Boulter, Andy Willoughby, Michael O'Neill, Anne O'Neill and Jo Colley - who are not represented here simply because their energies and their poems have been channelled into projects other than full collections.

This is particularly true of women writers (who constitute only a third of the poets in this book). The North East has always provided a forum for women writers. For many years *Writing Women* was produced from Newcastle, as is *Mslexia* today ; Diamond Twig and Vane Women publish poetry by women ; the Blue Room provides a venue and Gillian Allnutt's 'Inside Out', a thriving women's writing workshop. But poems in pamphlets, anthologies and first publications have not always been followed by longer books. As Linda France argued in her *Sixty Women Poets* (Bloodaxe, 1993), 'Many women are unable to take themselves seriously as writers until they reach a certain age, with the waning of family commitments alongside the waxing of self-confidence and considered abandon.' It seems that this is still the case in 2005. Even where women poets have a first small book or pamphlet it often takes a long time before they are ready to take the next step.

For different reasons, there are, regrettably, no Black poets in this book. Fred D'Aguiar and Jackie Kay have both been Northern Arts Literary Fellows ; Jack Mapanje teaches occasionally at the University of Newcastle. But none of these, alas, have been permanently resident in the region. For many years Teesside and Tyneside have enjoyed lively Urdu poetry scenes ; Ghazala Bashir was appointed Middlesbrough's first poet laureate in 1998. However, while English may be the first language of poets reading at North East musha'ara, Urdu is typically their first literary language. Finding a home for a book of Urdu poetry is especially difficult. Unfortunately there are no Urdu publishers in the region.

We asked each poet to submit 15 poems from which we made our final selection. We discussed each poet's work and arrived at shared decisions. We had no disagreements. For our own work, we followed the same process with each making the final selection from the other's work. Having the opportunity to read such a variety of work, and to sit over endless cups of coffee to talk about poetry was a privilege. In some cases it meant discovering a new voice, in others catching up on recent work.

Less than a quarter of these poets were born in the North East. Most (including the editors) moved here for work. This is consistent with the immigrant history of the region. But it is a wholly new feature of the region's cultural life. Historically, the region's native writers - Tom Pickard, Peter Flannery, Peter Terson, Rodney Pybus, Barry Unsworth, Jane Gardam (and of course Basil Bunting) - had to leave the region in order to be writers. These days, however, published writers move to the region because of the support that exists here for writing and for the sense of a community to which writers can belong.

Most recent poetry-publishing in the region has been done by poets in this book - Bloodaxe (Neil Astley), Diamond Twig (Julia Darling), *The Echo Room* (Brendan Cleary), *Ek Zuban* (Bob Beagrie) *IRON* (Peter Mortimer), *Liar, Inc* (Paul Summers), *Mudfog* (Maureen Almond, Bob Beagrie, Andy Croft, Gordon Hodgeon, Pauline Plummer, Mark Robinson), *Pig Press* (Richard Caddel), *Other Poetry* (Peter Armstrong, Richard Kell, Evangeline Patterson, Mick Standen), *Sand* (Kevin Cadwallender), *Scratch* (Mark Robinson), *Smokestack* (Andy Croft), *Stand* (Jon Silkin, Tony Harrison), *Vane Women* (Jackie Litherland, Marilyn Longstaff), *Writing Women*, (Cynthia Fuller).

Moreover, most of these poets have a history of involvement in the communities in which they live. Earning their living through community-based writing-residencies (including several with trades unions), public-art commissions, community writing projects in schools, prisons, libraries, teaching in adult education (more recently, in Higher Education), these writers may be described as organic intellectuals. Most of the poets in this book would describe themselves as being of the political left (at least four used to be members of the Communist Party). If most are published by the region's own presses it is because poets in the North East no longer need to look to London publishers for their work to be validated.

Like Howard Sergeant, we were not looking for poems with a 'North Country accent', rather for poems that work, that surprise, move, excite the reader. This is a book of poems from the North East, of the North East, for the North East, but not necessarily 'about' the North East. Anyway, 'the North' has many meanings ; this book contains just a few of them. Traditional form sits alongside experimental; comedy alongside philosophy, dialect alongside contemporary slang. The number of poets who write in non-Mandarin English is especially striking. So too is the interest in topography, poems about a specific place and time. A third of the poets in the book live in Newcastle, but this is not an overwhelmingly urban poetry. There is a lot more to the region than the Geordie Nation. Many of these poems are about the passing of old dispensations, bodies of knowledge, lost values, the ghosts the stir beneath the soil. It is a democratic poetry, generous and sad about the region's defeats, accessible without being facile. These poets are interested in the domestic and the historical, the Biblical and the everyday, in public life as well as the wintry, outdoor life of public spaces. They are equally comfortable addressing the local, the regional, the national and the international. They are a part of, and not apart from the communities they inhabit. This is the poetry of the 'imaginary republic' of the North East, confidently facing South without deferring to London. In short, these are poets who know their place. Away !

Cynthia Fuller and Andy Croft
Esh Winning and Middlesbrough
March 2006.

Note *We are grateful for the advice and assistance of Ann Caddel, Bev Robinson Jerry Slater, Lilian McSweeney, Paul McSweeney and Jackie Litherland, Carolyn Rowland-Jones, Raymond Reed, Lorna Tracy and Rodney Pybus, and Michael Mackmin and Martin Waterhouse, concerning the work of Richard Caddel, Julia Darling John Longden, Barry MacSweeney, Evangeline Paterson, Fred Reed, Jon Silkin, and Andrew Waterhouse respectively.*

To the Memory of Julia Darling

The Poems

Peter Bennet

David Burnett

Richard Caddel

Kevin Cadwallender

Valerie Laws

S. J. Litherland

John Longden

Marilyn Longstaff

Barry MacSweeney

Bill Martin

Peter Mortimer

Sean O'Brien

Evangeline Patterson

Pauline Plummer

Jon Silkin

Colin Simms

Michael Standen

Anne Stevenson

Subhadassi

Paul Summers

Andrew Waterhouse

Annie Wright

Gillian Allnutt

Romey Chaffer

heart note

because we for a while had been living there my heart

thought it was a house with cupboards and an open fire
and a door giving onto
an impossible steep twisted stair my heart

thought it could have small uncurtained windows it could go on
being there under its tiles for the swallows
every year

love was already living in the house my heart

thought when we got there it thought it was
a letterbox a back door opening to
a garden it could walk in

it was nothing we had put there but before us it was

apple willow and a wilderness of
rose thorn thick and dark
and light with its daylong delicate flowers my heart

thought it had roots it thought it could cover its roots
with straw it thought it could carry on
lighting its every morning fire

because we as love for a while had been living there

About Benwell

Perhaps there will always be yellow buses
passing and Presto's
and people with faces like broken promises

and shops full of stotties and butties and buckets and bubble bath
and bones for broth
where the poor may inherit the earth

and women who will
wade into the wind and waste with hope eternal
and kids like saplings planted by the Council

and William Armstrong's endless line
of bairns, whose names, in sandstone,
rehabilitate their streets of rag and bone

where bits of paper, bottle tops and Pepsi cans blow up and down
despondently, like souls on their own.
Perhaps there will always be unremembered men

and maps of Old Dunston and Metroland and the rough blown rain
and the riding down of the sun
towards Blaydon.

Benwell is part of Newcastle's West End and scene of some of the riots in September 1991. Lord Armstrong, founder of the firm that eventually became Vickers Armstrong, built many of the houses for his workers in the 1890s and the streets are reputedly named after his children, though in fact he had none. Dunston is on the opposite, south bank of the Tyne, as are Metroland, a permanent funfair in the Metro Shopping Centre, and Blaydon, celebrated in the song The Blaydon Races.

'The Old Town Hall and St Hilda's Church, Middlesbrough' by L. S. Lowry

I am, like the sky, alone.

St Hilda's poor spire pierces me.

As a pen, paper.

Church-wardens like to turn the word infinity upon the tongue.

Take their hats off to me.

The old town hall has settled, now, among its files.

Buff-coloured, faded, from the beginning full.

Mislaid.

A letter from the Board among Christmas cards.

Dear Sir, we write to advise you.

1959 already. Middlesbrough.

People forget me.

Like a street-lamp in summer.

Or they were born yesterday and do not know that during the war.

Village in County Durham, 1998

And now an angel passes like a bus, its scarlet side
too soiled with old advertisement

to be of use. Where men are
knocking down the old shirt factory

with ball and chain in the short December dusk, it will
break down.

In summer when the factory floor was strewn with dust –
-it must have been asbestos – and the door stove in

again, the kids, their pockets and an old pram
loaded to the brim with apples, came

to lob for dear life
till the windows lay like lustres in the sun.

Now, where the wings, in late December undistinguished as the
        sides of
buses, stall

there is a scattering of roof and ritual.

The Garden in Esh Winning

Go then into the unfabricated dark
With your four bare crooked tines, fork,
And get my grandmother out of that muddle of dock and dandelion
        root
And put an end to neglect
While the wind says only Esh Esh
In the late apple blossom, in the ash
And all the hills rush down to Durham
Where the petulant prince bishops dream

In purple vaults.
It's not the earth's fault,
Fork, but mine, that I for forty years of days and nights invented
        dragons
To guard my grandmother's bare arthritic bones
From my own finding. Now of all things I imagine a garden
Laid over, and dumb as, a disused coalmine.
In the north there are no salley gardens, no, nor bits of willow pattern
Plate to plead for me, no, only bones
Unmourned, the memory of the memory of a plane shot down
And its discolouration.
Who now humbly brings me my grandmother in pieces
Like Osiris,
Fork? Who eases out old sorrel gone to seed, old scallions?
Who pulls the purple columbines
Out of the not quite dark midsummer midnight? In the north the
        sky is green,
The long grass, partly shorn, lies down like a lion
And *something's happened to John*
And in this valley of discoloured bones
Ezekiel lies open to the wind, the fork-work done.
The Bible propped like an elbow on the ironing-board within
The house is full of visions, Gran,
Of what we are, were, always might have been.

My grandmother's son John was an RAF navigator, shot down over France in 1943.
The night it happened, she woke and sat up in bed saying 'Something's happened to
John'.

Barclays Bank and Lake Baikal

The bank walks in at half past seven, dressed and unembarrassed
by its sponsorship of Beethoven, the best

of music, *Hammerklavier*, here in its own town
Darlington.

Demidenko, Nikolai, in concert, self-exiled,
walks out of another world

like one who's wandered, handkerchief in hand, into the town
to watch the hammer of the auctioneer come down

and then, instead, plays Beethoven
as if he were alone.

He looks like Silas Marner so intent upon his two thick leather
            bags of gold
he lost the world

we live in: cough, cold, cufflink and the ache and pain
of bone.

It looks as if the light, Siberian, is breaking slowly over Lake Baikal,
as if our ship of fools

and bankers, borne upon the waters
of a bare

adagio, may founder in a quite uncalled for and unsponsored
sea of solitude.

But not tonight, dour Demidenko, dealer in another world's
dear gold —

for Darlington's recalled. At ten to ten
the bank picks up its leather bag, walks out again.

Arvo Pärt in Concert, Durham Cathedral, November 1998

Sea-otters will be calving soon about the Farnes.

Perhaps you'll go there, in your coat, tonight.
Perhaps you'll go to Coldingham

or Lindisfarne, or, landlocked, wait, as if
you too were

sandstone: wounded, worn by wind, rain, light.

O Lord, enlighten my heart which evil desires have darkened

where the imperturbable pillars stand.

For you have fidgeted through sermons.

Hard to sit still with all your insufficiency about you, isn't it?

But you will listen through your permeable skin as if
this music were

slow wounding, swearing in, osmosis.

Ebba, abbess of Coldingham, will find her nuns forsaken, fidgeting,

but you, as Cuthbert, suffering for all, will make straight
for the sea, to stand all night
waist-deep in it,

in praise and prayer,

in fret, is it, or under the stars' bare
scattering of thorns --

O Lord, give me tears and remembrance of death, and contrition –

until dawn. When you will kneel down on the sand.
Sea-otters will come to warm you then.

But you must be as sandstone.

Make of this music an Inner Farne where you may stand alone.

For it *is* Farne, from Celtic *ferann*, meaning land,

where monks will dig a well for you of wild fresh water,
where you'll find not wheat but barley growing on bare ground,
where you will build a wall so high around
your oratory, you'll know the sky, it only
a while

as instrumental, wearing-in of wind and water. Listen

then, you'll find your own skin, salt, intact
as Cuthbert after centuries of wandering, still
permeable –

O Lord, forsake me not –

and one, as Arvo Pärt in his coat, will stand before
the orchestra, the choir, as if he too had only now
walked out of water

new, renewable, knowing the comfort of sea-otters.

The lines in italics are taken from the text of Arvo Pärt's Litany, a setting of the 24 prayers attributed to St John Chrysostom for each hour of the day and night. St John Chrysostom, a hermit, became Patriarch of Constantinople in 398. While Cuthbert, born in 634, was a monk at Melrose Abbey, he visited the religious house at Coldingham, and it was there, according to legend, that he stood all night in the sea and in the morning was warmed by seals. From 664 he was Prior of Lindisfarne and, while Prior, spent three years living as a hermit on one of the nearby Farne Islands. In 685, against his will, he was made Bishop of Lindisfarne. He died and was buried there in 687. Because of Viking raids, the monks took Cuthbert's coffin and embarked in 873 on 'the wanderings', continuing until a final resting-place was found for the saint in 995, on the site of the present Durham Cathedral, which still contains his shrine.

Convent Girl

They wearied me with prayer.

In the darkening garden of the dene, I stared.

I sought him where the way was unprepared, a wild rose.

The old road with its white line will not come again,

nor my heart with its old-fashioned indicators,

but my riven father

who knows.

Maureen Almond

Beret

Berets straight girls *not*
slanted. Show your FCJ badges.
Don't eat in the street.
Wear gloves. Tunics below knees
please.   Now, repeat

after me. Yes Mother,
No Mother,
Three bags full.
Straighten your collars
I'll turn out ladies
if I don't turn out scholars

Your hem
must touch the ground
when you kneel down.
Have you taken it in
at the waist?
I want to hear a pin
drop.   Pick up that 'H'
you're not at home now

Did I blow the whistle?
Did I?
Walk on.

Booter

This is a ritual you dress down for
in your Sunday worst.
You get there after seven,
when it's cheap.
Call yourself a pensioner,
haggle over the price
of *War and Peace,*
get him down to fifty p.
It's all part of the game.

You trample over temporary cinders,
land cleared for extensions to a college
you're too old to attend.
It used to be a dog-track
You were too young to go to.
You try to blend in
but you have 'stuck-up, middle-class
cow', stamped on your forehead.

You pick up a Sinatra
because he's recently dead. And,
like the man says,
'it might be worth summat'
You ask if he'll take any less.
He says, 'Am bloody givin' it away
at a pound!' So you put it down -
crawl away like a shamed greyhound
whose just lost the big race.

You half-hear someone else's stake,
'Will yer take a quid
for that Wallace and Grommit alarm mate?'
That's where you went wrong,
You should have quoted the odds.

Will you take seventy p.
for this little statue
                    mate?'
'Can't come down any ferther Pet,
It's an Avon bottle - the collectable now, them'

At least he called you Pet.
A kid races past,
fast as an electric hare.
'A gorrim down! A gorrim down Dad!'

'Am proud a yer lad - mind, a bet
yer can gerram new
for worree was asken!'

A tick-tack man in a butcher's van
says he'll throw in some Cumberland
with the rindless back -
Can't say fairer than that.
After weeks of studying form
You decide to gamble.

You romp home,
see neighbours on patios,
buried in their *Times*
croissants, steaming cappuccinos.

You slide the run-around back
next to your ten-year-old Jag
Press the button for the automatic
up and over and the trap shuts.

You make tea and bacon 'sarnies'
Gloat over your winnings:

A fiver's worth of Chinese chicken,
War and Peace.

I know Exactly The Sort of Woman I'd Fall in Love With If I Were A Man.

(after Deryn Rees-Jones)

She would flambé and bubble like Tina
Turn her temperature to more than fifty
The rough wild husk of her voice would lift me
to way past boiling point. Oh this Prima
Donna of my fantasy, I've seen her
drooling at me. A hot chilli kiss she
blew, landed on my plate once, it missed me
by a spare rib, made my taste keener.

As for me, I'm already shimmering
in a thin glaze. I can turn up the heat
whenever I want to. I'm simmering,
waiting to be whisked along with her beat.
She doesn't know, but in the glimmering
of her eye, I'd be good enough to eat.

Trinkets

I suppose I was sent to you
as a kind of punishment was I?
Like gout.
I suppose the buzzing in your big toe
is down to me.
Well let me tell you,
I might have let the hornets out
but it wasn't me who stole fire
and kindled it to dragon's breath
in your big toe.

I didn't chain you to a rock
and prey on your foot

like a vulture.
I came to you
with a box of goodies
you could only have dreamed of.
Now everything but cold hope's escaped
from under our heavy bedclothes.

Friday Nights

By eight o'clock they're rounded up,
driven from the high reaches of the estate,
down into the centre.

There, they turn and turn again
between the Dun Cow and the Ketton Ox,
until finally they thread through
a narrow gap at the Cross Keys,
their breath rising like dust,
vaporising into the cold dusk.

One by one they're picked off,
caught round the neck,
made legless,
a Hustler's all that's needed
to remove their covering
which is hardly risen from their skin.

It's reckoned to take forty-six moves
to get them to a stripped state,
but they're ready for turning.
In three curved blows they'll be done,
which just leaves the marking.

A hustler is also a type of shearing comb used when the fleece is close to the skin.

Brian

My crumbling little man, my sandy idol
stripped down to just your underpants and socks;
each night you stack the cushions up in blocks,
a pyramid to mark out where you'll settle.
Way beyond the boundary of the table
I slide my eyes across your curves and bumps,
watch quietly till you slip to sleep in grunts
and sigh, content as any baby in a cradle.

It's when I see you spread like that, full stretch,
my love, my god, my sturdy little falcon,
your heels and toes hooked round the sofa's edge,
I realise you are my rhyme and reason,
my sun, my light, the cause of every breath.
Our couch will sail the waters into heaven.

New Year (2002)

On the moor road, sheep paw at frozen ground,
scratch for frosted grass in the late sun's shadow.
I feel as if someone's poked me in the eye with a hot stick,
lose sight of the flock, and woolly dreams of a good year.

We speed, me and my blind eye to Pickering,
I'm told, it's a conjunctival haemorrhage.
Whatever its name, this half-sightedness
sums up my two thousand and one odyssey.

At the 'Forest and Vale' we feast on tuna
and egg mayonnaise; the remains of afternoon tea.
I eat two triangles, it's all I can face.
What I want is a darkened space, a bed
in the annexe, deep as a cave.

The others huddle together in Sheila's room,
drink wine, wonder if I'll kill the rest of their party.
I close my eyes till sleep comes
and dreams escape, tied to the bellies of sheep.

Keith Armstrong

My Father Worked on Ships

My father worked on ships.
They spelked his hands,
dusted his eyes, his face, his lungs.

Those eyes that watered by the Tyne
stared out to sea
to see the world
in a tear of water, at the drop
of an old cloth cap.

For thirty weary winters
he grafted
through the snow and the wild winds
of loose change.

He was proud of those ships he built,
he was proud of the men he built with,
his dreams sailed with them:
the hull was his skull,
the cargo his brains.

His hopes rose and sunk
in the shipwrecked streets
of Wallsend
and I look at him now
this father of mine who worked on ships
and I feel proud
of his skeletal frame, this coastline
that moulded me
and my own sweet dreams.

He sits in his retiring chair,
dozing into the night.
There are storms in his head
and I wish him more love yet.

Sail with me,
breathe in me,
breathe that rough sea air old man,
and cough it up.

Rage, rage
against the dying
of this broken-backed town,
the spirit
of its broken-backed
ships.

The Jingling Geordie

Watch me go leaping in my youth
down Dog Leap Stairs,
down fire-scapes.
The Jingling Geordie
born in a brewery,
drinking the money
I dug out of the ground.

Cloth-cap in hand I go
marching in the jangling morning
to London gates.
Jingling Geordie
living in a hop-haze,
cadging from the Coppers
I went to the school with.

Older I get in my cage,
singling out a girl half my years
to hitch with.
Oh yes! I am the Jingling Geordie,
the one who pisses on himself,
wrenching out the telephone
his Father placed off the hook.

Listen to my canny old folk-songs;
they lilt and tilt into the dank alley,
into the howls of strays.
Oops! The Jingling Geordie
goes out on his town,
rocking and rolling a night away,
stacking it with the weary rest.

See my ghost in the discotheque,
in the dusty lights,
in the baccy rows.
Jingling Geordie,
dancing gambler,
betting he'll slip
back to the year when the Lads won the Cup.

Well I walk my kids to the Better Life,
reckoning up the rude words dripping
like gravy off me Granda's chin.
Whee! goes the Jingling Geordie:
figment of the gutter brain,
fool of the stumbling system,
emptying my veins into a rich men's-palace.

Folk Song for Thomas Spence

Down by the old Quayside,
I heard a young man cry,
Among the nets and ships he made his way.

As the keelboats buzzed along,
He sang a seagull's song;
He cried out for the Rights of you and me.

Oh lads, that man was Thomas Spence,
He gave up all his life
Just to be free.
Up and down the cobbled Side,
Struggling on through Broad Chare,
He shouted out his wares
For you and me.

Oh Lads, you should have seen him gan,
He was a man the likes you rarely see.
With a pamphlet in his hand,
And a poem at his command,
He haunts the Quayside still,
And his words sing.

His folks they both were Scots,
Sold socks and fishing nets,
Through the fog on the Tyne they plied their trade.
In this theatre of life,
The crying and the strife,
They tried to be decent and strong.

Oh lads, that man was Thomas Spence,
He gave up all his life
Just to be free.
Up and down the cobbled Side,
Struggling on through Broad Chare,
He shouted out his wares
For you and me.

Oh Lads, you should have seen him gan,
He was a man the likes you rarely see.
With a pamphlet in his hand,
And a poem at his command,
He haunts the Quayside still,
And his words sing.

An Oubliette for Kitty

There's a hole in this Newcastle welcome,
there's a beggar with a broken spine.
On Gallowgate, a heart is broken
and the ships have left the Tyne.

So what becomes of this History of Pain?
What is there left to hear?
The kids pour down the Pudding Chare lane
and drown a folksong in beer.

So here is an oubliette for you, Kitty,
somewhere to hide your face.
The blood is streaming from fresh wounds in our city
and old scars are all over the place.

There's this dirt from a history of darkness
and they've decked it in neon and glitz.
There are traders in penthouse apartments
on the Quayside where sailors once pissed.

So where are Hughie and Tommy, Kitty?,
the ghosts of Geordies past?
I don't want to drown you in pity
but I saw someone fall from the past.

So here is an oubliette for you, Kitty,
somewhere to hide your face.
The blood is streaming from fresh wounds in our city
and old scars are all over the place.

While they bomb the bridges of Belgrade,
they hand us a cluster of Culture
and tame Councillors flock in on a long cavalcade
to tug open the next civic sculpture.

And who can teach you a heritage?
Who can learn you a poem?
We're lost in a difficult, frightening, age
and no one can find what was home.

So here is an oubliette for you, Kitty,
somewhere to hide your face.
The blood is streaming from fresh wounds in our city
and old scars are all over the place.

So here is an oubliette for you, Kitty,
somewhere to hide your face.
The blood is streaming from fresh wounds in our city
and old scars are all over the place.

And Pigs Might Fly

(for Helmut Bugl)

On this evening flight,
necks stuck out,
we dart in formation
to a Stuttgart dream.
Complete strangers,
we share a common French wine
to celebrate clouds.
With your rough words,
you ask me what I do.
'Write poetry', I say,
and sign away a verse or two for you,
hovering in mid-air, between snow and sun.
'And you?' 'I breed pigs I do',
flying home from a swine seminar in Montreal.
To prove it, you sign me a photo of six of your litter,
the Swabian breed of Helmut Bugl.
It's a flying cultural exchange,
a rhyme for a slice of time.
The stars are sizzling in the thrilling sky
and, tonight, pigs might fly.
Tonight, pigs might fly.

Cuba, Crocodiles, Rain

It is raining on Crocodiles,
bullet-tears on the scales.
Here, where the balance of power has changed.
These banks of hardened green-backs, spread
stoned along the water's edge,
are caged
like old dictators,
reigns ended
as young Cuba
surrounds them.

Peter Armstrong

A Metamorphosis

Hearing the earth move above him
  and split along its memory of grain
  he could only raise one
whitefleshed, blackgrained arm

to the oncoming roof,
  as if to reach air with it,
  narrowing his hand to a leaf, regret
of the dark and the stiff

tree of his genealogy honing
  to a white shaft
  that now, a season after,
has broken ground, bending

to the open weather, a hand
  opening its thank-offering
  to air, lifting
a prayer from the black ground.

Her Rosary

(i.m. Mary Armstrong 1916-83)

Here is her rosary:
five sad mysteries in the hand,
five sorrowful decades

in the breath of a chant.
What hangs in their parabola
is the blue of her skies:
an element of promise,
a gift of healing.

What shows to the eye
is the maculate hand, the skin drawn tight
over a bone frame, sorrow clenched
on a featherweight chain.

To the grieving son
a neutral space,
to the feuding son
a peace-giving:

here is her rosary, her mother's
before hers, and now
a mesh of links, a fine tether
to hold us.

The Red-Funnelled Boat

Comrades, since it's evident
that the voices teasing us at nightfall
with their inklings of another island
where Jerusalem might be builded,
are at best of shady origin,
and more likely beg the question
of the demon in the synapse,

let's go line up at the jetty
for the red-funnelled boat to take us
by black-watered sea-lochs
to its approximate asylum,
- *aliéné, égalité, fraternité*
inscribed on the gateposts

and the inside of the inmates' foreheads –

where we might hope to be permitted,
under the benevolent dictatorship
of the monthly needle,
to establish our republic
of tweeds and decorum:
one last collective indulgence
in the dreams of the mind politic.

Between the ashlar ward-blocks
and the rusticated boundary,
the light will be democratic
on the backs of garden details
and the chronically second-sighted,
the electrodes reserved only
for those weeping over their Isaiah.

Tell those who come after
how we boarded in one body,
feeling, but not flinching at
the bow's one long incision
down the firth's dark mirror:
the red stump of its funnel lifted
as high as it was ploughing under.

*There was no mental hospital on the isle of Bute, so those needing one would be
taken, by Mac Braine's ferry (known for its red funnel) to Loch Gilphead. To go
mad, then, or to be peculiar, or odd, was to be 'ready for the red-funnelled boat'.
From an anecdote of Nicol Ferrier, Professor of Psychiatry at Newcastle, who grew
up on the isle.*

An Englishman in Glasgow

(for Steph and Alistair Wilson)

Let the rain be padding its fingers
    on the soft drum of a car
and the high-built crescents stretch
    into a temperate Bohemian dusk,
a lax, acceptant exegesis
    of the parable of Friday night.

I could go on circling that maze
    of greenery and presbyterian frontages,
the Kremlins and the Gormenghasts
    dreamed into a municipal park,
the reductionist bars stood preaching
    their one true work-ethic of drink,

could smuggle back across the border
    this weather-smudged contraband,
have the dormitory villagers
    stripping back their oak-beamed lounges
to the concrete ceiling,
    to the strip-lit nub of things,
hunched above their halves and chasers,
    dreaming accordions, republics.

From an Imaginary Republic

Over all the grizzled province
weather will be happening to brick,
the bronchitic natives going
hollower and hollower in the cheek,
like you've seen them, walking too quick
in drizzling library footage;

and the light that's collapsing
at the back of crees and prefabs,

will be found to have died
where the city gives the ghost up
in the brick-rubble back-lane
we all grew up in;

and were always nearly leaving,
rehearsing one last glance along
the yards and light-spilling doorways
before boarding for the fabled
promiscuous metropolis
where the arts and tarts were coupling

but have always found ourselves again
adrift across this outback
of the white-bricked chapels
and the closed Co-Operatives,
the flexing bed of fern
smoke reassembles on the air;

lyrical with drink
have litanied the pitfallen
and glorious relegations
on a night when the clubs
were awash with voices
and the Hammond Organ's thick vibrato;

 but tonight the dark and the drizzle
are whispering attrition
and a soft coast's slow erosion,
the fences rust along the border
of a northerly republic
and the crossing-gates jam open;

the one frost-bitten guard
croons softly in
a dialect that's frozen.

Among the Villages

Stumbling across them among thin pastures
and the gorse-grown relics of rail
you couldn't fail to find
the air heavy with elegy,
the locals wry, but incomprehensible.

Buses going other places
yielded brief epiphanies
through the blurred arc swabbed clear
in fogged upstairs windows,
of streets besieged by weather,
terraces shored against
the ebbing tide of trade,
but you knew all that:
that whole inheritance of shales and spoils
you'd sluice clean into the work of giants.
Maybe even knew this night:
the way the light at the gable corner
lights next to nothing,
that head-scarfed woman hurrying
from history to the neighbours.

The Club Organist at Enon

who, rising from a dream of Wurlitzers,
a blessed assembly on sprung maple,
wed Vienna to the City of God
    and we were Marching To Zion in 3/4 time.

O charism of foxtrots!
    the bright black & supple
    mirror of patent leather:
we were waltzing to Zion
    in a sabbath light,
that footloose trinitarian signature
    written by a miracle

through the white
sappy heartwood of our limbs,
Now; *One two three, One two three, One two three:*
  (wrapped in a maze of grace-notes
  go Caritas and Eros);
One two three, Together two three, Waltz two three
(through the sweet apocryphal circle
  of His judgement).

Bellingham

Farewell Secret Bellingham,
the capital of Nowhere;
Nowhere since it never seems
quite possible to go there
                  - Sean O'Brien.

Let it stay hidden there like strength
                - Philip Larkin.

Even Nowhere has its capital,
mispronounced by foreigners
who visit by an accident,
sunlight having camouflaged
the drifting kelp of coal-smoke.

Its histories will be going on,
the grey stone ticking over in the sun,
the four-wheel drives and pick-ups
collecting heat behind the windscreen.
Its grace-notes and its labours blur.

Beyond, there is the forest;
its deep green quilt drawn over
the sleeping figure of the border.
Hidden down its fire-breaks
the feral species muster.

But what were you expecting?
Grass is bending double
over the spoil-heaps of the giants,
and imperial roads gone native
lose themselves down farm-tracks.

Here a modest statuary
accommodates the weather,
and the names on stones and shop-fronts
negotiate from era
to different-spoken era.
The bus pulls out; the streetlights
flicker up and spell
You Are Where You Can Get.
The valley settles round that alphabet
hidden there like sense, initiate;

and the wind planes down the reservoir,
the broken wave-heads iridesce;
miles off on the trunk-road
headlights frame a sign-post;
they pan across your ceiling and they pass.

Neil Astley

A Month in the Country

The place is Islayev's estate in the country,
this framework his latest construction: "That nonsense
will harness the river, and give him the freedom
to grow what he wants. If he's working he's happy."
She turns to me, languid. His wife. And the woman
I've loved more than any. Natalya Petrovna.

"Now give me your arm," says Natalya Petrovna,
and raises my hopes of our walk in the country.
Though close she is distant, not there, for the woman
is watching Belyaev at work on some nonsense,
a kite for Verochka to fly. She'll be happy
resisting the wind's tug, its pulling for freedom.

In falling for him she surrenders her freedom:
Belyaev is loved by Natalya Petrovna.
She too is denied, and if nobody's happy
Islayev at least is transforming the country.
But now this lament is the worst of the nonsense,
this sadness like grief, to have lost such a woman!

I only exist in my love for this woman,
in playing a part that allows me no freedom.
She tells me I'm talking a lot of old nonsense,
my speeches are lost on Natalya Petrovna.
I can't live without her. This month in the country
her presence alone makes me more than just happy.

These words are Turgenev's, who thinks he is happy
reliving his *liaison* with Pauline, the woman
he never possessed, through his *Month in the Country.*
Her husband, his friend, would allow them some freedom,
Islayev's approach with Natalya Petrovna.
'Turgenev, you write such a load of old nonsense.'

These phrases are echoes recalling a nonsense.
They signify nothing. I cannot be happy
imagining her as Natalya Petrovna.
My dreams have me never quite reaching the woman.
Each line may be mine but I don't have the freedom
to change how it ends in *A Month in the Country.*

What nonsense it is with my love for the woman:
unhappy or happy, I give up my freedom.
Natalya Petrovna. I'd give her the country.

East of Easter

For years they came in wonder, filing past
his waxy russet-bearded face. Kazakhs
and Tadjiks saw their colossus, tall as
the Caucasus. Uzbeks and Oyruts gazed
on living legend, the titan who shook

the earth, whose speech made land and landlords quake.
His right hand held the sun, his left a beam
of moonlight flooding the mausoleum.
Awe-struck Ostyaks came from the north to look
at the hunter who'd slain their enemies

on the ice, clubbed the fur-traders like seals,
gave their blood-money and dogs to the poor.
Kirgiz men said Redbeard could overpower
the evil one, drive him beneath the seas
with his magic ring, and knowing no night,

he never slept, withered kulaks with light
from his glowing eyes. He rode a white horse
to lift Armenia's yoke, and stirred up wars
on an eagle's back, putting Whites to flight
from the air; stood atop an armoured car

fist raised at the Finland station, called for
action, with Trotsky now invisible
seen at his side by Petrograd people
welcoming the sealed train, when Commissar
Stalin ran to kiss his turned cheek, a sign

he was his dear disciple (the Georgian
plotting behind his back). When he suffered
heart arrest, he let himself be martyred,
tied with tubes to his deathbed like Aslan,
but breathing into a thousand statues

lifted up his stone-like fist in cities
all over Russia, held out for the day
he'd rise again, when medalled dwarfs would try
to pull him from plinth with ropes and pulleys,
bind him like Gulliver trussed on a truck,

parade him prone through the streets of Simbirsk.
Toy soldiers jerked to life then as he'd proph-
esied, switched off his life support, shut off
the flow of visitors. When the clockwork
generals came to the bed where he'd lain in

state since '24 they found not the man
but a shadow stain like the Turin shroud.
He melted like a wraith into a crowd
of waiting statues moving in a line
like androids, trailing rope and scaffolding.

Vladimir Ilyich in the van, standing
fist raised like an icon, marched his statues
out of Moscow. Where the Volga elbows

the Don, a thousand giants turned, stepping
the steppes like nightwalkers. So Lenin led

his lumbering host out of the promised land,
through the Aral seabed to Samarkand
where Uzbeks joined the horde. On they headed
east of Easter, till he rose: his red beard
caught the light, sun spoke of the dawn ahead.

The Dressing Station

That last Easter, we read Wilfred Owen
in English, History reached 1916.
They rammed the Rising down our throats
as Thatcher's task force gave 'a bloody nose'

to Argentina. Going back to school
after the break, Anne Sheehan played the fool
and flirted with the young guard on the train.
He gave us the old joke: 'Limerick Junction,

change here for Galway and America.'
Anne said 'Let me go with you, Rebecca'
in the play interval. She was backstage
giving me my wounds, circling a bandage

around my turbaned hair, for my male part
in the phoney war we were acting out.
Proud of the Red Cross on her head, my nurse
fastened my dressings tight with safety pins,

giggling when Sister called my crutch a *crotch*.
As Anne leant over me, her strapless watch
bobbed on her breast, the buttons strained to burst
from the starched blue uniform. I blushed

as she talked of going over the top
with me in France. After we'd all packed up,

we tuned our secret radio upstairs
to BBC News on the World Service
and heard a Falklands sheepman's crackly voice
attacking 'the Occupation Forces'
in Port Stanley. I forgot the lock on
the prop cupboard and got a dressing down

next morning. Gunmen could have broken in
and stolen all our weapons, said the nun.
Those hunger strikers were desperate fellows.
The H-Block men would kill for arms like ours.

The Road

The road was always out there, a white thread
across the valley, a scar she exposed
pulling back the blinds at daybreak. It drew
his eye, like a wound or missing limb, towards

the woods where cars emerged as far-off shapes
murmuring like wind through ancient water-pipes,
a low drone rising to the burning roar
of their old gas-range, as he watched them

move along the line of levée and field,
making for the island. At night the glow
of headlights and the distant hum
were comforting, as he felt her warm arms,

her steady breathing, hold him while they slept.
East was the city, from where, when war came,
the limping cars of refugees stumbled
along the road, their lights dimmed. In the dark

he listened for their wheezing, an engine's
cough like a poorly child, the heightened pitch
of a wrong approach, a gearbox wrenching
at the bend; he searched the night like an owl

expecting some disturbance, a scrabbling fox
at the wire, the worry of a lone plane
circling near, the uncertainty of cars

heading west. Months later, with some alarm,
they woke to a stuttering like small arms
from the island, then the road rumbling.
Dawn showed a line of trucks and APCs,

the grey troops of the government forces;
they saw a red Republican fighter
come in low to strafe the column, shockwaves
shaking all their windows. Yet both sides stayed

away from them, no one approached the house;
they watched the frontline as they worked the land,
a filmshow seen while stooped to milk the cows.
When silence came, they hoped to hear the cars,

but the road stayed motionless, overgrown
like a disused airstrip. It disappeared,
a skein of mist dispersed by morning sun,
a childhood memory she vaguely recalled

as he moved across her belly like rain
shadowing their fields, his tongue's trail glistening
on her milky stretchmarks. She drew him down
that way, where tawny hairs were growing wild.

For Want of a Nail

Their leaders bought blind, because of the cost;
the MiG 15s (ex-Afghan) wouldn't fly.
The ground troops halted, the battle was lost,
the breakaway republic doomed to die
for want of support, *for want of a nail.*
The warring factions kept up their attacks

on the besieged enclave. Their envoy's news
didn't reach them, something wrong with the fax
from the Geneva talks. Their Christmas truce
shot down, the town fell, *for want of a nail.*

The radio went off the air, the rebels
stormed the presidential palace, but the
federal forces basted them, in Goebbels'
phrase, because they needed guns not butter,
for greasing the wheels, *for want of a nail.*

The surgeon needed sleep: the drip-feed's seal
was faulty, someone left a swab inside.
The new heart failed, the rupture wouldn't heal.
They kept him on dialysis: he died
for want of a bed, *for want of a nail.*

The cargo shifted, the bow doors weren't closed.
The lorry hit a car and shed its load.
She'd be here if the council hadn't closed
the school, she had to cross the busy road,
victim of the cuts, *for want of a nail.*

The walkway fell fifty feet from the deck.
Rescuers were late, the ambulance stalled.
The owners said there'd been a safety check
last year, it wasn't the company's fault
that corners were cut, for want of a nail.

warnings not heeded, *for want of a nail,*
nor safeguards observed, *for want of a nail,*
usual precautions, *for want of a nail,*
normal procedures, *for want of a nail,*
no proper funding, *for want of a nail.*

The phone line broke, the deadline expired,
they stormed the plane, the hostages were shot.
The talks broke down, the army marksman fired.
They couldn't reach the trapped people, and not
for want of trying, *for want of a nail,*

disaster waited, *for want of a nail,*
the president killed, *for want of a nail,*
his aides couldn't help, *for want of a nail,*
the government fell, *for want of a nail,*
a spokesman claimed, *for want of a nail.*

Blackened Blues

A body bag unzipped itself
and slipped a no good body loose.
It toasted its own blackened health,
fired off a tirade of abuse,
death cries, its blackened body blues:

'Let cockerels crow the firestorm glow
when missiles cruise your streets at night.
Let heads and tails spin round with rounds
of red and yellow tracer light.
Death dances to the blackened blues.'

'When gunships home in on your homes
a crowded shelter's your best bet:
its infra red is easy meat
for a heat-seeking exocet.
Death cries your blackened body blues.'

'The curfew wakes at crack of dawn
when guns are chattering like cold teeth.
Let bullets sing out in the trees.
The convoy sighs without relief.
Death dances to the blackened blues.'

'Nowhere to run on a death march
when mortars pound the town ahead.
Children are slow. They're first to go
when snipers earn a pound a head.
Death cries their blackened body blues.'

'My fighters are all irregulars,
their semtex breath's like marzipan.
The safe areas are never safe
except to death's militiaman.
Death dances to the blackened blues.'

'The clampdown brings on a seizure,
the ceasefire holds in its breath.
The bread queue's panned with hot crossfire.
The unmarked van delivers death,
death cries, those blackened body blues.'

The Green Knight's Lament

(extract from The End of My Tether, ch. 27)

Even in the dark cavernous barrow, his green skin shone; he moved towards them purposefully, a great stooping figure, grassy hair spilling in a silky fan from his shoulders, his beard a tumbling nest of leaves. Stilling their instinct to back away, the green axe held out like Excalibur, all powerful.
 -Welcome, he said. You know the pact we pledged. We made our covenant, I bared my neck like Barleycorn to take your blade. Now take off your headgear, bow your heads that I may give you answer with my axe.
 -There must be some mistake, stammered Oliver de Foie.
 -It's Kernan you want, surely? said Hockle. He struck your
head off, he took what was yours.
 -No mistake, he responded. Kernan is a part of me, and I of him.My head was his head, he took it and I took it back, a twelvemonth gone, a year ago today. But you men took what was not yours, you killed my country; what you've done has cost the earth, my plants and people, my birds and beasts who were not yours to take. No general good was served, no one's interests but your own.
 -Where are we? asked Maw. Who are you, in God's name?
 -I am the Green Knight and the Green Man, Cernunnos and Kernan. I am foxglove and fleabane, cat's-ear and cowslip, hogweed and cow parsnip. I am harebell and hare's-foot clover, stork's bill and bird's-foot-trefoil. I am dove-foot crane's-bill and mouse-ear chickweed. I am bee orchid and dog-violet, dog-rose and dog's mercury. I am toad and toadflax.

He moved towards them.
-I am the linnet and bullfinch, the whistling lapwing. I am the spotted
flycatcher, the song thrush and tree sparrow. I am the barn owl and the grey
partridge. All these you killed.

I am the cornflower, the corn buttercup,
corncockle, corn gromwell, cornsalad,
corn parsley and lamb's succory.
I am fumitory and pheasant's eye,
shepherd's needle and thorow-wax.
I am the pink bindweed in the cornfield,
the bright red poppy, yellow corn crowsfoot,
broad-leaved spurge and red hemp-nettle.
I am the purple knapweed in the meadow,
bryony in the hedgerow, I am finch and warbler
darting among the dog roses.

I am weed knotgrass in the wheatfield
with six pink flower-spikes, food
for the red-yellow leaf beetle, no more.
I am the larvae of the leaf beetle, food
for farmland bird chicks, no more.
I am the weevil and rove beetle,
the larvae of moths and sawflies, food
for songbirds, not now, all killed,
bindweed, beetles, birds, all gone.

I am seed of weeds. I am seed-eating birds.
I am corn bunting, cirl bunting, yellowhammer.
I am the insects. I am the insect-eaters.
I am the hovering lark and fieldfare.
I am the vole, the shrew and the fieldmouse.
I am the owl and the kestrel.
I am marshes and wetland, all drained,
moorland and water meadows, all gone.
I am the cowslip on the chalk down,
the dropwort, the devil's-bit scabious,
dwarf sedge, burnt orchid and toadflax.
I am the clustered bellflower.

I am the chalk hill butterfly
feeding on the horseshoe vetch.
I am the marbled white, the chequered skipper,
adonis blue, pearl-bordered fritillary.
I am hay-rattle yellow in the hayfield,
the black knapweed, the wild daffodil.
I am the cowslip and the meadow buttercup,
the adder's tongue fern, the green-winged orchid.

I am the silent field of ryegrass too,
the silage field of ryegrass, no grass
but ryegrass, no plant permitted
but ryegrass, nothing but ryegrass.
No ploughman treads this empty space
where all the air a solemn stillness holds,
no beetle wheels his droning flight,
no drowsy tinklings lull the distant folds.
Where are the owls and insects?
Where are the finches and cornflowers,
mice and moths, beetles and butterflies?
Where are the people, the farmers
who lived off the land, who gave us our food,
people and plants, birds and beasts all one?
All gone, all gone, all driven from the land.

And why, you men of greed?
Your cash crops killed us off,
your fertilisers forced us out,
you poisoned with pesticides,
you looted the land, and why?
You pulled up the hedgerows,
made big farms bigger, rich men richer,
small farms fail, money out of misery.
You turned our land into badlands
where nothing grows but money.
When money fails, nothing left,
nothing left to grow. You took it all.
There's nothing, nothing, nothing left.
torrenting, her tongues of flame delighting

his tensed skin, an insect water-skater
licking water-lily lips, extinguishing

their long burn in light-play on water,
misting together, his hot spring sprinkling
into gentle spray, they rolled over

their river-bed, heads and tails lunging
in and out, each chasing the other,
paws and hooves a-fly, sinning tongues singing

 till they lay on the far side together,
rakehelly, no more damned changes to ring,
ram-wolf with civet cradled by tiger,

her jasper-yellow 'n' black stripes snaking
furred limbs around him, demon lover

ERRATA
Neil Astley poems

'The Road', p.59, first two lines should read:
   tuned to a higher frequency, his ears
   expecting some disturbance, a scrabbling fox

'For Want of a Nail': the last line of the first stanza on p.59 should be
the first line of the first stanza on p.60.

'The Green Knight's Lament' should end on p.64 with 'There's nothing,
nothing, nothing left'. The last line on p.64 and all the text on p.65 are
not from this poem and should have been deleted.

Liz Atkin

It didn't belong to Peter Pan

I watched the child
a girl of maybe six,
face crayoned in lipstick
teetering on her Mum's high heels

as she pulled
on the plastic mitt protruding
from rotten carpet, hauling
the deflated body of a sex doll
from its skip grave,

blonde nylon hair matted
with brick dust and cold tea.

As she dragged her by a foot
over to her watchful friends
this crumpled pink plastic skin
not much bigger than her

became in the evening sunshine
a grotesque, ill-fitting shadow.

Evacuees

During the early days of the war
they removed them from the city
to travel by train to rural Wales

and supposed safety from explosions.
I would have loved to see that train.
All carriage seats were taken out
since these particular passengers
either came complete with thrones
or preferred to stand. They say
Kings and the three fat Queens
went first class while Lords and Ladies
and certain heroes travelled second
with Lions and horses in the Guards van.
Winged Victory was reluctantly left
behind on the platform, her bronze
wings an impediment, but a triumphant
arm raised to wave goodbye despite.

Imagine those stony profiles
as they chugged slowly past,
straight from a Max Ernst dream,
there'd be no waving and no windows
open, just rigid folk brought down
to earth and not so heroic without
their plinths or a restaurant car,
heading not for a seaside holiday
but five years buried in a black Welsh hill.

Instructions

Take off the clothes that you're wearing
and stuff them to your shape, then make
your head using your head - adapt something
to resemble but pay careful attention
to detail, use a mirror or recent photograph.

Next place your effigy at the window
either sitting or standing whichever,
avert the head if not satisfied
with the likeness and place a book,

mug of coffee or newspaper nearby.
Once you've transferred money, housekeys
etcetera to the relevant pockets
you are free to go, free of your self
Take a last look at you in the window,
wave if you want to, and remember it's
too late to adjust glasses, fiddle
with the earring, the parting in pretend hair,

just go and hurry, don't hang around
since you are starting your new life
as stark naked as the day you were born.

Lakeland Colour

We used to pass this mill
that made blue.
Not the blue of lake or sky,
cornflower or periwinkle,
but a blue that bled
all over the road
and could be seen
on the hands and faces
of its knocked off workers.

I was reminded of this
years later,
seeing the illustrations
in an old Home Doctor
found second hand in Ulverstone,
for here was Blue Disease
with its faulty heart,
and Blue Ointment
for all human infestations,
even the Blue of Asphyxia
was illustrated alongside extreme cold,
and finally the Blue Pill,

a possible purge for poisoning
made of mercury, roses and liquorice
to be taken in the dark
and chased with a black draught.

I wonder if that mill
had been making these blues,
not azure, turquoise or ultramarine even,
and certainly not small cloth bags
of a blue that they said
would make white whiter than white.

The Biscuit Tins of England

are small airtight museums
for things that no longer need
to breathe, opened maybe twice
a year depending on location.

Absently packed by factory girls
each on her individual variety
Jam Sandwich Crème day after day
or Bourbons week by week,
filling the space, filling the tier
of Family Select Assortments

that become Christmas gifts
and lowly raffle prizes before
arrangement on 4 o'clock doilies.

Once the last favourite has gone
they come into their own
to house fossils and old photographs
not fit for the album, buttons,
letters and sewing bits. Some go to
garden sheds for seeds, screws
or sharp sand, others underbed

or wardrobe deep with secrets
and old nylons. A few are buried,
suburban time capsules containing
curled dead pets, exhibits and evidence
and one or two have even sailed,
the real ships biscuit with message,

and yet they long for the call,
not saucepans and railings this time,
but for the Biscuit Tins of England
to stack themselves high and solid
presenting rusting teatime faces.

One day

The sky above the pigeon lofts
is stippled daily
with spasmodic formation flying
by pampered birds with map pin eyes.

I prefer their city centre cousins
crowding the parks for pastie crumbs,
underfoot C.C.T.V. extras who,
by night are accidentally shut
in the shopping mall,
an airy aviary.
with stationary escalators,
switched off fountains
and an audience of rigid mannequins
behind their deceptive glass

as they soar and swoop
from level to empty level
showing us how it will be one day.

Bob Beagrie

Reincarnation

I was once an unruly patch of lawn
In a sheltered housing block, overdue
A visit from the Council gardener.

You were the path beside the wheelie bin
Running beneath Florrie's washing
With her true blue crocodile pegs.

Though once we were a crossword
Cracked by eleven every morning,
Our cryptics dunked in sweetly traded coffee

Sooner or later we'll be the credits
Of an Australian teen soap, rolling up
The screen just too fast to read.

Cook, The Bridge and The Big Man

I'm driving over the border, passed The Captain Cook
Dougy's in the back and Les Murray, fresh from clouds
Packs the rest of my small-town car, wears it like a turtle shell.
We both know he's into The Dreaming, suspect he's strayed there
Once or thrice, so we're taking him to see our Transporter
To persuade him to cross, as there are no trolls left
And Peg's just a myth to scare off truant kids.

So how do you cross that thing, in a ferry of sorts?
No man, on a flying carriage.
Where do you board?
We're already on.

I pay the ferryman's toll, Les says the crew seems amiable enough
As we set sail, suspended over the Tees cast at a low shining tide.
Riding the slow judder toward Samphire Batts we chew the fat
Of James Cook and cluck over his stroke of bad-storm luck
That left him God-fallen, cooked and eaten, first by Hawiians,
Now by us, and the rest of his home-town.
Grimm talk, but it is Halloween.

The gates swing open to the salted sunshine of riveted places,
That would much rather drift out to sea, with privets like gunwales,
And every shop wears a security grill. I start up the engine, drive onto
Terra Firma, with Les looking back and up at the alien skeleton, saying,
Well boys, Thanks for that. Got to be the weirdest bridge I ever crossed.

Ritual

Old Blakey looks like he's lived in Heretu forever
As he squats on Fish Sands at the foot of the steps
In bicycle clips and Lieutenant Columbo's mac
His iron aged bike leans against the south sea wall

He takes out a powder blue dustpan and brush
Sets to dusting the beach into a Lidl carrier bag
Leaves a neat two-foot square of flattened beige
With bristled plough-lines like a garden in Kyoto

Climbs up the steps with his bag quarter full
Mounts the bike and peddles past the Pot House
To sit at home and sift for the tide's favourite grain
The beautiful one; the one with the World in
.

Tourist

(after a visit to Boulby Mine)
You're as close to the Devil as you're ever likely to get.
Says the guide, as he takes you on a white-knuckle ride
In his transit van 800 meters beneath the seabed. Six miles out
under a darkening horizon, you stop at the working face
Sample the red heat, silent salt and dead air of the maze.

Down here sweat dries as soon as it appears, the natives
eye you from behind their beams, around a table of maps
playing Black Bitch, it's as obvious from your swan-neck
as it is from your dress that you don't speak the lingo
nor ken the currency of a full shift in hell.

Looking back into the pitch of converging chambers
beyond apple-core pillars and onion rings,
past geologist's marks and graffiti that reads;
The Rocket Man Is Tojo's Son, you catch a fat slice
of history from this fresh frontier where civilization's
know-how meets the Zechstein Sea.

Then the Odyssey back through sheer ages
of Sherwood Sandstone and Rotten Marl
through the bones of giants, through thoughts in stone
in bronze, through iron-edged livings to landscaped valleys
to simulacra, to a shepherd's sky over the road to bed.

Bruise

Your heart in your hands
The misjudged drop was such a scare
Landing your left buttock on the stair
Instead of the sole of your bare right foot.

A few hours after the tears
It appeared

Like a Svengali card
The ace of spades

Resting on the upper curve
Of the cheek
Where it sinks
Towards the cleft
Of a well fleshed peach.

Each night, in bed
I'd check the spread
Of its shorelines
Its shifting hues and moods.
Then kiss it better

Like a wild cat drinking
From the water's edge,
And scan the inklings
Of this paranormal barometer.
This action splat on a
Jackson Pollock picture.

On Monday the perfect flaw
Was a pair of lips,
Rouged and pouting
Straight out of a Man Ray print
Murmuring softly
From the shadows of the sheet
Hoc est corpus meum.

As I'd read and re-read
The illuminated page
Of silver leaf scores, tracing
Filigree streams of stretch marks
To their source in a script
More ancient than cuneiform.

On Tuesday the red spot of Jupiter
Slipped into an oil slick negligee

Devouring orbiting freckles and moles
In a wash of earth blood
Drowning mussels, gannets and gulls.
On Wednesday the blemish
Was the Aurora Borealis, reflected
In an oracle's far-seeing eye,
Framed by a golden sunset
Like a broken yolk speckled
With peppercorn cumuli.

On Thursday the darkness
Was half its original size
More a thumbprint ringed
By fine whorls of wood grain.

On Friday it was as hard as the
Valentine heart of a Spring nectarine.
By Saturday it had vanished
But for the faintest coffee stain
When you said over your full
Mug of Mocha, 'Hmmm...maybe
I should get a tattoo right there.'

The Were-Tongue

Last night
I never thought
I'd blunder preoccupied under
a bloated moon into a thoughtless phrase
and want to bite off my tongue at the root

as it stumbled
into an ambush that
had been brewing for days, spat back
under attack to see you retreat inside,
leaving the auto-pilot in charge.

That other
you to combat this
other me, the one with his paw
in his maw and what keen ears you have
Grandma, what a silver bullet glare
That cuts to
the quick like a lunar eclipse.
No bedtime stories snagged behind your eye tonight
under the hood of a red cloak I saw a white dwarf
implode as your glass of lemonade hit the deck.

And this morning
my reflection's got the bare-faced-were-
cheek to ask how long I expect to play this
bad guy painted black with a silent movie
moustache skulking suspiciously under my nose.

The Myth Making Workshop

Spent the day teaching school kids in Sunderland
How to enjoy words, roll 'em round the tongue
Like boiled sweets, feel their sugar-fizz like cola-bottles
Then gob 'em onto a page to make a picture of a worm
A dragon or a memory of a favourite place.
The girls got straight into it, but the boys, apart
From the one armed with a Parker pen, just stared
Full of the inevitable advance of puberty, each aware
Of the unlikely height and the strange shape of the girls
This term, but not trusting their own, each other's or anyone's
Words (fizzy or not) to name the sudden change;
Their feelings of dislocation, desire and repulsion
Whenever one of 'em glances over; to listen to this joker
Waffle about poetry, dragons or someone called Medusa.

Never Enough

Too much cholesterol in too many
bites of cake too many bargains in
too many window displays, too many
shoes to wear in one week & far too much sex
on today's t.v. too many carrier bags crammed
under the stairs too many scratch cards & coupons
stuffed into her purse not enough notes folded flat
to the lining lying back to back the picture faces
conspiring & not enough
change to make a
decent rattle.

Too many years of too many fags
sitting on her chest in too many queues
for a reduced perm & set that's had enough
of coping with too much
rain
Too much
sea wind
being kept under-wraps
by a history of headscarves & a season of hats.

Too long at the sink thinking
there's not enough days till the Christmas crush
& not enough days to save for next year's holidays
in Blackpool, The Lakes or the Costa del Sol
too many pinched days spent nibbling the corners
of never enough endless days to be basked away
on lie-lows like a babe in the shallows
& sipping too much sangria.

Not enough days & not enough days
not enough hands & not enough eyes
not enough sweet nothings poured into her ears
& not enough ears to hear the too many
tales of old wives on too much tamazipan
& not enough laughs while these not enough

days stretch into too many yesterdays & not enough
tomorrow's already filled too the brim with too many
spiders lurking in too many baths with too many
legs & far too much hair

& that bus driver's smile's missing too many
teeth from too many fights after too many
drinks or too many bites of his wife's fruit cake,
muttering to himself under his too much moustache
that he's spent too long squatting a double yellow line
behind too many arseholes driving too many cars
under too many middle-managers making too many cuts
& too many changes to the old bus routes.

 There's not enough seats or there's too many people,
too many sneezes & too many germs not enough
flu-jabs to deal with the threat of the expected epidemic
in the Christmas crush, there's not enough days,
& there's not enough days & she's beginning to feel
that its one of those days when she's lived one
too many of these not enough days.

Peter Bennet

Genealogy

Since yesterday, it seems, the maps have changed,
the church clock cannot tell the time,
the names you want have faded from the microfiche,
and from the xeroxed parish registers.

The village is beneath the town,
the town is underneath the city.

Just think, the letter from your ancestor
that would have made the whole thing clear, the task
so simple, put aside and never finished,
because a moth got in the inkwell.

Call it a day.

You'd starve, in any case, if you went back,
the past contains no sustenance,
the birthday cakes are grey with dust,
the orchards there grow only apple cores.

Look now, at the changing creature
here in the hedge, made out of leaves: its tiny
limbs reach out for recognition.

Its colour goes so suddenly from green
to splintering silver: can you see it, dare you touch?

Content

Time ripens in abundance, hanging
unplucked while he examines the horizon,
or shies selected stones at driftwood.

Since exile here, he understands
he is a figment of his own imagination.

His mind is now becoming like the ocean
on which he sometimes fancies glimpses
of distant ships, or makes some speck
a swimmer's head, small waves
the rocking angles of a swimmer's arms.

Solitude, and lack of tools or toys
do not constrain him: he can visit
all his wishes, walk or run, repeat his journeys,
act on impulses or cancel them,
and name things or decide to leave them nameless.

He is content to be passed over
by infrequent clouds, and birds
with gaudy wings and human voices.

He disregards the long-haul airliner
whose dreamy passengers can hardly see
his island, let alone
the threats to trespassers he has inscribed
in foliage across the broadest beach.

Filming the Life

Your sisters have agreed to drag their skirts
across the fields where trees are shrugging
coldly, as it is October,
towards the lane with hedges, and the gate
where gravel leads to wider gravel,
and damp-stains on the quoining of the manse.

We have the Bible on the hallstand,
adjacent to the wet umbrella,
and cabbage in a kitchen full of women.

The draughts at ankle-height across the flagstones
come from the hills on which your father wanders,
prising sermons from the mist and boulders.

Your role now is to find an upstairs room,
and be the ghost-child at a pointed window,
offering his breath to glass
in order to inscribe it, and then seeing
a darker world on which his name is weeping.

You are too sickly to grow old,
and will not live to see your pamphlets smoulder
in every bookshop of the revolution.

from The Long Pack XXI

This is your summer, and the oak tree
grips its leaves about my face.

The last Leveller that was shot to death:
a face of leaves
that stares back smiling at your own.

It took five tons of oak to smelt one ton

of iron, a skelp of land to feed one sheep.

For you, we ranting Angels might have turned
oak roots in the wards of earth
to unlock England for her cheated yeomanry.

The very shadow frighted you
and shook your kingdome.

Rout out the titled man in every hollow,
unfurling park land, dunning for his rents!
The substantiality of levelling is comming.

XXII

Sinne and transgression is finisht,
a meere riddle, that they
with all their humane learning cannot reade.

North Tyne, untarnished by the moon, I see
still flows stealthily by Houxty. A shield
of pasture there may yet contain
the like of that heraldic bull
whose glimmering stillness strengthened me, the night
we wove our stratagem within the wood.

Alan, that was my lost bride Helen's brother,
my father, busy as a gnat,
poor drunken Marjorie: their divers ends
I cannot know. Together with myself,
whose death you must be privy to,
this was our one flesh dwindled to its remnant.

Some beer, some scraps of bread and meat, a sword,
two knives, and one great pistol
my father brandished like the cuddy's jawbone
Samson hefted, owning neither shot nor powder:
these, with my silver whistle and a Bible,
comprised our final commonwealth.

Thou and thy Family are fed,
as the young ravens strangely.

Fairytale

The children dream a foray, and their bodies
follow on their hands and knees
out from the forest, under barbed wire fences.
The wind among the trees is scolding.

A company of white geese by the stream,
down where the lane goes through a farmyard
overhung and dark with oaks,
are moonlit so that they resemble
excisions from an older, radiant world.

These are dream geese, docile, and too beautiful
to raise their wings in clamour, or to scatter.

Breath keeps pace as bare soles, gladdening
to soft damp earth and smell of prey,
accelerate a measured run,
and this is good, and this is human nature.

Wolf-girls, wolf-boys, spread your arms
find balance, vocalise your hunger.

Each night the geese are there again, but stronger.

David Burnett

Alexandria 31 B.C.

After the procession, the trumpets
And the drums, the gilded chariots,
The trophies, the ships' beaks of bronze,
The swags of roses, the snow-tunicked slaves,
The maidens, each brow wreathed with leaves,
The magnificent, incomparable procession
That is the splendour and order of the city,
After it all, after the dream,
The exquisite and too brilliant dream,
With the plaster images of the gods,
The bad history and worse lies,
The deliverance, the triumph at Actium,
And the acclamations that mean nothing,
The grave chanting of the sober priests,
The libations and burnt offerings,
The baubles, the well watered wine,
The shying, refractory horses,
The surly, indifferent children,
The intense, insufferable heat, -
After it all, the Caesars and their crowns,
The neighbourhood is itself again,
Sheets hanging out to dry, the shouting,
The loud laughter in each stair,
The smell of cooking and new bread,

The ordures andf the waste, the stench and flies,
Men idle, spitting and throwing dice
Ogling and chaffing girls, a birth,
First things that are always first.

An Orkney Calendar

January
Crammed light. Its swathings. On the hill
Such light as is about the grail.

February
Fill dyke. And what will never fill, or fail,
Gun metal, pitiless, immovable.

March
Atlantics, and the driven wet
Americas of air, that weight.

April
Gulls stooping where the plough is laid,
The loamed flood lifting from the blade.

May
Miracles. Sven walking from the waves.
The one green tree with its leaves.

June
A swale of silver and its spill and race,
A bee swarm pulsing in the grass.

July
The oats' silence. And the seas',
A black fog trampling out each place.

August
A flail sings, loosening on stone
Each pure, gold vowel of the sun.

September
The sea' s fist, and its glut and freight:
A left shoe, oranges, a crate.

October
Candle end, and moth, and star.
Before words that they speak of here.

November
At Hoy, still, awful, terrible,
Within the air a lighted hill.

December
At Yule, star fire within the thorn,
A fish mouth stammering of corn.

The Olive Grove

A soil that fattens, and its weight
And glut, nets stretched between the boughs
And pressing in the chequered light
Upon each stooped and twisted trunk.
Each tree a miracle of leaf,
Entire and perfect in itself,
True, just, and apt, with nothing slack
Or waste: the timber joists, each cord
And fibre kindling, the flesh fruit
And oil and light, the sucked stone seed.
What other metaphor for you?
Where else for what we know by heart?

Late Autumn

Windfalls beneath the hedge. The rake
Snags in a fist of tousled leaves.
Upon the lawn burst husks and shells
With scarlet hips, the petals blown
And shredded from the blowsy rose.
Each juice sublimes. Sticky and soft.
And full the yellow plums gorge still.
Oils. Resins. Essences. The air
A musk you almost taste to breathe.
All afternoon a fragrance flaunts
That leans from every languid stalk
And sweetens the dry, shrivelled bents.
Such light. So still that nothing stirs.
The cricket fast asleep at noon.
In a hedge bottom the drowsed wasps.
The ancient Sabbath of the leaves
A lassitude that stills and weighs.
Unceasing ripening. Yet, day
By day, the shadows close and steal,
The sun ebbs, wastes and seeps away.
With the first frosts, rheumy and sweet
And parched, the last vines wither
On the stem. At dawn a sopping wet.
The damp. The rottenness. The mists.
Within the brush and in the ditch
A cloying, sickly, deathly smell.
An end of summer, and yet, still,
At noon the oven of the fields.
In the thinned shallows of the stream
The sliding gravels grate with light,
The trellis and the mellowed bricks
Burn hot as August in the sun.
Yet, still, the summer spends and spoils,
A fullness loosening itself.

Each day a lessening to less,
A weariness, a pulse that fails,
And in the dusk a heavy moon,
Each silence, and a gold that rusts.

Summer Snow

At mid-day, suddenly, in summer
Within the air flake drifting upon flake.

To build such darkness out of air,
Such snow, and its breathed nothingness.

At noon the sun itself an emptiness.
Ash everywhere. In the ash tufts of hair.

Upon the skin a film, a bitterness
And smell that nothing rubs away.

Not snow, and its pure nothingness,
But in the air a sweat of oil and soot.

In each flake all we know and are,
The nothingness of all we build.

Each flake that is still, too, of God,
Upon the skin, upon the mouth, the tongue.

Listen. The last hour of the world.
Look. Taste. And do not look away.

Richard Caddel

For Tom

Dear head, four days ahead of love's day
I bring you love. Not that you lack that,
heart, or music, living far beyond stars
close in our hearts memory and moving

hard as you did then under my hand.
Never still, your humour and sharp mind
returned bright now, little carer. So I
stumble to rest missing you, not twenty.

From Wreay Churchyard

What of memory, a
               film not
wound on properly, cold
               daylight.

Pine trees, then, for
               memory, a
black plastic sheet
               flapping. Pinecones

of stone. Letter B
                 stray in the
glass, larksong, fire
                   forgotten, it was

Spring in the far
                 hills, it was
time.

Going Home

for John Riley

What in the world we see
is what's important. There
the days seemed shorter and our hearts
spun with the compass under

trees, magnificent pointers
out of galaxies. Continental drift,
an appointment we were late for,
an old friend missed.

Larksong Signal

Arcane and isolate breathing
acts of faith – longstone
to blind fiddler. High song
patient in rain. *Sing it –*

no ideas but in tunes –
'sounds we haven't heard
that the birds know about' –
writing on air for dear life

Nightstory

Together, for warmth. To-
gether, in gale and
flood and sore throat.
Together in evening

light. Breath fought for
together. Breath and
speech won at what
cost together. Lying

awake together under stars
under years under
writer and knowing
together in shared light.

Nocturne in Black and White

for Lucy

I sit here as light
goes, thinking of you
crossing mountains at
night – stars

so close and bright
you could've touched
them. Or
so it felt, like *'Where*

Stars Fall'– a place
neither of us yet know
reaching our hands to
touch, towards it.

Ramsons

a calm, a
     red sun low
in my driving mirror.
     pale moon.
smell I can't drop, or
     song, chance, wild
garlic, a weather
     beaten sail

Shiner : Moves Towards Winter

Weather moves towards
winter seen through bright
glass and streaming.
At night each star tokens

a little calm, we dare
a dark spoon of hope.
Whatever – it's a gift, this
looking forward and back

and holding loss and
distance and between us
a night time smile of here, and
now touching of fragile arms.

Stars on a partly cloudy night

Throstles feeding – their neighbours basking in evening light
on the ground, or in midgy air, or by puddles. Teasels & hogweed

stand stiffly upright, in moral purity, listening. A terrier,
head cocked to one side, awaits his call. Moon is an owl, rising

alert for signs of prey, combing the copse low over beechwood,
near the surface of the undergrowth. Heartbeat racing – animals

running or hopping or standing or lying down. The moon
at intervals caught behind cloud – a planet in step with us

for a few feet as we go home - too tired and breathless – to
the next listening point, hearts spinning like toys to the sky.

Kevin Cadwallender

Baz Nativity

A virgin birth
On Boxing Day
Christ knew where the Father was,
Baz was born bloody
And cursed,

The umbilical cord
Twisted about his neck,
Blue with cold rage
And daring
God to take him....

If he were hard enough.

Magi backing away .
Not wanting any trouble.

Baz inherits a Dad

When Baz's Mam got married
Baz got a Dad,
I remember his tears
Burns cut his mucky cheeks,
The first time he was strapped.

He showed me the welts
Of skin underneath his jumper,

I told hjm my sjster had headlice
To cheer him up.
We went to point at her
As she wailed under the fine-tooth comb.

He said,
'It's great Kev,
I've never had a Dad
Who beats you like a Dad should'

I lay awake thinking about those words
But couldn't grasp the logic.

My head itched through thinking too much.

Baz Lex Talio Nis

Bullied once too often
in the juniors
and dreading the
final bell.

On that long march home
not daring to look back,
leering voices scuffling
at my haversack straps.

Yells and commotion
cry-baby calls
mocking my misery
and coward's yellow
colouring my guts.
Turning to face
my demons
and seeing Baz
dervishing his
towel bag into

the enemy ranks,
I charged too
and we routed
them all.
Baz grinning like a maniac
at my mute appreciation,
escorted me to my house
saluted and sounded the all clear.

Stopping only once
To empty the brick from his towel bag.

The Building Trade

Julian is an existentialist. he works on a building site
with Tom the labourer, Fred the brickie and Bob the hod carrier.
it works like this: Tom fills Bob's hod up with bricks,
Bob carries them to Fred and Fred builds a wall.
Julian's job is to help the bricks understand their own reality.

Tom has ham sandwiches for lunch, Bob has cheese and Fred has egg.
Julian doesn't have lunch as he feels this is saying 'no'
to a society which insists on social imperatives such as lunch.

Sometimes the bricks argue with Julian saying
"But we have the right to freedom"
Julian smiles, "man is condemned to freedom"
"But we are bricks" they cry, "why do you oppress us?"
some days the walls just don't get built at all.
Julian doesn't sleep well.
he dreams of a mass uprising of bricks,
of boundaries collapsing all over suburbia,
of Sunday morning street warfare with flymos
and hovers clashing over disputed inches of turf,
of middle-class landowners with nothing to keep
their mortgages in. . .
secretly,

Tom practises hod carrying
Bob practises bricklaying
and Fred is doing a night class in sociology.
Julian is an existentialist and lives outside
of the restrictions placed upon him by the
constant problem of having no self to esteem
and no self to be 'ish' with
this however does not prevent his sleeping
with the gaffer's daughter who has
a Btec in Freudian hairdressing,
which means that everytime
she cuts someone's hair
they look like a dick.

The French Connection

Here Kev, you do writing
write us a poem
will yer?
To Julie
she sez she'll
giz it if yer can.

Din't use nee
big words mind
and nowt too puffy
just enough to, ye knaa,
get me end away.

How... it's just like
that police bloke
from Jersey in France,
innit,
yer knaa
Bergerac.

Cyrano de Bergerac.

Tracy's True Colours

Tracy has two babies,
one black, one white,
calls them her own private 'toon army',
takes them to sit in the stands.
One of them was once kissed by Kevin Keegan
on a day when the press were invited.
Tracy spends her child benefit
on season tickets and 'babygros',
breast feeds behind the opposition goal,
has a tattoo on her wrist of a magpie,
collects autographs like silver paper,
precious little names glued
on the walls of her nest.
Waiting for the landlord to come
and fix the gas fire,
decided her kids would be
better off in the care
of rugby union supporters.
Left a scribbled note;
black biro on white and
two kids wrapped in
a hand knitted scarf
in away colours.

Baz and the Freedom of the Press

Full of Hell,
Baz gatecrashes the chip-shop,
bringing down on the counter a greasy
newspaper bearing a colour image
of a topless model.

'It's a fucking disgrace, you should
watch what you're selling,
I bought them chips for my little girl'

The chip-shop owner is
caught somewhere between
bemused and terrified and
pours two lots of vinegar
on some wifie's tail-end.

He stutters meekly,
'But..but.. I only sell chips!'
Baz rumbles on about guards in Auschwitz
and then explodes,
'Bloody typical,
I bet you're a Tory,
Only a bloody Tory rag
would print this filth
and only a Tory would
wrap up my little girl's chips
in pornography.

'But....but.. '

The chip-shop queue
are nodding their agreement
and checking their wrappings
for nudes.

The poor bastard is sweating now
and apologising, he offers Baz
a free Fish and Chip lunch.
Baz graciously accepts the offer.
The queue warmly applauds his exit

Outside I remind Baz
that he hasn't got a little girl
and he reminds me
who's got the free lunch.

Marooned

for Seema

That summer was haywire;
a battered maroon volkswagon
and 'the Rye' blistering our
way to Dillon's doorstep.
Heavy headed in the 'Diggers',
we sold our wedding bands
and burned the certificate
in a stainless steel sink.
Now, we grow cosy out of choice;
exchanging vows in private,
Turning into the family we
always hoped for but guarded against.

Drinking alone
like the old days,
I no longer feel the pull of movement,
Finding inertia desirable in the
tracing of your spine.

I tear the back off a beermat
and write your name carefully,
I don't want to get it wrong.

George Charlton

Sea Coal

This is the coal coast. Where Seaham tilts seawards
Splintered suns float on the North Sea's pressure
Compounding best coal squeezed from strata

Between seafloor and rockbed. Below,
Sunken eyes lie back exhausted;
Cold currents unpick the sinews of men

Who rippled in earnest, coaling Imperial flotillas:
Both bone-cage and bulkhead fronds
Have fossilised in sea-salt.

Underwater siftings are washing
From the stokehold of the sea, poor nuts,
For sea coal burns badly, gives off meagre heat.

It has become derelict treasure salvaged
Out of an undertow. Coal has produced
Its own decay; coal-pickers who scrounge

Bent-backed on the water-fringe balance
Sacks on the cross-bars of clapped-out bikes,
Stretch their spines and look out gazing –

There, dead things have come from the sea to tell
Bleached tales to the hard-up and out of work,
Rumouring of desolation riding the slack.

Nightshift Workers

They have come from a factory
Where fluorescent strips flared all night

And ears grew numb to machinery.
They are going home to working wives,

To cooling beds at breakfast time,
Undressing fatigue from their skin like clothes.

Later to wake at four and taste teeth
Soft as fur in their mouths.

They live in a dislocation of hours
Inside-out like socks pulled on in darkness

Waking when the day is over.
They are always at an ebb, unlike others

Going out to work in the morning
Where sun and moon shine in the sky together.

Gateshead Grammar

There must be hundreds like us now,
Born since the war, brought up
In terraced streets near factory yards
And on expansive council estates.

We were the ones who stayed on at school
In academic quarantine. Others
Took apprenticeships in the skilled trades
And left us indoors to finish homework.

And we didn't notice it at first –
The literature that wasn't written

For us: passing an exam
Was an exercise in its own right.
To live like Spartans, think like monks
Had something heroic about it...
Now we dress carefully, and at
Introductions in expensive restaurants

Suppress the local accent in our voice,
Not to give ourselves away.
And little by little we go home less
To parents who seem to have fostered us.

We are like those bankrupt millionaires
With our own social success stories
And personal failures. Remaindered
Fashions at give-away prices.

The Lost Boys

They are here in quayside bars
By moonlight, their South American mustachios
Reminiscent of the places they'd take off to
If they could, career prospects blown.

Outside, a wall-eyed moon hangs round
In a night of green fog, and the ghostly ships
Await their embarkation
For the pale relief of the guano islands.

The water, not far off, keeps up
A muffled agitation with itself
Like advice given by acquaintances
Who could not grow up or settle down.

They have loved a lot of people
In their time, too many perhaps
To have done themselves good,

And appear not to have changed in years
As they sit at tables like the gods
In postures of exhaustion. Fatigue
Has smudged their eyes; their public bar democracy
And franchise lasts till closing time.

The Girlhood of Iseult

Clearly, I can see your past:
The isolated lodge
On the old road to the coast;
The girls, all sisters, younger
Than yourself -white knees, white
Ankle socks startle the grass.

There is an old horse, bridled,
And about to be saddled;
A dismantled motorbike
In the shade of the wall;
And the girls are at play
With maimed dolls, or matches.

I can see you stand apart,
Raised hand to your brow –
A salute to the strength of light.
You are wearing a light-checked girl's
Summer frock, pre-puberty's last,
As you turn your gaze to the fields,

To the shipyard cranes as far
As the sea, charting the course
Of the river. At the drop
Of a match the first crop's
Stooks will suddenly catch, the air
Smear with a watery glaze.

Benton Static

Whatever it has to mean, it has to do
With the fact that the generator
Has its own life to live, humming
Its own tune, mirthful, atonal;
With the tall whitethorn hedges
Thickening in season
As they have done for centuries.

It has something to do with a hidden paddock
Orphaned at the end of an unadopted lane,
New grass growing back at the edges,
The clover-munching sheep grazing there;
And an amateur gardener standing at ease
Resting the tip of his hoe
On a green raft adrift in leafy suburbs.

Somehow my own house is involved in it,
Its useless chimneystacks reduced,
The curtains drawn in the children's room
Already. And my neighbour:
His skill as a tradesman, the sizeable
Mortgage, like me, he inherits; his own business
Run from the back of a second hand van.

Above all it has something to do
With this enduring northern twilight,
A blackbird's uninterrupted song
In the midst of deep shrubbery.
It is two men on a pavement,
Strangers in passing, acknowledging
One another's solitary presence.

Brendan Cleary

The Exchange Visit

Well I woke up this morning
& I was in Czechoslovakia
a peaceful suburb of Prague
to be exact

it had rained
so the lawns all glittered
& I had a splitting head
from too much 80% Vodka
well presumably so --

the whole thing is a mystery
because now I talk the language
I have a Czech wife
three handsome healthy Czech children
for the moment their names escape me
a Czech house with a Czech roof
overlooking a Czech swimming pool

what luxury!

it's really quite some existence
I've carved out for myself
& I've read Kafka in the original
& all my old favourites like Philip Marlowe
in handy pocket-sized Czech translations

still I have a job remembering
how I fell asleep
beneath the shadow
of the lame cow
at the edge of Mulligan's field
in the drizzle
in the breezes whirling tractor blades
in the old sod

yes I have a job recollecting
how I woke like this hungover
in this suburb of Prague
which thankfully is very handy
to all of the shops

what utter luxury!

Newcastle is Benidorm

girls in Friday exit routes
in flimsy skirts & skimpy t shirts
all brandish castanets
& form a human party chain
to dance through Eldon Square

with the skill & dexterity
of bullfighters depicted
on trinkets & souvenir ashtrays
the' lads' in the bravado after hours
hover in doorways makin' moves

& safe sex hasn't been invented
& all the bars tonight were hivin'
& the sky's the colour of sun tan lotion
& i' d give a million to be so neutral
& everywhere has become a haze
of free offers & tabloid slogans

& disco rhythms insidious & thumping
& the crowd from the Pizza house jumping
into litter bins & pissin' on windows
selling fridge freezers & community singing
& groping hands & fumbling tongues at bus stops
& football arguments & the ringing
of alarm bells set off for 'high jinks'
& the stale boke on the floor of the Bacchus tavern
& all down the cubicles in nightclubs - stinks
& there will never be an armed uprising
against the Capitaist Conspiracy here
or anywhere else for that matter -
what a crying shame!...

'Here we go, Here we go, Here we go'......

Are you lonesome tonight?

this bar's too fuckin' bright!
the mood!, the atmosphere's not right!

you used to touch just about anything
& it would become adorable

now i'm drunk & want to give you a ring
& when I drink, as you know, I'm deporable

when I drink I want to go back
just back, anywhere! after a stack

of pints, rums, tequila slammers I'm reeling
these charades make me wonder if feeling

is just what happens on the T. V.
- the only thing that helps is my bed

& I could phone you now it's way past 3
you might say: 'Christ, thought someone was dead'

I might say: 'no, worse than that, it's me'.....

Unhappy Hour

So I asked her why she left,
it was because I am so ugly.

So I drink here at twice the price
with my desperate sad compatriots.

Him over there in the baseball cap,
that's Eric, his wife fell under a bus

& Big Arnold's mum has got cancer
& Rosie in the corner has lost it

by 6 most nights speaking in tongues.
But these people are my friends

& they matter, drunk in slum basements,
stumbling heartbroken in the sticks.

We drink here at twice the price,
it's our own glorious sad republic.

People are my friends & they matter....

The Death of Maria

There's this line from an old David Bowie album:
'learning to live with somebody's depression'.

That's me, I used to think, on the sofa by the telly.
We'd sit there night after night amid the adverts

& usually I'd be daydreaming of escaping it all.
I even invented an imaginery lover in my head, Maria.

She was Italian, sophisticated, bisexual & best of all
everytime I walked into a room she'd swoon.

But Maria kept fading away when Dynasty was on
or Family Fortunes for a laugh, she receded slowly

until the day you waved the electric bill in my face
& Maria just about disintegrated. Bits of Maria

all over the kitchen, swallowed by our rituals. A shame.
A very deep, hurtful shame, if the truth be known.

Long before I made Maria up I used to dream about you....

The Wedding

for Jonathan Richman

A black taxi from some posh territory outside Sheffield
down in my wedding gear half-blocked to The Leadmill

& Norman Hobbs had put me on the guest list, Jonathan
so I was led through the punters by doormen & you smiled

& wiped yourself with a towel & I wanted to mention
how on Norman's wife's birthday you strummed guitar

in among the waves at Tynemouth in rolled-up jeans
so we shook hands & I headed back to shenanigans

in the hotel where the Captain & Sarah danced slow
to their special song which I think was Wet Wet Wet

but should have been 'It ain't me babe' as 2 weeks later
she cut up all his trousers & shirts into tiny strips & left

so he verbally abused her dad who was a Wednesday fan
& years later he still watches out for them to be stuffed.

The Second Coming

The usual pre-match warm-up at Tommy's,
waterpipes in his Black Hole of Calcutta flat
& now this disturbing news of Rosser's forklift
& Stevie Close looks like Nosfratu The Vampire
saying 'it's grave' & i'm imagining the funeral,
like Gerry Moran he'll have The Eagles played,
Hotel California, the epic guitar solo at the end
& with his legs all mangled Rosser will be laughing
up in Heaven with all the other mediocre strikers
& just then Micky Miler spews up on the touchline
& that's just putting his boots on & i'm wincing,
looking forlorn to the allotments for a miracle
& low & behold one comes in the shape of Rosser,
boots over shoulder, humming in the sun.

Bob Cooper

In Wrynose Bottom

And now my teeth are chattering. The rain
smattering on my hood, stinging my nose,
as the clouds, like raggedy old dishcloths
left in a full washing up bowl, uncurl.
Homesick Roman soldiers straggled down here,
tinkers, leech gatherers, road menders, cooks,
stumbled along. They all got just as wet.
Shivered as they walked by the flooding beck,
cursed their luck. Tomorrow, like yesterday,
old Fords may get their radiators refilled,
there may be sun, lark's song, a quiet stroll,
someone may just stand, finish off their film.
But right now, the truth, I don't really care.
God, this is an awful place. So empty.

On The Newcastle Metro

And there with the overcoats,
smooth hair, gloves,
where people crowd in, crowd out,
like pollen, an unconsidered touch
of perfume, cashmere,
stays with me on the escalator,
sunlit.

The Day Frankie Nearly Died

It's six in the evening, the streetlights coming on,
though the Cathedral clock struck three minutes ago,
and I've already been to The City Vaults,
had a Tetley's, bought 20 Silk Cut,
then glanced in at The Blackie Boy,
where Tommy behind the bar said he hadn't seen you,
and there was Frankie near The Imperial,
pissed as usual, lighting a roll-up and trying to sing,
but he didn't see me so that was OK

while the *Marxism Today* guy crossed over again –
the old one with the pony-tail and tartan D.M.'s
who I'd try to ignore outside The Beehive
until he mentioned oppression and I'd got onto Stalin,
though he hadn't heard of Akhmatova or Mandlestam,
and he'd interrupted, said poetry was unproductive,
but, still in full flow, I'd switched to the Prague Spring,
flowers in the gun-barrels of tanks, then Jan Palach –
while Frankie sang on, to brighten up even your darkest night –
and I was reading Baudelaire when Palach curled up in flames,
Les Fleurs Du Mal for the first time, and a woman's hair
as rich as tobacco that I'd loved to have smoked, inhaled –
and now hearing again that hard-left tone as Frankie relights his tab,
holds his bottle like a microphone and continues to croon,
You just call out my name ... while the finger-wagging starts
and Frankie shouts over to me as the shoving begins

when this police car pulls up and they get out,
pull on their caps, then stand each side of Frankie –
and I'm sure they're going to lift him – but this Socialist guy
gets hold of the Safeway Cognac, steps to one side,
turns his back, stuffs a hanky in the top,
tips it, lights it – though no-one else notices –
then throws it at the car, and it doesn't explode
until Frankie falls over – or is he pushed –
then everything flares, purple blossoming light
and I see you over the road, running to them,

wrapping your coat round Frankie's hair,
shouting something so loud at the night
and our faces, like the Vltava, frozen over.

Andy Croft

The Neon Thrush

in memory of Paul Hogarth

I leant against the car-park wall
    When frost was neon-pink,
Weighed down by bags of shopping full
    Of New Year food and drink,
And tangled spools of tape uncurled
    Among the car-park litter,
A silent sound-track for a world
    Grown old and cold and bitter.

The freezing car-park might have made
    A fitting year's-end figure,
The word made skin and bones, clichéd
    As Winter's iron rigor -
But all at once a voice arose
    Among the shopping trolleys,
A song with which to juxtapose
    The century's human follies.

Confused by car-park neon lights
    To sing the coming dawn,
It sang instead the death-bed rites
    Of vanities unborn.
False dawn, false start, O stupid bird !
    An uninvited heckler,
Appropriate to this absurd
    And gloomy *fin de siécle.*

115

A proper Y2K poseur !
   As if to disregard
The deadened senses of the year
   It sang this false aubade.
This night is like a two-faced dream,
   The century's paradigm,
Where artless Nature can't redeem
   What humans do in time.

31 December 2000

Dives and Lazarus

As it fell out upon a day
   Rich Dives he held a feast,
And he invited all his friends
   And gentry of the best.

They made themselves a national plan
   To better the nation's health,
And help themselves to the public purse
   To better their private wealth.

Then Lazarus laid him down and down
   And down at Dives' door,
'Some meat, some drink, brother Dives,
   Bestow upon the poor !'

But Dives was a busy man,
   And Dives locked his door,
For England is a friendless land
   If you are old and poor.

Then Dives sent his tabloid dogs
   To bite him as he lay,
And print their teeth marks on his flesh
   And hound him on his way.

And Dives sent his merry men
  To spin *The World at One,*
And lick his weeping sores until
  It seemed his sores were gone.

And Lazarus he was hungry,
  And Lazarus he was old,
And Lazarus wasn't in BUPA
  So Lazarus he went cold.

And so it fell out upon a day
  Poor Lazarus sicken'd and died,
And Dives threw his corpse away
  Before his blood had dried.

And Lazarus he went straight to hell
  To burn for ever more,
For there is always the Devil to pay
  If you are sick and poor.

And it fell out upon a day
  That Dives sicken'd and died
And Dives he went straight to heaven
  (Which now's been PFId).

For Dives was a rich man
  And rich men know what's their's,
And when they've taken that they want
  To take the poor man's shares.

The rich will always feast and dine
  While others want for more ;
Unless the poor throw off the rich
  The rich will keep them poor.

And public medicine will not thrive
  While there is private health,
And there'll be no cure for England's ills
  While there is private wealth.

from Great North : Mile 1-2

'There must be a job gannin' in Sooth Sheels !' (voice of spectator)

The crowd is still too dense to pick up pace,
  You have to watch your step at every step,
And though your breathing's good you can't quite place
  The feeling in your knee as on you schlep
Towards the City Centre, past the Quayside,
  And up towards the bridge, the gateway South,
A fleshy flood-tide running to the seaside
  To meet the river foaming at the mouth,
Via Jarrow, Hebburn, Harton, up to Westoe,
  And all the pitless, pitiless estates
Where living is a well-thumbed manifesto
  In praise of unredeemed one party states.
Now Britain has its first North-East PM,
  But power's no longer weighed in tons of coal
Or block votes from the Durham NUM
  And 6.8% are on the dole.
Where public loss flows into private gain
  The River Tyne conjoins the Acheron,
And private profit meets with public pain,
  And Government-North-East is known as GO-NE !
Below, the swollen, muddy river flows ;
  Above, the pealing city's Sunday bells ;
And linking heaven and earth's a bridge that goes
  Across to Gateshead, where the angel dwells.

This is tomorrow's Guardian front page,
  The usual Tyne Bridge long-lens/aerial photo,
One of those half-true clichés which our age
  Believes can show what Britain is in toto -
As though the last two decades of defeat,
  Industrial neglect, decay, decline,
Could be redeemed by 80,000 feet
  In unison across the River Tyne.
Like Glasgow junkies, say, or Eton scholars
  Seen waving wads of starred GCSEs,
Or striped-shirt traders selling us for dollars,

Ibiza clubbers stoned on whizz and Es ;
Like England fans who drink in foreign bars,
  Or vigilantes looking for a nonce,
Redundant miners doing up old cars,
  Or like New Labour branches in Provence,
  Such images suggest we understand
  Our neighbours rather better than we do,
Until we see ourselves at second-hand
  And think the sepia images are true :
The Boro red, Toon Army/Maccam stripes,
  Brown ale, brown bread and avacado peas,
And all the browned-off, browning calotypes
  That separate the Tyne, the Wear, the Tees.

Part Mardi Gras, part May Day march, part Mela,
  This bannerless and minerless Big Meeting
Is like a weird, post-modern Miners' Gala
  (Without the beer, the speeches or the eating) ;
Our sweat's not spent to make the world's improvement,
  Our sponsors' banners aren't quite so exalted,
But right now we're not that much of a movement -
  This is the forward march of labour halted !
This carnival North-East's a mummer's play
  Where old Misrule rides round on Shank's mare,
The world's turned upside-down for just one day
  And every tortoise gets to beat the hare ;
A race with over 40,000 losers
  Where every loser knows themselves a hero,
The biggest heroes are the wheel-chair users,
  And Newcastle is Rio de Janeiro !
There's something in this sweating, chugging throng
  Of runners caught in Northern monochrome,
A place and time that's yours, where you belong,
  That makes you feel as though you're almost home.
Well not quite home - there's still a long way yet,
  (11.1 miles to be exact)
A lot more miles of agony and sweat
  Until your knee is well and truly knacked.

Methuselah's Losers

A quick one-two, a turn, a screaming shot,
   Back off the post, a run through the defence
To knock it straight back in, and though we've not
   Yet touched the ball, we're one-nil down against
A team whose youth and energy subdues us
And makes us feel a bunch of hopeless losers.

Because Methuselah's too long to go
   On Third Division league and fixture lists
We play as Losers and/or Meths - as though
   We only lose because we're always pissed !
There's better teams than us made up of boozers,
And being sober's no help to the Losers.

At least we are consistent ; losing streaks
   Like ours take years and years of bloody training,
It's hard to be this bad, you need technique ;
   So please don't get me wrong, we're not complaining,
We don't think being useless helps excuse us,
It's just that practice makes us perfect losers !

You do not have to win to feel the buzz
   Of sweat, testosterone and self-display ;
Part circus show (including clowns like us)
   Part theatre, part athletics, part ballet,
A game designed for gents that's played by bruisers
Who are long past their prime (just like Meths Losers)

Who, stuck in boring meetings, traffic lights
   And check-out queues, replay the games we've played
On Sunday mornings or on Thursday nights,
   The well-timed tackles, passes, goals we've made,
The unrecorded triumphs which enthuse us
Enough to turn out weekly for the Losers.

I like defeat, its sweaty, human smell,
    Familiar as a much replayed own goal
Or spannered shot ; this losing fits me well
    (Just like our too-tight strip !) and on the whole
I think a winning sequence would confuse us,
At least you know just where you are with losers.

While those who can afford it, cheer success
    Via satellite TV and sponsors' boxes,
On sweaty 5-a-side courts we transgress
    The age's most unbending orthodoxies :
To be the worst ! The thought somehow renews us :
Down with success ! And up with all the losers !

Not coming first's an honourable aim
    When winning is the only Good ; there's pride
In coming last, in losing every game,
    In being always on the losing side.
The games we really should have won accuse us :
Success belongs to others, not to losers.

Let's hear it then for those who're past their best ;
    Without us there would not be many winners,
We're here to make the numbers up, the Rest,
    To teach the art of losing to beginners ;
Their shiny, bright successes just amuse us,
For even winners have to play with losers.

So here's to hopeless losers everywhere
    Who know we're stuffed before we even start,
Who live with disappointment and despair,
    Who turn defeat into a kind of art ;
An army of dissenters and refusers,
We'd change the world - if we weren't such good losers !

Just as Blue

A breezeless, sunny, Summer day
  At Brooke House Farm, and I'm just four
Or five, a town-mouse come to stay,
  Homesick perhaps, and not so sure
About this world that's fierce and strange
  And full of things from story-books :
The giant oven in the range,
  The furnace doors I must not touch,

The home-made broom outside the door,
  The baking smells of gingerbread,
And everywhere the friendly, raw
  Tobacco smell of Uncle Fred ;
The cellar with its froggy holes,
  A fox head stuffed with marble eyes,
The fences hung with rats and moles ;
  The piglet wriggles in the sties,

The shippon gloom of dust and straw,
  The diesel stink of old machines,
The high-pitched smell of fresh manure,
  The dairy's chapel quiet, its clean
And polished, buttered, sunshine taste ;
  The angry, barking dogs on chains
Whose unleashed fury must be faced
  If I'm to venture down the lane.

But here, against the haystack sides,
  A ladder climbs to heaven knows where,
A stair up which, half terrified,
  I slither backwards into air,
Till half way up the clouds unfold
  Their magic carpet in the skies,
A square of blue enframed with gold,
  A vast and roofless blue surprise.
How close the sky appears from here.
  No child could ever paint such blue

As this, an endless, hurting, clear
  And lovely, lonely, trespassed view.
Within this blue I've built a den,
  A musty house of bales of straw
To keep out stupid one-eyed hens,
  And hungry wolves outside the door.

 How dreamy still and quiet it seems,
  As though the giant world is curled
Asleep and I'm inside a dream
  Of bean-stalks far above the world,
Where hay bales might be spun to gold,
  And happy endings are all true,
Where little pigs do not grow old,
  And skies are always just as blue.

As if I've had this dream before,
  Down tunnels made with itching legs
I reach to find, within the straw,
  A clutch of warm and feathered eggs,
Like magic beans which only grow
  When all the grown-ups are in bed,
Which lead to where all children know
  They grind your bones to make their bread.

The sleepy world below now stirs -
  The milking stalls' electric hum,
A distant tractor's muddy purrs,
  The background mumble of the glum
Suspicious cows, as they're pursued
  By Fe-fi-fo-ing dogs and men.
It's time to leave this solitude,
  The giant world's awake again.

Outfaced

'At 50, everyone has the face he deserves' (George Orwell)

'My shaving razor's cold and it stings' (The Monkees)

Near fifty years you've watched this long-lost twin
  Who watches from the bathroom mirror's glass,
A well-known stranger underneath the skin
  Who never lets a bleary morning pass
Without reminding you you're past your best,
  And that you have already reached the stage
When nothing you can do will help arrest
  The thinning hair and thickening lines of age.

Strange ritual game that starts each working day !
  In which you race each other to the sink
And while you scrape away the stubble-grey
  You stare each other out and never blink.
It's hard to say which anxious lines you've earned
  And which were given like a patronymic,
And anyway by now you should have learned
  Your understudy is a natural mimic.

There's clearly something in this mirror face
  That somehow says you really do not mind
If strangers want to put you in your place
  Announcing who your fizzog brings to mind.
When you were younger, people used to stretch
  Across the railway carriage aisle and say,
'You're Michael Palin's double !' (Cheese Shop sketch),
  'You're just like Michael Yorke in *Cabaret* !'

James Taylor (*Two Lane Blacktop*) was OK,
  But you knew it was getting time to worry
When like a dreaded loop from Groundhog Day
  Two strangers said you looked just like Bill Murray.
To think of all the men you could have been,
  Instead of this one life in which you're trapped.

(And if Bill Murray's your Platonic twin
   The Man Who Knew Too Little seems more apt).

Although some children from Years 5 and 6
   Once said you made a perfect matching pair
With David Ginola ! (without the tricks,
   The skill, the style, the good looks, or the hair),
The parallel's now usually some old codger
   Who always seems to win it by a nose –
Phil Thompson, Gerard Depardieu and Bodger –
   A balding race of ageing Cyranos.

 And recently you've met the helpful folk
   Who stop you at the bar to offer gladly,
'You are the spitting image of that bloke,
   The ugly one, from Men Behaving Badly'.
These days you really do not want to think
   What monsters they will soon mistake you for –
Something from *Men in Black* or *Monsters Inc?*
   Hell Raiser II, the thing from *Alien IV?*

But as you rinse the shaving foam away
   There is no doppelganger more bizarre
Than this old mug who mirrors your dismay
   And lets you know just who and what you are ;
Although you can't escape this stranger's stare
   Or hope that you could ever take his place,
He knows exactly just how much despair
   Dismay and disappointment you both face.

Edge

Easy to see why they thought it was flat
   On such a bright and windless day.
This was the view from Mount Ararat,
   The world a perfect circle of grey,
A bright, spinning coin in the palm of the hand

Contained by the sharp horizon's rim,
   A bucket of sunlight, full to the brim
With all that we know and understand.
Easy too to see why they thought
   This flattened, silver, well-scrubbed flood
Was made for them, each fish they caught
   A salty covenant from God,
Revealed in every rainbow scale,
   A promise that the sea would hold
   The hidden gold with which it's shoaled,
And harvest seas would never fail.

Hard to remember the first surprise
   When the morning was edged by the black silhouettes
Of ravenous long-ships, the fisherman's eyes
   When the round world was caught in his nets,
Violent and strange, too heavy to land,
   Too huge to be thrown back over the side,
   An edgeless map, washed up by the tide,
Shaped like a footprint found in the sand.

Easy to see on a day like today
   Why we believe that the world is a sphere,
As the tankers edge their oily way
   Along the slow horizon's frontier
Beyond the curving slope of the earth;
   And why we know we can't disown
   The promise that we're not alone
Painted in rainbow oils on the surf.

Beyond the mirrored edge of all
   We think we understand or know
The unacknowledged monsters crawl
   In the amniotic undertow,
The nightmare, hungry things that creep
   Slowly up the pebbled shores
   Of headlands washed by ocean snores
Where watching cliff-top sentries sleep.

The world's not flat but curved with longing,
    An endless, cambered plain of foam
We whittle smooth by our belonging,
    Ringed by the harbour lights of home,
From where we scan the skies above
    The submerged kingdoms of the blood,
    The unfathomed mountains of the flood
For our returning human loves.

Julia Darling

Be Kind

Be kind to white male southern students
who in post-acne anxiousness lumber
down the narrow pedestrian walkway
on their way to slowly open bank accounts.

Be tolerant. Even though they keep
meeting each other, neighing like donkeys,
swinging their half-cut hair and strappy bags,
standing in heavy clumps.

Don't think about their parents in Surrey,
or blame them for bending
your windscreen wipers, or roaring rude words
when even the birds sleep.

Or shudder at their purchases in corner shops,
Pot Noodles, Fray Bentos, Vesta and peas.
Or imagine their corner of a communal fridge,
their lonely anglepoises, their non-stick milk pans.

Perhaps they are homesick, worrying about
their parents' divorces, and yesterday's essay.
Or have agonising lovebites on tender shoulders.
Or are wishing they had gone to Exeter, or Bath.

So don't attack them on your bicycle,
grazing their shins as you pass,
not saying sorry.

They don't all vote Conservative
and pull their trousers down.

A Happy Childhood

When I was young I used to open drawers
in College Street; your life was folded there.
I'd reach in with my hungry wanting paws,
take anything I felt inclined to wear.

I knew that yours was mine and that your things
were free. I could take scarves or foxy stoles,
dress up in pointed shoes, your Sunday Best
your veils, your musky scents, your silks and voiles.

That's how you always made me feel inside,
as if each drawer in you was open wide.
Even dreams and thoughts were not denied.
I stole those too. You never seemed to mind.

But now I'm old, I know how much things cost.
I'd give them back, but most of it is lost.

Too Heavy

Dear Doctor,
I am writing to complain about these words
you have given me, that I carry in my bag
lymphatic, nodal, progressive, metastatic

They must be made of lead. I haul them everywhere.
I've cricked my neck, I'm bent
with the weight of them
palliative, metabolic, recurrent.

And when I get them out and put them on the table
they tick like bombs and overpower my own
sweet tasting words
orange, bus, coffee, June
I've been leaving them

crumpled up in pedal bins
where they fester and complain.
diamorphine, biopsy, inflammatory.

And then you say
Where are your words Mrs Patient?
What have you done with your words?

Or worse, you give me that dewy look
Poor Mrs Patient has lost all her words, but shush,
don't upset her. I've got spares in the files.
Thank god for files.

So I was wondering,
Dear Doctor, if I could have
a locker,
my own locker
with a key.
I could collect them
one at a time,
and lay them on a plate
morphine-based, diagnostically,

with a garnish of
lollypop, monkey, lip.

A Waiting Room In August

We've made an art of it.
Our skin waits like a drum,
hands folded, unopened.
Eyes are low watt light bulbs

in unused rooms.
Our shoulders cook slowly,
in dusky rays of light.
This morning we polished
our shoes, so that they should wait

smartly. Our wigs lie patiently
on our dignified heads.
Our mouths are ironed.

Acute ears listen for
the call of our names
across the room of
green chairs and walls.

Our names, those dear consonants
and syllables, that welcomed us
when we began,
before we learnt to wait.

Call us to the double doors
where the busy nurses go!
Haven't we waited long enough?
Haven't we waited beautifully?

Chemotherapy

I did not imagine being bald
at forty four. I didn't have a plan.
Perhaps a scar or two from growing old,
hot flushes. I'd sit fluttering a fan.

But I am bald, and hardly ever walk
by day. I'm the invalid of these rooms,
stirring soups, awake in the half dark,
not answering the phone when it rings.

I never thought that life could get this small,
that I would care so much about a cup,
the taste of tea, the texture of a shawl,
and whether or not I should get up.

I'm not unhappy. I have learnt to drift
and sip. The smallest things are gifts.

Things That Should Never Have Happened

I should never have eaten avocado
or pizza. I should have stayed with pies,

cabbage, neaps. And why did I
travel to Spain and Morocco?

I should have remained on this island
drinking beer, not wine. I should not

have navigated tunnels and crossed bridges.
I was better off in a home made boat

in a small harbour, catching crabs,
boarding insignificant trains, using Tippex.

Carrier bags have not improved my life
neither has gourmet cat food.

And I could have done without the menopause,
motorway service stations, nylon tights,

long corridors, imitation fires, imported apples.
And the past. I could have done without the past.

Satsumas

She is gliding out of Marks and Spencers,
carrying a clematis, a pound of satsumas.
It's just after five. Her legs are heavy.

There is the bus station, green wrought iron,
a woman in blue, selling the Big Issue,
a long coated man with a face like a lion.

She sees the stone angel that flies from a column.
And a child is laughing, a bell is ringing;
the bones of the city breath in a rhythm.
The starlings gather. She peels a satsuma
seeing a bank that was once a tea room,
before that a hairdresser, before that a lane.

She is bulging with maps, with lost streets,
threaded through her like silver. Stone faces
look from the cornices. Perhaps she is turning

into stone? *It's alright*, she says out loud
to the closing shops. *I'm still here. Actually*
dropping her bag of satsumas

watching them fall onto the tarmac, rolling
bright and orange, against the grey.
Living fruit and stone. The kernel of things.

Probably Sunday

One daughter is sleeping, her face unbuttoned.
She's dreaming of wardrobes, of sharp gold shoes.

Downstairs her mother writes her will
and studies investments, orders the past.

The mother's lover is at the computer
shooting dragons and snakes in a watery cave.

Another daughter runs a manicured finger
down a list of queens, memorising their deaths.

The dog barks in the hallway and the cat
examines a spider, then kills it.

We are baking potatoes, it's probably Sunday.
We are an English family in an endless terrace.

Alistair Elliot

Old Bewick

We come for a day of peace: the wick
of bees, the ripples widening on a rock
scratched by fingers that never fondled iron,
the lumpy mattress of moor, with cairns for buttons,
the curves of Cheviot and marine horizons.

We learn the place was given as a reward
to a Northumbrian who killed Malcolm the Third,
Macbeth's successor: crime and death
to delight, instruct and move. We thread the gate
onto the common, dazed by northern heat.

A mile to Blawearie. Something quicker than time
and rain has broken the grey abandoned farm:
somebody has been practising war. We eat
in sycamore shade, staying under cover
when a helicopter rises and slides over.

Three fleas hang on the skyline, trailing ropes
or legs or smoke. They hide and hop
over our heads, scattering turds of sound.
The curlews have to cry a little louder
to keep a territory on the Border.

For this is still the Debatable Land. In cities,
in rooms, you can forget the competition.
Here in the heather, when our earth lies open
and the sun takes it, you feel the very ground
of fighting, the fatal impulse to defend.

135

At Appleby Horse Fair

The young men stand in the River Eden
half-naked, splashing and washing their horses
to sell up there on the skyline,
but also parading
themselves, their thin teenage torsos,
their skeletons hardly hidden, their red skin.

Barefoot on the bed of the stony river
in soaking trousers, they appear to
be doing just as they want:
shouting unintelligible
words which then they squirt on
pinto backsides in green detergent.

But when the ponies regain their colours,
the lads shorten their grasp on a headrope,
jump on a back, and file
off up the hill in silence.
Selling your friends is a hard job;
it helps to do it with style.

MCMVI

In Memoriam James Adam Elliot, MD ChB (Edinburgh)
Glencoul, August 1901 - Clatterbridge, August 1991

The postman used to shout across the loch
till they rowed over. Once it was for Will,
from Carnegie. 'He's somewhere on the hill
getting our dinner. Who's this Carnegie?' 'Rich.'

Will was fifteen, the eldest, trying to teach
my father (five) his letters. In Glencoul
their lonely house was technically a school.
Their textbook might have been the Pentateuch.

Carnegie offered a fiver and a bookcase
for the School Library. So when Will came back
with the pony, the muzzle-loader and a carcase,
the boys composed a letter. They sent the cheque
to a bookshop, with two clippings from the *Herald:*
Everyman's Library Classics a Shilling Each,
and someone's Hundred Best Books of the World.
They'd fetch them in the boat, from Kyle, next week.

The boys have disappeared: the teacher, Will,
in France, of the same plague as Pericles;
my namesake died when No-Man threw a shell;
my father, of Medea's skin disease.

The books may well survive. The one I'd like,
perhaps on a tray in the rain now, marked '10p',
is *Vanity Fair,* in which the boy got stuck
half up the tree of knowledge. I would look
for the words he read, to everybody's glee,
'He was a man of charming gravy-tea.'

The Love of Horses

The lost people of Atlantis must have sent us
This weather, full of dying breaths.
The horses add to it, panting as we climb
The tearful slope;
So do the formally lamenting sheep,
Who miss their lambs and know who is to blame.

I'm on a highland garron, disgraceful Caesar
Whom everyone loves: a steaming nicotine-
Stained character with a black mane
And a humorous stolid look,
The sort that always tries to be last in line
But runs up hills with a dead weight on its back.

The fields were terraced by the people of Calroust
In the Middle Ages, and later walled. One field

Stops us; we cannot pass, because
It holds a mare and foal. In fact, the mare
Has already singled out my Caesar
Hung her head over the wall and met his eyes.

Solemn, they haven't noticed we too are silent,
To watch the very gentle slow approach
Of the two flaring noses;
Putting their long thin faces side by side
They discreetly snuff each other's essences.
This taking of breath - what could be more polite?

In a trance of unfamiliar fumes, they dream
(Looking judiciously over each other's shoulder)
On the art of overlapping forms,
On the truthfulness of odours, the grace of necks,
Round haunches, crooked legs, and have just reached
The aching loneliness of farms.

When Helen says cheerily, 'Oh, he's such a Lothario,
Caesar - but she's a thoroughbred and in season.
We'll have to go round.' I thought the mare
Knew a good horse when he smelled one. On we trot,
Thinking he might not ever again smell her.
That small rain from Atlantis tangs of salt.

Facing South

for Tony Harrison

Happiness, therefore, must be some form of theoria.
                         - Aristotle, Nicomachean Ethics, X,8
Theoria: . . . a looking at, viewing, beholding. . . 'to go
abroad to see the world' (Herodotus) . . . 2. of the mind,
contemplation, speculation, philosophic reasoning. . . theory. . .
II. the being a spectator at the theatre or the games. . .
                     - Liddell & Scott, A Greek-English Lexicon

Sat at my desk, I face the way I would
migrate: sunwards along this cobbled lane,
over the poplar trees of Elmfield Road,
across the Town Moor, up the mud-grey Tyne,
screaming with other swifts along the spine
of man-made England, eating airy food
and dozing in slow circles over Spain. . .
to the great desert where they still wear woad.

I had to buy an Apollo window-blind
to shut that out - the interesting sky
pours vagueness into the unresting mind
more than the prettiest-coloured passer-by,
more than the cars mysteriously left
unlocked by jolly women and dour men –
-so many people unafraid of theft –
I have to watch till they come back again.

I never saw a thief here. The one thing
that pricks our quiet bubble is the .roar
of comment from St James's - the fans sing
inaudibly, but bellow when we score.
Horror seems far away: our car-alarms
play the continuo of crime; we feel
the needles hovering near our neighbours' arms;
the viruses float in; but peace is real.

We suffer some illusion of control
in watching: so, the passenger keeps the car
safe if she watches the white line unroll;
the watching fans 'support' the football star;
watching the world wag past our café chair
gives us a sense of ownership: we share
some of that passing chic or savoir faire,
forgetting we are only who we are.

I must shut all that out. I want to make
these verbal systems in my workshop here.
Watching the world's a job too big to take:
I want to make small worlds that will cohere.
We have both travelled; south, east, west. I go
north now, quite near, where on the first of May
our earth relaxes and its rivers flow:
there I want nothing but to stay, and stay.

I could fly further; I've been free for years,
but don't migrate, for always there outside
in all the infinite other hemispheres
there'd be more sights from which I'd have to hide:
I'd have to take the blind, to blot out views
that would distract the wandering inner sight,
that pleasure Aristotle says we choose:
the blank I look at as I sit and write.

Linda France

North and South

Back in 1962 the world was
A foreign place I was just beginning
To feel at home in. I'd mouth and tongue sounds
My ears heard – Mam's clipped consonants, big sisters'
Sing-song vowels. And people understood.

Then one night was a dream of a red room
With wheels that kept me awake, stars spelling
South. South. South, where it never snowed and we
Would live in a nice new house and I would
Go to a nice new school.
No one warned me.

Hamworthy Primary was full of kids
With straw between their teeth that made them sound
Like lazy cows. Where I came from the talk
Was quick as flocking birds. We laughed out loud –
-No sneering behind hands, with rolling eyes.
Who's her? I cried inarticulate tears.

To survive, I had no choice but to try
To make my mouth echo back their fat *ain'ts,*
Become a chewing cow; or at least pretend.
I parroted their slow accents, even
Though the long feathers never really fit.
I plucked them out, the first chance I got;
But discovered I'd also lost, mid-flight,
My native accent I thought was bone.

In its place was this anonymous voice,
That sounds, to me, as if it belongs to
Someone else; feels two or three sizes too large.
The words and the spaces between the words
Ring with false echoes, false compass points.

Caracole

All my friends dreamed of a Pony Club heaven,
hosts of horses, well-groomed angels, chestnut,
roan, any nine-year-old girl would burn for.
Black Beauty left me frosty as a paddock
in winter. I never even had a bike.
But Paradise was Saturday night down
at the Labour Club, dashing white sergeants,
men in lipstick and sequins, stallion-eyed,
a clarinet playing *Moon River* over and over
until someone called Time switched the lights on
and everyone's face was yellow and singing.

The horses I liked were the ones at the front
my father backed, with thoroughbred names,
hooped and chequered jockeys and the flutter
of luck on their noses. I'd feel
their steaming breath quicken to silver
in my palm when Dad cantered home
from the bookies at tea-time.

And aren't I my father's daughter, a filly
who jumps and jumps and stays the course,
galloping across fields on a pony
I stole from a man named Shanks, putting
my shirt on the dazzle of chance,
no saddle, a loose rein?
And isn't heaven a saloon with plenty
of hooch and honky-tonk, flamingo women
singing like angels for all us gauchos
who'll go to bed with our boots on,
buckskin sun nuzzling the flat horizon?

The Meat Factory

The smell of raw meat is Chanel No.5.
It feels as if I'm right at home here
among the viscera, the flesh made new
and candy pink.
Dressed in disinfectant blue,
wellingtons, caps and rubber gloves, everyone
squelches on the tiled floor, stripping the willow
of troughs of offal to the dying chords
of the slaughterhouse next door.
Eggs are slotted
into the sockets of blushing, marbled pies.
Sausages are sleeved into cuff-linked lines.
Antique machines prick pat-a-cake pies,
six at a time for my baby and me.

Like summer rain, blood is never very far
away, the colour of the heart, the lights,
the sweet sweet breads.   .
Let me tell you, I've got the glad eye
for the boss of the chicken room, snowy with feathers
that tickle your gizzard, women cackling,
their fingers plucking. My skin is savoury
bumps. .
Lunchtimes we go upstairs to the canteen,
carnal with smoke and greasy newsprint, and eat
anything at all with gravy, counting
the notes in our paypackets, already
twistin' the gnawed bone of Friday night away.

Mess With It

'If you don't know what jazz is, don't mess with it.'
FATS WALLER

It creeps up behind you on all fours,
a reed between its teeth, so quiet
you barely notice. Until it's too late:
smoky breath tickles your neck keening
its sweetness and you toss back your head
in red surrender. The blood beneath your skin
runs hot as sex, cold as death. You borrow
its velvet pelt, watching your face lost
in the mirror of its Spanish eyes.
If you have to ask what it is,
you'll probably never know.

It's a secret for anyone with ears,
an inkling to dance like an oyster
with a black pearl heart. The sea
isn't deep enough for its blue.
It swims you till your lips are salt
and crazy. Never was an ache more
beautiful; like the love you fall into
too easy. If you don't know what it is,
don't mess with it.

It will score your belly with gorgeous claws,
tug your guts into tight cords.
You'll lose yourself in its glorious bite
and no one will believe the height
of your eyes. It will love you then leave you
with just a brush of silver on the rim
of your high-hat. And when the sun goes down
you'll catch yourself swaying to the fragrance
of sweating lilies, blowing their white horns
as if there was no tomorrow.
There isn't. You know what it is.
Love it while it lasts. Mess with it.

If Love Was Jazz

If love was jazz,
I'd be dazzled
By its razzmatazz.

If love was a sax
I'd melt in its brassy flame
Like wax.

If love was a guitar,
I'd pluck its six strings,
Eight to the bar.

If love was a trombone,
I'd feel its slow
Slide, right down my backbone.

If love was a drum,
I'd be caught in its snare,
Kept under its thumb.

If love was a trumpet,
I'd blow it.

If love was jazz,
I'd sing its praises,
Like Larkin has.

But love isn't jazz.
It's an organ recital.
Eminently worthy,
Not nearly as vital.

If love was jazz,
I'd always want more.
I'd be a regular
On that smoky dance-floor.

The Lady's Mantle Letter

She will write him a letter to tell him
  how cool and wet her garden is this July,
    how beautiful the alchemilla is,
      a strange citrus, petal-less froth above
        the green nearly-circles of the fanned leaves.

They are the shape of its other name –
  Lady's Mantle – an outspread cloak, pleats
    stitched with pearls of dew, scallop-edged;
      designed for wrapping and unwrapping,
        a honey-scented aphrodisiac.

'Alchemilla' is after 'alchemy' –
    the magic water it breathes through its leaves
      part of the ancient recipe for melting
        metals into gold. She will tell him
        what waiting is and what it isn't.

She will write him a letter to tell him
  these things because she's feeling inside out
    and he's not there to unwrap her, wrap her
      in his pashmina arms; and because
        it's him she's thinking about when, by chance,

she places three stems of purple crane's bill
  in the same vase and catches the shock
    of both flowers growing more alive,
      their colours spilling into something new.
      She will tell him how soft the rain is.

The End of August

The pink hollyhocks announce themselves
to the valley. The lower blooms are waving
their creased dark flags. The tight buds
right at the top will never open.

For twenty miles square there's no stock.
Only a single dog, barking for the collie on heat
over the fell. And the hollyhocks
at the window, smelling of nothing, swaying.

Stagshaw Dhamma

Somewhere in Thailand a golden statue
of David Beckham kicking the air, hair
keeping the secret of his eyes, is set
before the temple Buddha. The monks
don't know his name but the Abbot says
football is religion to millions and the truth,
if you look, is everywhere.
In a field
in the North of England I am looking
at the everywhere all around me.
The land is high and wide, so many shades
of green. It is one with the weather
and what we call time but is really the truth
telling itself over and over and us
listening to it,
hanging on the edge
of the golden light and the earth rising
up to meet it and the sheep who are eating it,
black faces chewing, fat hearts beating
beneath the floating highway of pylons,
the sky-soaked purr of a plane sailing past
the wideopen eye of a brimming moon.

The Simultaneous Dress

The trick with a simultaneous dress
       is that you wear it underneath your skin
and let it show through, like a fancy vest
       under net. What you get is what you think.

You needn't go shopping for tailor-made
       or off-the-peg as you can't try it on
and then take it off. It's just there – the grace
       of breath. Call it alive. Love it or not.

It isn't what's known as wearing your heart
       on your sleeve: your bones remember your dreams
and they change the world around you. Your last
       days won't be spent twitching every seam and crease.

All you really own is the light it holds
in its endless, simultaneous folds.

Cynthia Fuller

Her Story

Inside my head a woman
walking on a dusty road,
bare feet over baked earth,
flies hang in the heat.
Ahead the road bends.
I watch her.
There will be a gun-crack.
She will crumple,
a bundle of rags.
I will not be there.

I could write about the way
a fly tracks the black crack
of her mouth, about her hands
hardening in the sun.
I could write about what waits
at the beginning of her journey,
like a story.

I write the words.
I am not there.

I want to write
that she turns the corner,
finds water, shelter,
faces lifting, greeting,
home –
but that is not her story.

Adult Education

Spry the white-haired man with memories –
Mosley's fascists in Whitechapel – years
behind him giving an authority
over me to whom he is shyly deferring.

Tentative and beautiful with age,
skin sculpts an eggshell edge of bone,
a heavy-lidded grace, her eyes kindle,
light, with her mind's bold flight.

My life is a shallow pool.
I dredge the silt for shells
to offer these whose lives
stretch back behind them like the sea.

Easy Rider

Because her innocence alarmed me
(At 63 her eyes were wide and blue)
I took my mother to see *Easy Rider*.
'You don't think people are like that really?'
The shiny carapace I'd grown at twenty
creaked, but held. I had to think it.

I'd like to phone her now to say
'Sorry about that film.' We could laugh.
Cry maybe, twenty-five years on.
I could admit how I avoid the films
that sear my eyes with hate, with hurt.
I could admit my search for candle flames
in darkness, how wrong I was, that what
I took for innocence was hope.

Radicals

for HWJ, 1907-67

It was a campaign – playing records
loud enough to burst into the pauses
between *Workers' Play Time* and *Mrs Dale's Diary,*
threatening my dad's wireless cocoon.
And don't criticise what you can't understand.
The words hardened his mouth to metal,
drove him further back into silence.
A zealot, humming, I knew I was right.
The times they are a- changin'.
I spat rage on to the page in poems.
Politicians lied, parents were complacent.
My world shivered in soldiers' hands.

Touché, Dad, if you could see me now
your mouth would give one of those rare smiles.
The politicians are still lying.
I switch them off, adrift in the modern
on a ramshackle raft while
the old road is rapidly fading.
I'm avoiding the rapids, ignoring the fast track,
the whirlpools of quick information.
Paddling upstream, against the current,
I cling to the old wood of this craft
solid and outmoded as faith.

Carter's Garden

The spade's thin edge bites through turf,
turns back the cover on moist knots of worms,
insect legs scrabbling from the light.
Crouching to loosen soil from roots
I feel him there behind me breathing, close.

I work my fingers hard, watch
the clods' fine crumble, try to recover
my rhythm, the flutter of his breath
not sound, not touch, a stirring.
If I turn he'll curl back into air.

He watches me disinter small relics,
smashed glass, the cinders from his fire.
He knows the secret of the wire
snaking rootlike just below the surface,
the flaking shafts of six- inch nails.

His beds and dumps have made the contours, soil
rich on the right, the left stubborn with humps.
The day I dug into the mound
I called a grave – dog-sized – he watched
from the doorway, distant from my fear.

Keeping an eye on me in his garden –
my skin's shiver tells me he's there
behind me, benign – today he lets me see
across the slant of the spade's dark bar,
the flicker of his paler shadow slipping free.

Buried

The clang of boots on stone, the engine's shunt
between the shaft and ovens, steam from the baths
sending hot clean clouds into the coaldust air;
shift by shift men drawn from close terraced rows
down to the deep drifts – this should have left a scar;
the clatter and wrench, the jostle of tubs,
the jag and scrape of low-roofed passages,
the seep of dust, hands bruising a living.

If drowned villages can sound their muffled bells
under the sea, listen, for beneath
these impassive contours where field's return
to field erased it all – some giant hand folding
the earth right over – deep under its grassy cover
the colliery's clamour will be echoing still.

Sleep

I watch your sleep. It is an unquiet sea
where currents pull you into pain.
You stretch your hands against, towards, speak
in a nightmare language whose words slip
out of meaning, breaking, dissolving.
I watch your troubled sleep, watch over you
as if I could protect you, could turn
wild-cat fierce against what would harm you,
or with the gentlest touch could comfort you.

I think my love is only a small boat
out there on the dark water, tossing.
But the timbers are tight, curved smooth
to the swell, the restless motion.
In the night's immensity it will float.

Desmond Graham

The Accompanist

Knucklebones as big as chestnuts
playing the harmonium while I sang
hitching my short trousers
breathless at the high Cs,
for all the ferrets in my rib cage
piping out the 'Benedictus'
with a final squeeze,

Miss Grinstead, in half-mits pedalling,
pulling at the diapason
like a war-film stoker with a battered engine
full steam ahead,
and the bag of sugared almonds
past the last note
wrapped and tied to give me.

My father waited every Sunday
for her hands to fall like fish
on the bass part,
tear a stop out,
for her to pedal on
right through the floor,
but she was my accompanist,

I knew that if I broke
at a high note,
wobbled out of breath
with her playing,
if only with a clash of heartbreak
right across the keyboard
she would cover up.

She is learning her hands

She is learning her hands
like a flute player
with the little finger perched
on an inch of thin air
above the last stop.

She is playing arpeggios slowly
each finger depressing
a hammer of air
onto silence.
She has perfect pitch.

She is examining the find
of her hand's back,
levelled for the light's fall,
her rosetta stone
with the clue to creation.

She is closing her hands
on the feel of her fingers,
discovering cushions of palm,
seeing how far you can come
without skin touching.

She is tucking her thumb
between index and middle finger,
cat's tongue
left out
when she curls into sleep.

She is learning the space
between what the eyes see
and the hands grasp,
-assured of an arm's length
five fingers' dimensions.
   She is timing the gaps
within touch
testing one hand with another,
finding what touches is touched,
like a lover.

Prospero

He has covered the backs and shoulders
of half the former Gallowgate End
of the Toon Army and all the bikers
who sailed with him for the small time,
Prospero – Tattoo Artist;

his designs are legion: dragons wound
round the rib cage, purple tongues of passion
peeping out as snakes between the thighs;
a city side of Calibans he has transformed
with speech in the biceps, pectorals.

On Saturdays in summer you can hear
behind closed curtains sounds of the old days,
Zeppelin, Zappa, a whiff of dope and joss stick
clings to his leathers, a steam of pinks
and purples lights the evening sky.

Miranda long since left him.
Ferdinand wouldn't give a toss
to work for such a wanker.
Gonzalo runs the perfect commonwealth
in the cafe on the corner.

He has one place left to cover:
the deft left hand he always uses.
The north wind blows a sound
like great waves falling from St James's -
-the *Toon Army* is calling for its freedom -

he lifts his implement and we hear buzzing,
the pigeons leave his attic by the broken pane,
right-handed he inscribes a single letter,
'M'.

Rosalind

has legs long enough to make it
up the hill before anyone can tell
whether she is man or woman.

Rosalind ties up her hair and back,
puts on a beret, dun coat and ancient
trainers so no one knows her sex.

When Rosalind's at home, alone,
high above street lamps, higher than pigeons
camped in the treetop below,

she lets her hair down like Rapunzel,
all the way, then handful over heavy handful,
climbs back up to reach herself.

Rosalind is a translator, translates
from silence into thought; translates
back all the gabbled chatter

which surrounds her in the daytime
into what it really means: she is mistress
of all languages extending beyond talk.

Then, in the morning, she will lace
her big brown boots, pin up her hair,
and take her whole self with her everywhere.

The Pound of Flesh

The old synagogue turned to photographic
studio, neat vans with logo Antonio's-
zipping off to all parts piled high with mags;
Salvation Army, closed to visitors except
on Sundays when the silver instruments parade
downhill their tinsel and the abstemious
double-lock large cars; St Paul's,
the school and church set out with razor wire
and double fencing like a prison, the great bells
clockwork; the City Mission, where still the cheapest
cup of tea for miles is drunk by locals
out for the free heating; and that woman,
orange knitted hat pulled tight, check skirt
a sort of marmalade below what once
was herringbone, the thinnest sort of tweed,
a finger on the doorbell, no light upstairs,
but she still looking, waiting for the footfall
and the heavy route to where the signs declare
in front of faded curtains: Spiritualist Church;
and opposite, the Post Office where she queues
each Monday for her pound of flesh.

Jackie Hardy

Whale-watching on the Alpha Beta

This sea-horse is a bucking bronco
in a tidal race. My tranche is ten

to twelve o'clock, a piece of cake
that tilts time back, and forth.

In flotsom, my eyes imagine fluke
and fin, each white horse a hurry

of feeding gulls. For hours nothing
bigger than a harbour porpoise,

a colony of common seals. In and out
of islands, the sea frenzies with guillemots;

the air flocks with fulmers, shags,
shearwaters as thick as midges

on the Isle of Mull. The crew bait
me with fishermen's tales, the ones

that got away; yesterday's pod of orca
heading north, the school of dolphins

leaping to a rendezvous, the young minke
who nudged the dinghy while they watched.

Resentment rises like a stream
of diver's bubbles. Then I saw it –

distant, a back, a graceful arc, no more.
'Nine o'clock', I scream. We wait.

I win the Mars bar dangling from the mast,
seasoned now with spray, a sweetener

for sighting the day's first whale.
Today, the first and last.

Throbbing up the loch, past the cottage
with the bright pink roof, once

the captain's place, I stow memories:
my minke, a Mars bar, a sunburned face.

Correspondence

Your third letter arrives
and I read it through
three times. You write
of gardenias;
their awesome scent.
Gardenias and the garden,
the light and the heat,
the light and the shadows,
colours, smells and how lightly
life impinges in the garden.

I reply with leaden skies;
snowdrops. How they lie
drift after drift on the bankside
beneath the castle.
The way the wind whips
their fragile necks; pearl heads.
Even under heavy clouds
such a sweet perfume.
Galanthus nivalis.
How you will miss them this year.

Through my window

sidles morning
with birdsong;

the all-day drub of traffic,
sometimes softened
by the shush of rain;

at owl-light
an eerie toowhoo or two,
the harsh rasp of a dog fox;

and in the dead of night
when the wind is loud,
the whine of ghosts
caught in the telegraph wires.

Tony Harrison

Newcastle is Peru

'Correct your maps: Newcastle is Peru!'
(John Cleveland)

'Venient annis saecula seris,
Quibus Oceanus vincula rerum
Laxet & ingens pateat tellus,
Tethysque novos detegat orbes,
Nec sit terris ultima Thule.'
(Seneca, Medea, 375-9)

For defending in our Civil Wars
the King's against the better cause,
Newcastle got its motto: FORTIT-
ER TRIUMPHANS DEFENDIT.
After Nigeria and Prague I come
back near to where I started from,
all my defences broken down
on nine or ten *Newcastle Brown.*

A sudden, stiff September breeze
blows off the sea along the quays
and chills us; autumn and I need
your shoulder with a desperate need.
A clumsy effort at control,
I faff with paper chips and coal,
and rake out with elaborate fuss
one whole summer's detritus.

A good draught and the fire roars
like muted Disney dinosaurs,
and last week's Sunday paper glows
yellowish, its urgent prose,
like flies across a carcass, spreads
and fattens on the voiceless dead.
A picture shows lobbed mortar bombs
smashing down Onitsha homes.

The fire sucks in the first cold air
under the coverage of massacre.
The fire chatters, almost flies,
a full-fledged bird of paradise.
I lay down, dizzy, drunk, alone,
life circling life like the Eddystone
dark sea, but lighting nothing; sense
nor centre, nor circumference.

 A life-long, sick sixpennyworth
of appalling motion round the Earth;
scared, moonrocketing till Pop-
eye and blurred planets stop;
Switchback; Helter Skelter; Reel;
the Blackpool Pleasure Beach Big Wheel,
its million coloured lightbulbs one
red halo like an empty sun.

The *Caterpillar;* Hunslet Feast;
one hand on my first woman's breast;
darkness; acceleration so
we're desperate with vertigo;
then chained in solitary *Chair-*
a-planes through whistling air
as all the known Leeds landmarks blur
to something dark and circular.

Venus, Vulcan, Cupid stare
out vacantly on City Square,
and *Deus iuvat impigros*
above the bank where God helps those
who help themselves, declares
Leeds purposeful in its affairs.
Mercator, miles, school chapel glass
transparencies to blood and brass.

And *Self Help* Samuel Smiles was said
to have waltzed round our first bed
in our partitioned ballroom flat
with hardly room to swing a cat.
Worthies! Loiners! O King Dick
Oastler and his rhetoric,
and William Hey, the first to show
syphilis *in utero.*

O highlife crocodiles that went
round one palm tree in the bare cement!
The dizziness! That spiral stair
up St Vitus's Cathedral; there
the golden cockerel and great Prague
before us like a catalogue;
slides. Bloodless mementos, all
Time-Life International.

 And now with vistas like Earl Grey's
I look out over life and praise
from my unsteady, sea-view plinth
each dark turn of the labyrinth
that might like a river suddenly
wind its widening banks into the sea
and Newcastle is Newcastle is New-
castle is Peru!

Swirled detritus and driftwood pass
in state the 1880 *Sas-* .
inena Cold Storage Co.,
and Neptune gazes at the Tyne's flow
sea wards, where the sea-winds 'boast

and bluster' at the North East coast,
the sluggish Tyne meandering through
the staithes and shipyards of Peru. .

Shadow girders faced with sun
shimmer like heaped bullion.
Commerce and contraceptives glide
and circle on the turning tide;
Plain, Gossamer and *Fetherlite*
and US *Trojan,* knotted tight,
ferry their unborn semen, free
for ever from discovery.

Discovery! Slaves, now trains,
like *spirochetes* through dark brains,
tunnel the Andes, spiralling for zinc
and silver, gold and lead; drink
still makes me giddy; my mind whirls
through all my wanderings and girls
to one last city, whose black crest
shows all the universe at rest.

At rest! That last red flash
as life's last ember turns to ash
and riddled dusts drop through the grate
around the heart. O celebrate,
as panic screws up each charged nerve.
to cornering the next sharp swerve,
Earth, people, planets as they move
with all the gravity of love.

 First this Victorian terrace, where
small scars of the last World War –
those wrought iron railings made
into shrapnel and grenade,
acanthus leaf and fleur-de-lys,
victorious artillery –
are enough reminder that we brave
harsh opposition when we love.

This cluttered room, its chandelier
still spinning from the evening's beer,
this poor, embattled fortress, this strong-
-hold of love, that can't last long
against the world's bold cannonade
of loveless warfare and cold trade,
this bed, this fire, and lastly us,
naked, bold, adventurous.

Discovery! wart, mole, spot,
like outcrops on a snowfield, dot
these slopes of flesh my fingers ski
with circular dexterity.
This moment when my hand strays
your body like an endless maze,
returning and returning, you,
O you; you also are Peru.

And just as distant. Flashing stars
drop to the ashpit through the bars.
I'm back in Africa, at ease
under the splashed shade of four trees,
watching a muscled woman heave
huge headloads of dead wood; one bare leaf
for covering wilts in the heat,
curls, then flutters to her flat, cracked feet.

And round each complex of thatched huts
is a man-high cactus hedge that shuts
out intruders and the mortars thud
like a migraine in the compound mud.
Night comes, and as drunk as hell
I watch the heavens and fireflies, and can't tell,
here at my Shangri-la, Pankshin,
where insects end and stars begin.

My fingerprints still lined with coal
send cold shudders through my soul.
Each whorl, my love-, my long life-line,
mine, inalienably mine,
lead off my body as they press
onwards into nothingness.
I see my grimy fingers smudge
everything they feel or touch.

The fire I laid and lit to draw
you downstairs to the second floor,
flickers and struts upon my bed.
And I'm left gazing at a full-page spread
of aggressively fine bosoms, nude
and tanned almost to negritude,
 in the Colour Supplement's Test
Yourself for Cancer of the Breast.

Durham

'St Cuthbert's shrine,
founded 999'
(mnemonic)

ANARCHY and GROW YOUR OWN
whitewashed on to crumbling stone
fade in the drizzle. There's a man
handcuffed to warders in a black sedan.
A butcher dumps a sodden sack
of sheep pelts off his bloodied back,
then hangs the morning's killings out,
cup-cum-muzzle on each snout.

I've watched where this 'distinguished see'
takes off into infinity,
among transistor antennae,
and student smokers getting high,
and visiting Norwegian choirs
in raptures over Durham's spires,
lifers, rapists, thieves, ant-size
circle and circle at their exercise.

And Quasimodo's bird's-eye view
of big wigs and their retinue,
a five car Rolls Royce motorcade
of judgement draped in Town Hall braid,
I've watched the golden maces sweep
from courtrooms to the Castle keep
through winding Durham, the elect
before whom ids must genuflect.

But some stay standing and at one
God's irritating carrillon
brings you to me;. I feel like the hunch-
-back taking you for lunch;
then bed. All afternoon two church-
-high prison helicopters search
for escapees down by the Wear
and seem as though they're coming here.

Listen! Their choppers guillotine
all the enemies there've ever been
of Church and State, including me
for taking this small liberty.
Liberal, lover, communist,
Czechoslovakia, Cuba, grist,
grist for the power-driven mill
weltering in overkill.

And England? Quiet Durham? Threat
smokes off our lives like steam off wet
subsidences when summer rain

drenches the workings. You complain
that the machinery of sudden death,
Fascism, the hot bad breath
of Powers down small countries' necks
shouldn't interfere with sex.

They *are* sex, love, we must include
all these in love's beatitude.
Bad weather and the public mess
drive us to private tenderness,
though I wonder if together we,
alone two hours, can ever be
love's anti-bodies in the sick,
sick body politic.

At best we're medieval masons, skilled
but anonymous within our guild,
at worst defendants hooded in a car
charged with something sinister.
On the status quo's huge edifice
we're just excrescences that kiss,
cathedral gargoyles that obtrude
their acts of 'moral turpitude'.
But turpitude still keeps me warm
in foul weather as I head for home
down New Elvet, through the town,
past the butcher closing down,
hearing the belfry jumble time
out over Durham. As I climb
rain blankets the pithills, mist
the chalkings of the anarchist.

I wait for the six-five Plymouth train
glowering at Durham. First rain,
then hail, like teeth spit from a skull,
then fog obliterate it. As we pull
out of the station through the dusk and fog,
there, lighting up, is Durham, dog
chasing its own cropped tail,
University, Cathedral, Gaol.

Facing North

'The North begins inside.'

(Louis MacNeice)

God knows why of all rooms I'd to choose
the dark one facing North for me to write,
liking as I do air, light and views,
though there's air in the North Wind that rocks the light
I have to keep on, all year round, all day;
nor why, despite a climate I profess to hate,
and years spent overseas, I stay,
and, when I start to pack, procrastinate.

The North Wind's part of it and when it blows
my shutters rattle and the front door slams
like memory shutting out half what it knows.
Here I poured huge passion into aerogrammes,
the lightest paper loaded with new hope
that made the old pain seem, on looking back,
seen through the wrong end of the telescope
making it so small I soon lost track.

The window's open to the winter's chill,
to air, to breezes and strong gusts that blow
my paper lantern nothing will keep still
and let me make things happen in its O.
When the circle, where my hand moves over white
with red and green advances on black ink,
first swung like this it gave me such a fright
I felt I was on a ship about to sink.

Now years of struggle make me concentrate
when it throws up images of planets hurled,
still glowing, off their courses, and a state
where there's no gravity to hold the world.
I have to hold on when I think such things
and weather out these feelings so that when
the wind drops and the light no longer swings
I can focus on an Earth that still has men,

in this flooded orchestra where elbow grease,
deep thought, long practice and much sweat
gave me some inkling of an inner peace
I'd never found with women till I met
the one I wrote all those air letters for
and she's the one I'm needing as I see
the North Wind once more strip my sycamore
and whip the last leaves off my elder tree.

Now when the wind flays my wild garden of its green
and blows, whistling through the flues, its old reminder
of the two cold poles all places are between,
though where she lives the climate's a lot kinder,
and starts the lightbulb swinging to and fro,
and keeps it swinging, switched off, back and forth,
I feel the writing room I'm leaving grow
dark, and then darker with the whole view North.

Passer

His knuckle tattoos say: *Nothing and Futile:*

I'll kick in his knackers, boot straight to his bollocks.
I'll twist his tackle, he'll not toss off tomorrow!
His nob'll be naff for wanking for weeks!

Sigurd of sickbursts, brew-belcher, *Brown Ale,*
What *lot* or *dom* do such dickheads lust after?
Spewdom for starters, the Sat' day excesses
lack and lacunae in lad-lore and lager,
livid at life, lashing out in lads' lingo,
Newky Nirvanas, the nightly negations,
the doubled-up drunkard heaving his *humous.*

But soaks' slop's sustaining to the spuggy survivor:
the spuggy picks over the piss-artist's spew,
the *passer* picks over the piss-artist's puke,
unsqueamish in Corfu at squid-rings in sick slosh,
never nauseous on North roads at Niagaras of Newky,
slices of carrot in school crayon sunbursts,
Tandoori and *Tennants*, late nosh and Newky
devoured in the dawnlight, sluiced on to sidewalks,
kebab bits and *Carlsberg* gob-cacked, cataracted,
slivers of sleevers from last midnight's mêlée
tested for taste just in case they were juicy.
There's no lust for poison in the spuggy's spare spirit.
It's flight-feather fodder, spew is for spuggies.

Over boulders of gneiss, the bust kneecaps of Lenin,
the star-gazing eyes of horizontaled old Stalins,
pecking places for the *passer* (posh Latin for spuggy)
berries that bounce off the cracked busts and bronzes,
red hawthorn, pyracantha, the fruits of the May.
Look there, though, the spuggy, Bede's old soul
        symbol,
dodging the juggernauts to banquet on boke-bits.
The spuggy's the spirit Bede saw in brief transit
from darkness to darkness via being as banquet.
The scrabbled Cyrillic spuggies leave with birdclawfeet
's nowt spirit-lifting, but nowt nay-saying neither.
Spuggies sing as the light lifts, serenade the sun's
        sinking.

All meadhalls are measured by men at their margins,
the glee by the gloomfast, the song by the silence,
Sprechgesang by splutterings, Strad string by stranglers,
Puccini by punch-ups, *Tosca* by torture,
Callas by cattleprods, kilowatts to the cunt,
violins by the violence, cellos by the chokings,
the cabaret by the carton, built in the Bull Ring,
the paean by piss-artists, the beercan berserker
barracking the bardic, putting the boot in,
cornflakes or kippers by cranking the rack cogs,

snap crackle pop with the same in some cellar,
Gloucester's eyes acted by such deeds done daily,
curtain calls by kids kipping on kerbsides.
The scop scours the ruins for scraps of lost rhythms.
He once wrote *The Ruin* but on his returning
The Ruin is ruined, the writing has rotted,
the penmanship perished in fungoids or flamemarks.
There's no going back to piece it together
he looks through the lacunae to see Leeds and London,
the sacked scriptoria marked Stasi—Top Secret.
The *scop* of *The Ruin* felt like the *passer*
scop, spuggy, *passer*, the sorrowful sparrow
condemned to rewriting the gaps in *The Ruin.*

The willow herb waves once more on the wallstones.
The scop's messy mss. slashed with lacunae,
rubbler hyphen rebuilder, a walker of wallstones,
the *Wreacca-scop* walking Rome's empire in ruins,
pig troughs inscribed IMPERATOR or DIVUS,
cannibalized columns from Corbridge now Christian
upholding church masonry not a Mithraeum.
You might well bewail, in the wattle/daub era,
what the giants have built, but their buildings are broken.
If such great constructions should come to the ground,
barracks and bath-house go for a Burton,
it buttered the Brits up to crave their conversion,
made all things regarded vain, vanishing, frail.
Now Socialist strongholds collapse into commerce,
sold at streetmarkets collected as kitsch,
military medals a marketed melée.

Canta mihi aliquid. Nescio, inquit, cantare.

 Now ask that Caedmon to sing the collapses,
the megaliths ruined like the Romans before them,

The *Wreacca* met Caedmon and said: Fuck off,
         Caedmon!
Now Caedmon couldn't say: Cunt! back, now could
         he?

Initial Illumination

Farne cormorants with catches in their beaks
shower fishcale confetti on the shining sea.
The first bright weather here for many weeks
for my Sunday G-Day train bound for Dundee,
off to St Andrew's to record a reading,
doubtful, in these dark days, what poems can do,
and watching the mists round Lindisfarne receding
my doubt extends to Dark Age Good Book too.
Eadfrith the Saxon scribe/illuminator
incorporated cormorants I'm seeing fly
round the same island thirteen centuries later
into the In principio's initial I.
Billfrith's begemmed and jewelled boards got looted
by raiders gung-ho for booty and berserk,
the sort of soldiery that's still recruited
to do today's dictators' dirty work,
but the initials in St John and in St Mark
graced with local cormorants in ages,
we of a darker still keep calling Dark,
survive in those illuminated pages.
The word of God so beautifully scripted
by Eadfrith and Billfrith the anchorite
Pentagon conners have once again conscripted
to gloss the cross on the precision sight.
Candlepower, steady hand, gold leaf, a brush
were all that Eadfrith had to beautify
the word of God much bandied by George Bush
whose word illuminated midnight sky
and confused the Baghdad cock who was betrayed
by bombs into believing day was dawning
and crowed his heart out at the deadly raid
and didn't live to greet the proper morning.
Now with noonday headlights in Kuwait
and the burial of the blackened in Baghdad
let them remember, all those who celebrate,
that their good news is someone else's bad
or the light will never dawn on poor Mankind.

Is it open-armed at all that victory V,
that insular initial intertwined
with slack-necked cormorants from black laquered sea,
with trumpets bulled and bellicose and blowing
for what men claim as victories in their wars,
with the fire-hailing cock and all those crowing
who don't yet smell the dunghill at their claws?

Fig on the Tyne

FOR SIANI, ON HER BIRTHDAY

My life and garden, both transforming,
thanks to you, and global warming;
started today to intertwine
tasting my first fig on the Tyne.

When I heard scientists predict
there'd be apricots and peaches picked
in Britain's South, and *pinot noir*
where the rhubarb fields of Yorkshire are,
the pithill *pinot* from lush vines.
ripening on demolished mines,
a Rossington *viognier,*
Sheffield *shiraz,* Grimethorpe *gamay,*
fancy made a sun-kissed fiction: -
Dionysus redeeming dereliction.
Dionysus! Wishful thinking,
sitting in Doncaster drinking
in Southern sun that lasts all day
a local Donny vin du pays.
No sommelier worth his salt'll spurn
Gewurtztraminer from Wath-on-Dearne!
No longer would we need to traipse
through airports to the lands of grapes.
No more queuing at Heathrow
when we grow all they used to grow.

There'll come a day no Loiner needs
to go beyond the *caves* of Leeds
to sup champagne that's bottled where
they throw their empties in the Aire.
The South creeps Northwards, some say sweeps,
swapping *Beaujolais nouveau* for neaps.
This vision of Yorkshire by the Med
no doubt won't come till I'm long dead.
Torridity in Tyne and Wear
won't come till I'm no longer here.
Predictions for this land of plenty
start, at the soonest, 2020,
which is cutting it a wee bit fine
if I'm to bask beside the Tyne.
Sometimes I have to fantasize
I'm living under bluer skies,
but today I had a little sign
here in Newcastle-upon-Tyne.
Not just that this year's birds are late
leaving the North-East to migrate,
they linger, O they're welcome, they
still sing for me at break of day.
Some prophets that I've read believe
there'll come a day the birds don't leave.

The sign I mean was true but small
and grown against my garden wall.
If the scientists' prediction
isn't all just wishful fiction,
I thought once, why, if Leeds grows wine,
can't I grow a fig tree on the Tyne?
Why not, if the River Aire's
going to wind through wine hectares,
assume the scientists really know
and plant something that needs sun to grow,
more sun than usually comes its way
in Newcastle or Whitley Bay,
and here, on Tyneside, I'll install
a fig on my least sun-starved wall,

and wait for global warming to produce
figs oozing with full taste and juice.
'Fig trees don't grow in my native land'
wrote Lawrence, when his work was banned.
The climate's changing, figs do grow
(and franker paintings go on show!)
though not like San Gervasio,
where the starved Midlander Brit
found figs as 'fissure', 'yoni', 'slit'.
All those eyesores and black spots
bulldozed flat in his native Notts,
wait the creeping South's advance
to metamorphose into France.

The climate he was restless for
would come up to his own front door.
I tell him now, the man who grew
one Northern fig, that it's not true:
If you want figs, stay put in Notts,
trust global warming, you'll have lots.
In parts of Europe blessed with sun
I've picked hundreds. Now, here, one.
I've roamed about in similar fashion
seeking Southern fruit and passion.
His restlessness fed into mine
though I've always come back to the Tyne.
Though my life's been a different story.
I've been 'ὸ ποιητης' and 'Il Signore'.
Places where he used to go,
Italy, New Mexico,
I've also been to, half-inclined
to leave everything at home behind,
then on Guatavita's shores I found
gold everywhere just on the ground.
I come to El Dorado and I find
exactly what I'd left behind!
Too busy being Pissarro
ever to let my garden grow
anything but those tough weeds

I've known in Newcastle or Leeds,
this gold I came to look upon
with an 'O my America' of Donne,
this El Dorado in my head,
when I found it, only led,
after all the searches I got high on
to the El Dorado dandelion.
That was my discovery,
poet/Pissarro of the *piss-en-lit!*
All that we search for when we roam
is nowhere if not here at home.
I picked one for you, and pressed the head
of that Andean piss-a-bed,
and now this one fig I discover
I want to share with you, my lover.
I never thought that it would grow
when I planted it ten years ago.
I decided this was what I'd do
about the same time I'd met you.
I watched it grow and much away
feared it'd die, but now, today,
September 20, '99,
your birthday, love, here on the Tyne,
not flooded yet in Grecian sun,
I picked one fig from it, just one!
I picked the first fig that I'd grown
but tasted its sweet flesh alone,
when I'd wanted, O so much, to share
the fig with one who wasn't there,
you with whom I hope to see
years of figs from that same tree,
I'd wanted here to cut in two
one half for me, one half for you,
to celebrate the first sweet sign
of global ripening on the Tyne
and with the first of my Tyne figs
celebrate you're 46!

I never thought the tree would root

let alone produce a fruit,
I've seen it, like our love, survive
from when you were only 35.
That's almost the length of time it took
to pick this first ripe fig to suck.
My heart too has felt the South,
that puts this fig into my mouth,
warm my heart's North at a time
life's forecast as a colder clime,
and, in the heart's depths, it renewed
love in life's last latitude.
And now today you're 46
and far from the first of our sweet figs.

I've watched it ripen from where I sit
at the kitchen table candle-lit.
I've watched it ripen at each meal.
Facing the autumn now I feel,
as reflected candle on the wall's
flickering, licking the fig, like you my balls,
so lost without you, that I've plucked
the sweetest fig I've ever sucked.
Such flavour, sweetness! Half's a feast
though ripened in the chill North-East
ripened through gales and CFCs
warming the globe a few degrees,
and by the shredded ozone layer
and, I confess, my loving care.
(Because my fig tree's far from Greece
I protect it now with garden fleece.)

I ate my half and then thought yours,
 like kids leave cake for Santa Claus,
should be left out on a plate all night
with the half-burnt candle left alight,
so tomorrow, when I woke, I'd know
you'd come to me from Tokyo,
where, as I picked, you'd been performing
among typhoons born of global warming

Goneril in Shakespeare's *Lear*.
But I know you won't be here,
to share the fig picked from my wall
with a ripeness that we know is all.
But so it wouldn't go to waste,
and longing for my favourite taste,
just as Kent said his *Alack*
(Act V, scene iii) I ate the black/
deep ruby bit I'd left for you
just as your corpse came into view.
May the both halves that I've eaten,
like 'an ounce of civet', sweeten
my imagination when I brood
alone on this bleak latitude,
trying to make my simple rhyme
obey the weight of this sad time,
but honour, too, rare days of joy
that death or distance can't destroy.
In Japan your curtain falls
and all the corpses take their calls.
Happy birthday! I'd raise a glass,
if those prophecies had come to pass,
of Bradford bubbly or Leeds *Mumm,*
though unhappy that you couldn't come,
being borne with Regan on a bier
as the deaths piled up in *Lear,*
to the sweetest woman that I've known
 most welcome to the figs I've grown.
Next September if you're freer,
and raised from the corpse-pile of *King Lear*
we'll celebrate your birthday here
with storm-ripened fruit. 46
leaves life enough for future figs,
and I still hope to suck a few
though this year I turned 62!
May whatever's left in yours and mine
bring figs like my first fig on the Tyne.

W. N. Herbert

Touching Lot's Wife

It's that God again; the sort of deity
who doesn't need to use our viruses,
our gases or our bombs, when He feels
like searing out some thousands of us.
Can't you recognise His handwriting in
that angular strafe of lightning? Any
graphologist would say: 'Dominating, but
creative.' That Geordie mother is
impersonating him right now, stabbing at
the little vertical loaf that was Lot's wife,
showing to her daughters how
this whole world billows at Jahweh's whorl.
I shudder too, still believing it's not nice
to touch art, wondering: would that finger,
placed on her children's tongues, taste
of more than her own salt? For this
vast canvas has that old God's finger-
print all over it, stirring the too-hot
porridge that was Sodom - or Gomorrah,
she's not saying. Maybe it's too near to home
to ask why this great foundry of souls
was lit and then put out, as if
the generations were a flicking switch:
ON the keyboard kids, OFF the coal-caked miners.
It looks like a fleet of dreadnoughts, gone
down burning in some massive Corryvreckan.
The father stands to one side, slightly
bored by all this dried-up daubing,
like squares of camouflage

between us and the work-starved streets,
maybe abashed by Lot's daughters being
first offered up to would-be angel-rapers
then lying with Lot anyway, drunken in the fells,
to give life to Moab and Ben-ammi.
Perhaps one daughter no longer equals one angel,
and no one's seed now seems to need such
preserving. Is he too noting the hot
invisible spirtle this kind of God employs
for destroying His bowl of bad men?

The painting has stopped quivering.
The nuclear unit leaves, leaving me
to see something further, not Lot's wife as
the original fag-hag, caught in a blash
of oceanic sperm, nor the Jackson Pollock that
John Martin made of his sky, but
a single fingerprint, filling the frame,
composed of myriads of salty fingertips:
a whole city pointing, identifying by
their uncowed need to touch, their own refusal
to dodge or budge or be extinguished.

Garibaldi's Head

_a læg se græge wulf _e bewiste _ret heafod, and mid his twam
fotum hæfde _aet hæfod beclypped, grædig and hungrig, and for
or Gode ne dorste _æs heafdes abyrian, [ac] heold hit wid deor. '
ÆLFRIC's Life of St Edmund

Kick it down the hill, you blue-brained kids,
bury it deep in the nearest to woods
that Blaydon's got.
Thank your longest straw there's not
a red-shirt she-wolf hereabout
to dig the head of the patriot up,
put her paw upon it, and treat it like her pup.
Gather up the flies from his trunk of liberty,
mash them into biscuit mix and nibble for your tea
on the very idea
of beatifying radicals in stone.
Statues should be admirals, aristocrats, Homerical;
a foreign common hero is just tastelessly chimerical.
Bury deep the thousand-headed mob-dog's bone.

But Garibaldi's head will not be good, stay hidden;
though you dunk it into duck-pond,
though you muddle it with midden,
it still serenades the severed moon, a hopeful sound;
although you've tried
stuffing up your doctrines with bog rhetoric and pride,
society's the pitch you can't punt the head outside

of. Coffin up his torso in an estuarial pile,
blue-plaque his genteel Tynemouth lodgings,
wear your retriever's newsprint smile,
explain he was a royalist and full of moral fudgings,
clench your fist:
remember how King Edmund's corpse united with his head;
God darned his throat together, left a single scarlet thread.

That's the common hue that still repairs the trousers
on faith's arse, grind down your teeth with biting
as you will, but you're ageing Tory towsers
and you'll never pass for vikings
now, still less sharks.
Having lied through plenty daylights you can lie there in the dark
and listen through the illness for the three sharp barks
you know, despite the knowledge that your noodle's growing mouldy,
mean 'Bring me the head of Guiseppe Garibaldi!'

*'In 1868, a statue of Garibaldi was erected on Summerhouse Hill. The statue was
slightly larger than life size, and showed Garibaldi, holding the telescope and wear-
ing the sword with which he'd been presented in 1854, looking eastward down the
Tyne. The statue was sculpted by George Burn of Newcastle.*
*About 1900 the statue was toppled from its plinth and rolled, broken, down the
hill. Due to this the head, exhibited here, shows signs of damage. It was found in a
builder's yard in Blaydon in 1941, and donated to the library in 1977.'*
— Inscription in Blaydon Library

Bede's World

On the metro to the monastery I ping out
a filling whilst picking my teeth with a pen top,
pop it back into place and bite down hard.
It stays. I get off at Bede Station and make
pilgrimage through industrial estate;
by dual carriageway I walk me along.

Soon there is no pavement, just a track
around the timber yard and over a weak bridge:
'BUY AN OUNCE AND YOU'LL BE STONED ALL DAY'
grey spraypaint on its blue metal side advises.
Instead I visit Bede's World.

A longhair,
more gonk than monk, meditates with plastic bag
in the grounds of St Paul's, while I pass

an Asian couple in matching sky-blue
grinding gently together in the lane by the Don
where the kitchen garden would have sloped.

I have gone the long way round to get in
to the eighth century it seems, looking back
over the wall at cranes and drums and half-
empty car-parks hemmed in by a fence of pylons
and the lack of ships in Tyne Port.

The kids, who may not be alright, have kicked
in the floodlights, taking out portions
of fourteenth century with them. I check out
the interior for lumps of vinescrolling
and the Jarrow lectures: 'The Codex Amiatinus
and the Byzantine element in the Northumbrian
Renaissance', 'Early Christianity in Pictland'.

The women minding the church's shop have
an engrossing rosary of others' ailments
to recite, filling the site with a locality
its surroundings continue to deny.

The museum most of all – with its salmon-
pastel round of brick and paddle-pool blue
of fountain, more atrium than cloister,
more Roman than Catholic – is not here.

 Inside you pick up telephones to hear
the Gododdin spoken in Old Welsh,
like cricket results or the weather,
and think how fleetingly theme parks catch
the attention of their visitors, like

a swallow flying into a hospital ward,
full of a terror shared by those in every bed,
battering itself off too much glass before
finding a way back out into the world.

Outside, withies and wattles prevail,
old breeds of hog and sheep and bull
from Ronaldsay and other outer zones
are clustered in the dark age hollow,
emmer, spelt and einkorn grow together in
the one authentic field, while a timber hall
and grubenhaus are being copied from
genuine remains.

        Only this incompletion
seems real: the workmen's radio tuned in
to a golden hour as None approaches is
as dependable as Bede's voice singing
'Ter hora trina uoluitur'; the photocopied
labels on the fences as trustworthy as
the copy of his Historia displayed
indoors as a superb example of Insular
miniscule script.

        Only our discrepancies
are real here; our marches in the face
of parliament, our writings in despite
of the vikings, even our theme parks
in the midst of recession, are bits
picked out from the sad mixture flowing
between black mud banks and made our own.

The Manuscript of Feathers

Saint and hermit send
each other news by seagull.
They never meet.
They never speak.
They do not discuss
the date of Easter.

Cuthbert on Farne is tempted
by the fur of sea-otters: it is like
the detached pudenda of the mermaids.
The moon is like their breasts:
it presses coldly on the shut balls of his eyes,
it fills their sockets with softness.

Herebericht is safe within his lake,
islanded from demons, speaks
with the freshwater fish about
the scent of home, its wholeness
of moss and quartz.
After this they offer themselves
to the roasting tongue of his cooking stone.

Cuthbert is beset again by gold:
coins of it leap from the evening waters
and cover his raggedy blanket,
every inch chinking with
a drowned king's hoard.
Otters sit outside his hut
and toast him with sunken wine.

Herebericht has visions of apocalypse
in which the world is reduced to islands,
in which the sea is flame,
in which each human sits, naked, sweating, watching
the tide eat at their shorelines.
He sniffs at the pebbles.
They smell jaspery.
They smell of Heaven.

The gull they send between them
carries no messages
scrolled around its leg.
Instead it is itself illuminated:
every feather written on in script
which only they can read.

Song of the Longboat Boys

Well we've been sailing all day through the ice and snow,
we've got this little wooden compass tells us where to go;
now some folks say we like to ravish and rage
but a viking's got a right to earn a living wage
in
> *Northumberland thumber thumberberland*
> *Northumberland thumber thumberberland.*

Well our boss is Erik Bloodaxe he's a bit of a dork:
he wants to settle down in this place called York,
but we're all far too young we wanna filch and fight
and gan oot wi the lasses on a Saturday night
in the

> *Bigg Bigg Bigg Bigg Mar-ket Biggbigg Mar-ket*
> *Bigg Bigg Bigg Bigg Mar-ket Biggbigg Mar-ket.*

Well we hear there's aal these lads who like to dress in gray
and sing their Christmas carols in the kirk aal day:
they get a lot of leather and they call it a book,
then they cover it in gold - we'd like to take a look
in
> *Lindisfarne disfarne Lindisdisfarne*
> *Lindisfarne disfarne Lindisdisfarne.*

Well Olaf's got an axe and Gunnar's got a spear
and you oughta see our boat cause we made it last year;
we're gonna crack your skull and burn your neighbourhood
but then we'll build this cool store and sell you bits of wood
in

> *Northumberland thumber thumberberland*
> *Northumberland thumber thumberberland*
> *Northumberland thumber thumberberland*
> *Northumberland thumber thumberberland...*

(Continue until interrupted by a chorus of Geordies):

'Woh! We're gannin to IKEA! Doodleoodleoodoo...
Woh! We're gan to buy some flat-packs! Doodleoodleoodoo...'

A Breakfast Wreath

Walking down Newgate Street on a Saturday morning
I saw a rasher of fatty bacon lying curled
on the pavement like an ear and thought:

who'd rather have bacon when they could have earholes,
an audience of thousands falling as accidental as snow,
and what if snow is not an accident?

I thought of Mary Trewhitt in St Andrews graveyard
since 1783, on whom all the snow has already fallen:
who'd listen to her smothered story?

Just 45 when Francis the shipbuilder
dropped dead on Christmas Day, and then their son
at 29, and 'Likewise are deposited here

Two Infant Children' of her daughter Jane.
What Novocastrian would stop to hear her?
Even I will not be back: my capacity

to maintain a habit is so poor
as my grandfather's Norwegian guitar knows,
as volumes on the Gaelic and Italian languages mutely
            witness from my book shelves;

as the tobacco fields of Virginia,
the tea fields of Darjeeling, the cannabis crops of Morocco
and the barley fields of Moray can all attest.

But for the sake of Vincent Van Pig, whose poor lug lies
on the corner of Newgate and St Andrews Streets
(formerly Darn Close and I'm sure he thought so too),

and for your sake, Mary, I place
on your grave these metaphoric flowers:
the fried eggs of yellow flags and narcissi,

the sausages of bullrushes and
the black puddings of dark violets,
the bacon rashers of roses and peonies.

Bite on this wreath with your single tooth
as the pavement jaws of Newcastle
chew on the city, and do not haunt me.

 After a while we have to go away
carrying the milky, unformed souls
and such nourishment as we are thrown.

We're given so small a role in our dissolution
it surprises us to learn
that it exceeds our personality

as a city exceeds the habits
of its inhabitants. So take the ghost
of that pig and board your husband's ship:

it's been waiting for you these two hundred years,
floating in an ebb-tide of the ears
of the listening dead, and the flowers

of the unlistening living. Sail into the foundations
of everything we try to build on grief,
sail into those stones, and do not haunt me.

The Entry of Don Quixote into Newcastle upon Tyne

He comes by Lambretta over the Tyne Bridge
with a lamppost for a lance, having just crashed
a transit van into the Angel of the North
declaring 'Protect the South from drear Boreas.'
The compressed, and screeching van still follows
with Oliver Hardy at the wheel, his Panchez,
still dressed in his coonskins à la *The Fighting Kentuckians,*
with a soundtrack of Handel via Zappa blaring
from a large rectangular megaphone.
Quixote, played as always by Peter O'Toole
as in *The Man of La Mancha*, ignores
the drivers who hiss, 'Don't sing!'
Having just slung seventeen bowling balls
at the Metro Centre-as-Leviathan and
attempted to liberate the pensioners from
the singalong at Harry Ramsden's,
he steps on the northern shore of the Tyne.

And has the crap beaten out of him at once by lasses
outside *The Pitcher and Piano* on a Friday night
for singing madrigals in Foreign.
He is thrown out of the Civic Centre
for interrupting every marriage ceremony with,
'Think of the unborn: give Limbo a chance.'
He is moved on from the War Memorial for yelling at
the frieze of marching dead, those who answered 'The Call',
'Look! Look the other way!' while Ollie
drops a vast banana skin before them.
He is given a cup of tea in St Thomas the Martyr's
for explaining they shouldn't 'Hate Evil'
as their slogan advises. He charges the Magpies during
a crucial fixture, convinced that eleven
cannot be a lucky number. Quixote is played,
as always, by Miguel de Unamuno.
The Toon Army chant 'Get back, get back,
get back to Le Pays Basque!'

He is chased by a herd of Range Rovers from Acorn Road
for attempting to give the rather plush contents of *Oxfam*
to the man selling *Big Issues* opposite,
then releasing tilapia and witch sole down
the drain outside Taylor's fish shop.
He is thrown out of an architectural salvage company
for brandishing a lump of wormy wood
and shouting, 'This is the stool
of Ignatius de Loyola: I can smell upon it
the buttocks of my physician father!'
He delivers a skipful of cigarette butts to the tenants
of the yuppified Wills Building; tries
launching Hardy down the slipway at Swan Hunters;
mans the reconstructed section of Hadrian's Wall
exhorting the Scandi-looking passers-by
to 'help defend us from these monstrous Picts'.
He breaks into the Formica factory with a petition
signed by obviously-fictitious anteaters
demanding they stop extracting formic acid from
queen ants just for kitchen worktops.

Quixote is played as always by Pierre Menard:
the queen ants squeak, 'Now write something by Borges!'
His Dulcinea is a lollypop lady in North Shields
sighted trailing the disk of her lollypop along the pavement
until it sparks, and puffing on a Regal. Just for her
he joins in the medieval joust at Tynemouth Priory
a little too vigorously, armed only
with a magican-opener and a melamine ladle.
While Hardy winces and eats a kipper stotty,
he has the crap beaten out of him yet again.

Firth of Tyne

1

Because I'm not at home here yet I walk
out to the rocks that jaw the estuary;
because I can't yet find that comfort of a curve,
the harbour shelf at Broughty Ferry,
I have to climb out on the names
that hold some flotsam of my own
known sounds, from *shiels* to *midden,*
to strut my crossbreed stuff,
part-scaly gull part-capon, to try to crow
this current roost into

the comforts of significance: my perch above
the Fish Quay, my extinguished beacon,
my lightless top of the ex-approach to haven,
before the gravel and the sleech
decided to shift the cheeks of their arse –
-the Old High Light as square and squat
as I feel now, sinking my weight within me
to keep from slipping on these stones.

2

Hot sand and iodine fades
to the bearded rock and blue-eyed mussel shells,
to white crabs lying on their little backs,
which give way in turn to the drying beige
of barnacle-acned boulders and
the pop-footing, bladder-smearing
step-ways and bird-pools where
you can slither but you cannot stay.
Usurping the Prior's Seat I stand
but have no previous these seabirds can recall.

This is not the Tay however much I think of when
Dennis Cheape and I went out for a slew
in his new first-flush-of-profits power-wedge,
rescuing a drift-boat from

the Castle Rock, though that might count
for something with the ghosts drowned here
who take the air at tides like these:
the *Betsey Cairn,* the *Craigneuk,*
the *Ardwell* and the *Friendship,*
the steamer Stanley and, cut upon these rocks
a hundred years ago, the

3
And this is not the Firth of Tyne,
however much I map my own place on it
or how loud the echoes bark:
shields for shelter, middens for
the blackened stink
of wrack and rock and wreck.

Or half-forgotten Collingwood for our
old Camperdown, both admirals of
the pitted cannon, the public bar, the park,
significant victories the names of which
elude us now: blank gaper south
standing for the opposite of liberty
who greets the daily Danish and
Norwegian ships, three keels of which
were once a raiding host, and are now
the sum of shoppers that we can entice.

4
Past the coastguard station there's
the smell of cigarettes from cars,
of ice-cream van exhaust fumes;
the look of plastic strewn in grass,
that fades but never rots, the soft
nibs of rain on tarmac and your skin:
it feels like stars just starting to appear.

Old ladies slump in open-doored estates
in a row of cars that cup the horizon,
pointed at the North Sea like they park
down the front, down the Ferry,
reading *Tullies*, eating chips, just like
Bill Raeper saw that year
he wintered in Sardinia: beneath the *nuraghi,*
the little towers of the dead precursors, were
cars pointed out to sea, in darkness,
in the rain, the small blue glows of TVs on in them,
cars that flickered with the dead.

Chronicle of Ronny Gill

(for Joan Johnston)

Poor Ronny Gill is missing and
they'll never track him doon:
hear them shouting in the shadows
and the tunnels of the Toon —
-there's a mannie stood at Monument
his job is just to croon
Ronny Gill

They've searched in aal the cellars and
they've looked in each saloon,
they dragged the Tyne to Blaydon
and they foond a silver spoon
that's never known the knackered mooth
of the man that has to croon
Ronny Gill

Some say he's gone to Metroville
some say he's on the moon,
some say he used to be a man
and now he's a baboon
but there's a gentleman at Monument
whose task is just to croon
Ronny Gill

Some say he's wor Pied Piper
some say he's Daniel Boone
and the Alamo won't let him go
until he names that tune
and there's a long lost soul at Monument
that's howling like a loon
Ronny Gill

When did he leave where did he go
and will he be back soon?
For coal and Keegan, ships like rats,
he's danced them from wor Toon
and left a man at Monument
with a single speech balloon
Ronny Gill

Norah Hill

Autumn

Someone had stuck a feather in the ground –
-perhaps a child. Akin to what that man
did thirty years ago. I had to call
and check the claims. To do with benefits.

How frail – I see him now – how old; without
a penny to his name. Yet he got up
somehow – I tried to stop him, but, all gasps,
up he would get. He hauled his thin legs up

out of the battered chair. What had I said?
We weren't like social workers; only did
the money side of things, but if we knew
some Course or Scheme or private Welfare place

that might be worth the candle, we would tell
the person being visited. Maybe
he'd mentioned that he wrote to friends a lot,
and maybe I'd said, 'I like writing, too.'

Happen I said I wrote some poetry.
I sometimes wrote a number down to ring
for English classes. How it came about
I can't remember now. What never fades

is the thick book of famous odes they used
to learn by heart, with exercises in.
It might have been his Gran's. It weighed a ton.
This tatty tome he crawled upstairs to fetch

might turn out educational at last.
He wanted me to have it, seeing, like,
he saw I'd like it, liking poetry.
I stand beside the feather, wondering where

his grave is; if he died much later than
he brushed my early quill. The old and young
are skilled in this coarse kindness. Kneeling down
to scan the verses time and brambles hide,

I have uncovered vines. Not young or old,
it's hard to learn of fruit in lichened codes.
I mean I understand enough to say
amen when claiming kin is what I think

I'm being trained about in mossy cracks;
strangers the doctors cannot mend, get up.

Moses Carpenter, a Mohawk Indian, travelled with Sequah, a quack doctor.
Almost a quarter of Middlesbrough attended his funeral. He was buried in
Linthorpe Cemetery in 1889, the year Linthorpe Pottery closed down. St. Luke's
day, the feast of the Beloved Physician, falls on October 22nd.

Sometimes I Stand

From the back bedroom, you can see the house he lived in,
the old man I hardly remember.
Sometimes I stand,
looking across glass shards cemented onto yard walls,
video-protectors, microwave-guardians.
He never locked his door, in summer
propped it wide for bairns and tramps.
They learned a lot in that musty dump: the right
proportion of crushed seed to water,
how to create special paste for sickly birds.
Dozens of cages he had all over, budgies, exotic beauties.
It broadened bairns, skills not dinned in at school,

how to balance proper amounts of food
on twigs through narrow bars.

Nowadays, of course, you can't let children wander off,
not into houses with filthy windows,
any road, and no woman about.
You hear such things.
They hear all sorts, the kids I make walk close to me,
not skipping on too far –
the unmistakeable, demented canary of car alarms,
the simple racket of familiar pop programmes – -
not the possible rustling of bright wings in dark corers
dappled with radiance imagining itself through
threadbare curtains
the back-yard creeper dances behind.

Ormesby Hall

Three times I have been close to this lavender,
these harvest fields. That first time, two ladies in
tweed costumes shook hands on lichened steps; murmured
English greetings on a sixth-form outing: the Colonel's
good lady and the History mistress
talking over 'Aut Disce Aut Discede'
on our berets, their quiet perfumes mingling.

Next time's a bit lonely. A special day they
didn't charge admission. Something to do with
Heritage. Strange in my own town, back after
twenty years, I strolled round cordoned beds and chintz
window-seats, white roses plain on black sideboards.
I took a frail friend once. This little mansion -
a member of the National Trust, she'd done

the vast ones – revived her with small surprises;

pamphlets of poems the lady of the house
once wrote. (She'd been advanced; in summer dusks had
Shakespeare on the lawn.) Across the cups, tiny
enough for toys, but meant to sip real coffee
from, I sensed through snowy frills and crested panes
the horses' pull and stench in ripening grain.

Doggy Market

Framed in the back of his tilted van,
the tissue-rustling Ornament man.
Pallid madonna in neat blue cloak,
china Alsatian with heart of oak.
St. Joseph and a duck in pot —
He'll take a fiver for the lot.

Was it a fiver he said? He'll tell
you what he'll do. Now these could sell
for twenty up the town,
but friends
he's known for years – for these he bends
the rules. He'll not take more -
go on, you'll call him soft – than four.

"Then wrap 'em up", he tells the lad,
"for that young lady looking sad",
and Granny cheers up a bit
to know her perm is such a hit.

A convex mirror weighs a ton.
It nearly blinds you in the sun.
A lady in a crinoline,
a shepherdess who's very thin,
a toddler kneeling on a stand
with touching prayers and chubby hand.
A tenner for the lot includes
a flight of geese and tasteful nudes.
I often stood by Statue Stan
as Mam walked on with Aunty Ann.
They only wandered round the stalls,

linking their arms, but something falls
on them when I recall the mess
of cabbage stalks, to grow and bless,
dustings of something opened out of sight,
sprinklings of something clean in tarnished light.

Town Hall Concert

Middlesbrough January 2nd 2002

'*He was, at twenty, undeniably the most handsome Jew in Vienna. It was said that
when he entered a ballroom, women had been known to swoon for love of him,*"
Naomi Jacob, *That Wild Lie,* (1930)-

Below the blaze of priceless chandeliers,
the cherished daughters swirl to violins.
The chaperones hunt husbands in the beaux.
A hundred yards from here, dim doorways hide
a schoolgirl with two bairns she can't recall
the fathers of. She's buying heroin.

The ice is vile tonight. Car-drivers come
by bus, and half the seats booked up for months
are vacant. It feels lonely and we're cold.
If they were still alive, our Mam and Dad,
they'd give each other little cards today.
Exactly sixty years ago they wed

five minutes' walk from here, in that old church
they still have incense in. The fragrance, though,
which comes about me when I sing my songs –
-when the Transporter Bridge is dust and air,
it will be here. It will be everywhere.
I have been here before, but not like this.

This balcony was full of parents then.
My mother lived for the brief moment when
the Music mistress with her little stick
gave a sharp signal, and the choir rose,
dozens of girls as one. She used to sigh.
'The cream of English womanhood in bud

on one sweet stem! Those blouses bloom like May!'
'Happen that's how that lass turned out a bard.'
That's what I'd sometimes see them thinking, aunts.
Our Dad, he got his navy suit out for
that Speech day every year. When we got home,
he and our Mam, they sparkled up and said

how well she'd spoken, that Old Girl that got
to Cambridge, or the Head of some big firm.
'What tributes that great scholar paid', Mam beamed,
'to your good teachers! Think how blessed you are.'
What would they make of this I'm sprinkled with?
I'm thinking of the fecund dews between

rehearsals in the morning and the Night,
Half-Days not like the ones the Borough grants
for Princess Margaret's wedding, or the sort
to do with outings on Ascension Day.
A flaccid pause that's out of tune with time
we called at cousins in we didn't visit much.

Those funny shadows, now, between the run
through of the anthems and the Night itself:
Till now I didn't think so much of them,
not subject, so to speak, to subjects; not
a theme for poetry – a pallid lull
we felt unharnessed in, and slack and strange.

I see they weren't just that, and what I see
is what's not there, an absence I can't leave
unmourned, unreprimanded; can't unknow
what didn't nudge a longing to its source.

Whoever wasn't there has come at last.
I can't make out his face or maybe her's,

this angel who has taken my strong hand,
the blacksmith heritage which doesn't go
so well with laurels as the navy suit.
She comes at last – or he – and warms my hand,
my little fingers and my little legs.
I put my hand in his, or maybe Mam's.

This lady or this gentle man has led
this little child to the big window's stain.
In those white socks and these black shoes I stand,
and this soft messenger attends me till .
sun brings the many-coloured mayors to life.
In these dark shades and those bright hues I wait.

I do not think this man will go away.
The gentle lady will not leave me here
beneath the gaping dragons on the beams.
I think they'll stay beside me till I speak
like Caedmon who was shy and couldn't sing
or put to death the prose in golden chains.

Gordon Hodgeon

For November

At the affair's end
here is a love-letter,
a last fling of the sap
to the sun, a world away.
Burn this and remember.

We warm hands and faces,
blind with the blink of light.
We become all flame, the image
roped to the broken chair.
We have the gift of fire,
its babbling tongues.
We have to eat all winter.

Potato Sellers - Cleveland

Through wasted lands, the major routes
display, in lay-by, on grass verge,
the advance guards, these far-flung ends
of profit, enterprise, advantage.

Fifty miles north the Wall's abandoned,
poems and sheep and not a toss for Rome;
twenty miles south the squat of Fylingdales
warning the riggs and cairns of what's to come.

And here these foot-men have to live, and now,
without a hope of proper work or pride,
a laid-on, paid-off, casual regiment
that's bought and sold and taken for a ride.
Such forlorn openings, some general's joke
among the derelicts of heavy losses.
A bag's price standard, shelter plastic sheet,
killed hours to breathe in luck's exhausted gases.

Cold furnaces stand cracked, the speechless din
of radio-babble towers another day
till watch ends, lights out, nothing to report.
A kestrel beats time to its dangled prey.

A Cold Spell

First light, there's no mistaking
the blackbird in its garden,
the bright nail of its beak
stabbed at a horizon
of ice-scraped branches,
with the promise of harm
in its birthright clamour,
claiming sufficient ground
or else or else or else.

Such a cold spell, so early,
stretched out from northern Russia
across the fields, yards, gardens
deep with buried hopes,
marching the dialects of blackbirds
to fill these English roads at dawn
with the stiff queues of refugees.

The bitter season's greetings,
blackbird in a garden of snow,
hugged in a cast-off jersey
always too tight at the neck
like a conscience, like a uniform.
Again the innocent's part,
the preparation for birth,
the requisition of death.
I, says the blackbird.

At twilight an exchange of fire,
sortie and retreat, low swoops
over borders, the trampled lawns
that were their playgrounds.
Children called in
who will never come.

Back home, in the warm,
do not doubt the blackbird,
bred for the implacable future,
dug in under the hedge
against this next long night.

In Conference

I am looking out, the window
to a wider understanding
beyond all this paper talk
on the fifth floor of *The Imperial*
and there is clear evidence that
these Harrogate chimney pots
are in charge, manage the great sky
and its unknowing hosts,
their swell and their migration.

Though it is done without a flicker,
laid down with the stones,
without questioning of destiny,
a century of smokefall
dark on the parapets up here
for us all to admire,
at the top, in the *Empire Suite,*
the unchanging arrogance
of crowns on high-set heads.

If the sun screams of fire or the clouds
shake in revolutionary dance,
these chimney pots are in charge, they manage
the great sky, at whose eye-rim
a green tide lifts. Hills, woods and dales.
There we learn to swim, begin in that flesh
to speak the language of the deep,
welcome its overwhelm, the toppling at last
of chimney pots, this Harrogate regime.

The Strap

Leather strap on the back door nail.
He'd belt us if we were naughty,
but never. We didn't know.
Never was future, moon-landings, our own cars.
Strap - shiny till you got close, saw
the cracks and scabby bits. His chin was like that
before he shaved. Hot water from the geyser,
the brush and shaving stick. And he kept on
looking and stroking. I do that with my beard.
Good lads most the time, our mum said.
Wouldn't have let him use it anyway.
But never. I sometimes think
just once he'd have enjoyed it, realised
he could do something. Not just work,
snooker, Woodbines, the pictures.

Thought I saw him once with another woman
five rows in front, got up, went home, forgot.
Did he? Did I dream?
Did the thought of her bare arm cross his mind
when the second ulcer burst?
By then mum and dad had moved and we
had wives and kids and lived away. The strap
went in the bin.
I wish they had had more excitement.
My kids look at me.
I wonder what they'll wish they'd wished for me
when it's quite safe, doesn't matter anyway.

No Ice

for John Macleod

Glenlivet 12, cheers,
no water thanks, no ice.

There's just me in the bar,
I don't ask twice.
The barman knows my taste
and fills my glass
without a second glance
to make this long night pass.
The others left the warmth,
the light, my company
on some wild goose hunt
for divinity.

Some new-born baby
in the pub-yard shed,
I don't know yet
if it's alive or dead
or what on God's earth
it is doing there
with two dead tractors
and a cracked-up chair.

They soon come back,
they're shivering with cold,
then by the open fire
the tale gets told.
I hear the yearly nonsense
about stars and sheep,
voices from up the sky,
it makes a wise man weep.

They do still look amazed
and they are really nice
to everyone. Won't last,
I get my order in, precise:

Glenlivet 12, cheers,
no water thanks, no ice.

Waiting

Late January, under the church wall's height
the snowdrops struggle out, their papery white
as sparse and pale as hairs left in my head.
Their anchors are the chalked lines of the dead.

The year that's gone, so far from what we guessed,
the worst much worse, the good far from the best,
the new graves not those that we had predicted,
our choice of plot by these that much restricted.

Now, as the footpaths open up and stick
swings round and thwacks to raise the bramble's sneck,
the gales sweep in and turn the fields to flood,
the resurrected sheep are fleeced in mud.

These summaries of day in winter's long
and whining *tenebrae*, that lights-out song,
these snowdrops rise, their paper white as bone,
brief IOUs, on which I could write down

the debts I owe you, love, this time of year
when hope and joy get trampled under fear,
attraction shrinks all shrivelled in the cold
and passion hugs its blanket damp with mould.

The dead beat grasses lying in my way
will lift their seed-heads to the longest day,
so everything will come to one who waits
with fading snowdrops by the churchyard gates.

Richard Kell

Walking with Matron

In the Nilgiris, a platoon of Christ's cadets
with uniform shirts and topee helmets, we were
marched under tropical leaves by Matron, singing
'Stand up, stand up for Jesus'. She led us firmly
out of the hooting shadows to revelations
of sky and mountain, precipices with slow white
ropes of water dropping three thousand feet to the
empty plain, and we rested there in the silence
that calmed her voice as she told us about the one
sheep that was lost and found. We filled our handkerchiefs
with tea berries, put beetles like gems in boxes
velveted with moss. On the way back I managed
not to crunch my peppermint: it dissolved on my
tongue like a sliver of ice, and my bitten mouth
was cool and peaceful. But near the school we halted,
while Matron lifted her walking-stick and battered
a small brown snake to death, her spectacles glowing.

Sabbath Triptych

Music by Wagner: horns and violins
propose the condonation of his sins
who honoured God the Logos. Mr Smith
would rather have a car to tinker with,
a hedge to trim, and God the Mechanist –
aloof, the cosmos ticking on his wrist.
Between the radio and electric shears,

myself and two Jehovah's Witnesses
contending on the doorstep. 'It's all here
in black and white, the prophecies are clear'
they tell me, shaking dust off, snapping God
the Father in a briefcase. Overhead
the unclouded sunlight equably surveys
its colours redisposed a thousand ways.

The Balance

Always the one that will not let me be –
when I would overflow (the mind free,
the heart ready to love, the voice to sing),
reminds me with its prudent nagging tongue

that life is such and such: the free mind,
the loving heart and singing voice are kind;
so plan, cherish, be provident, pay the bills:

the horses lumber, but the tiger kills.

Always the one that will not let me change –
when I'd be careful, sympathize, arrange
(the voice level, the mind about to freeze),
recalls what goodness tamed no longer sees,

that life is such and such: the frozen mind
and level voice are to themselves unkind;
then play, be prodigal, give joy its head:

the fountain's reckless, but the cistern's dead.

The Chain of Being

Attracted by the fidget and the chirp,
a cat is eyeing a blackbird on his perch
deep in an apple tree. Her lifting tail
electrically writhes and flicks. Elate
with atavistic ravening, she walks
the paling like a rope, then, hooking claws
in bark, begins her stealthy climb. I know
the bird as if the garden were his own,
and he's the one I feel for. Why should pets,
now strangers to the jungle and the steppe,
be fondly understood when they attack
live meat as well as chunks of Kit-e-Kat?
Predictably, the feathered pal retires
by air, the furry one by land. All's right,
as Pippa sang – or is till panic tugs
compulsively at scores of tiny guts:
sharp cries attest a universal law,
the trees and bushes fill, and over all
except the Boeing miles above, where lips
are moist with mutton, peas, potato, Pils,
I see the hovering hawk, whose majesty
is founded on the humble kin he eats.

Currents

(i.m. Tony Baynes)

You showed me your poem mourning
a friend who floated down the Tyne;
told me during our only walk,
the kinked flood briefly lit by sun,
about those black twistings
that hurt your mind year after year.
Last night the news came
of your soaked body: now
I think of words, bridges,
deadly waters finally coupling.

Valerie Laws

'Your Great-Grandma would have been good at Maths.'

Slice after slice, she has dished up her sleep to them,
keeping only the smallest piece for herself.
Now, tiredness keeps her warm, like fur.
         She's up before dawn, alone,
to make a shirt before breakfast
or there will be no dinner. A simple daily sum.

Small dead sighs from the just-cold range:
white linen gathers the light, and makes it gleam.
         She warms her eyes at it.
Her thickened fingers barely feel the needle
as it slips like a fish through the cloth –
tiny stitches unroll in hundreds, like eggs
         piped from a queen bee's sting.

Obedient as ironing, the shirt takes shape.
Into it, she sews her thirteen children
her man's shipyard thirst for beer
his rages and spent wage packets
and strangely, her luxury, numbers,
dancing through the needleholes in daisychains,
playing their tricks like toddlers in her head
         as she knocks back bread,
            hefts steaming sheets from the copper,
            leads the range with silver black.

Upstairs, bairns call, his braces drag
on floorboards. The shirt is finished,
fit for man to wear and woman to wash.
Her child, my grandma, takes it,
runs down the road for the money:
her survival, then her twins', then
my luxurious education, and
my children's choice-filled lives:

       while she begins her working day.

Bones from a Medic's Dustbin

I hold this human spine like a rosary of bone,
fingering the winged vertebrae.
I stack them to nest snugly
in totem poles of little trolls;
spread them to examine
the delicate neck rings,
the beaky thoracic vertebrae
which held the ribs, the massive
cushions of the lumbar bones
which carried, strained and ached,
and the shield-shaped pelvic bone
like the head of a knobby snake.

I fit it to my body all the way up;
at least my size, and closer to me now
than ever lovers were. But all my touching
of this body's stem can't tell me
whether man or woman, young or old,
but I can guess, poor, and probably Third World,
dark as their bones are milky
like white Aero. Western skeletons
cannot be bought and sold.

I think of this spine cocked to one side
to hoist a child, bent under hot, hard work,
twisted by pain, stretched out in sleep
and hope that once some fingers counted
the bumps in the living back, gently as mine do now.

The heart does not break when bones do

My heart used to beat in the swift,
sharp tap of my high heels,
pecking out the rhythm of my blood. Now
heart and feet are out of step,
out of tune: my halting, muffled feet
pluck painful notes, to the percussion
of two sticks; a patter of uncertain rain.

But the heart does not break
when bones do. It holds firm
at the core, sound as an apple,
candid as a barn owl's
heart-shaped, apple-slice face.

My heart still hammers out the powerful beat
That used to find expression in my feet.

Nantucket, 1810

Laudanum strokes me throat to womb, warm
As a lover, my lover, who's cold as the sea
And the wet, wild wind. Somewhere, nowhere,
His harpoon thrusts into the hot muscle
Of the whale's heart, the final spurt
Of scalding blood and sperm oil splattering
The white foam, his head. All I have of him
Is the memory of his face before the sea
Scoured it, three children born three years

Apart, and six inches of cold hard plaster.
'He's-at-homes', we call them, we whalers' wives,
Perhaps already widows months ago. We work
As man and wife, mother and father, visit
Each other, talk business, wear our Quaker black,
Make money. At night, like them, I close my lips
Around the bottle's neck, feel that rush of heat,
Reach for him, my he's-at-home, hard
But dead: the only part death cannot stiffen
When a body rolls with the humpback waves.

Deeper than laudanum, deeper than harpoons
Can penetrate, deeper than six inches can reach
In me, thick water closes over him in my dreams.
He may come back briefly, a stranger, older,
Rougher, the real man with his hot demands
Seeming less real than the figure of his manhood
Which shares my nights, my bed, my life,
Which never leaves me for that whore, the sea.

Quantum Sheep

A Haik-Ewe

Spray painted on the backs of live sheep, who rewrote the poem as they moved
about. Project funded by Arts Council North East, December 2002-June
2003. Over 8 billion combinations possible.

Clouds graze the sky;
below sheep drift gentle
over fields, soft mirrors
warm white snow.

Three of the poems generated:

Snow clouds the sky,
Gentle sheep graze;
Soft white mirrors below
Drift warm.

Warm drift, graze gentle,
White below the sky;
Soft sheep, mirrors,
Snow clouds.

Sheep below drift,
Soft snow clouds;
Warm mirrors graze
White, the sky gentle.

S. J. Litherland

A Story about Cricket

I'm sure Hera looked down from Olympus
and spotted someone like you. (I'm sure
she did.) Bored with your work, herding

a few goats and sheep, taking time out
to play the lyre and sing. And she came
down to offer celestial conversation,

watching as you talked: your slim build,
bare arms, still hands, one wrist braceleted
with a woven rainbow thread, the single

ring on your finger; discovered your humour
defending yourself with deft strokes
flourished like a Gower of those times,

before the game was shaped from mood
and movement; you, displaying fair curls
like his as you talk, curls she hadn't

noticed until you touched them, your fair
beard hiding your youth, blue eyes hiding
your intensity most of the time.

Hera couldn't force you like Zeus
or seduce you like Aphrodite,
dreamt instead of her immortal soul

snaking into yours as you conversed.
That's what she dreamt. I know she did.
Powerless to touch you or your mind,

the man behind the mind, desiring the soul
inside the man where you are both equal.
This is a most conventional story.

Actually, you spotted her unaware,
noticed her inability to see you,
her naked face innocent of coquetry.

Hera caught in a moment of neglect.
You were the one watching who threw
a question, eyes sharp with attention

she suddenly saw and faltered at.
The Fates had delivered to her door
a beautiful young man. She couldn't

believe her luck except he was mortal.
Hera talked to her not-yet-cricketing
shepherd, dreamt of desire like a snake-

clasp coupling, desire where poetry
and music meet and hold fast, where
seamlessly we change into each other

leaving ourselves on the outside like clothes.
But don't think I'm Hera. This is only
a story about the beginning of cricket.

How it started as an art of conversation,
a wish of seduction, a compromise
of attraction, a sport they think

began among shepherds by a wicket gate
without the intervention of the goddess.
After five days Hera devised a game

in your image, of courtly strategy
and attack, tactics and defence,
above all, of fair play and deference

to a question of judgement, where
her soul and yours are the players
held together and apart by the rules.

Poetry as a Chinese Jar Moving in its Stillness

We were talking of poetry. Eliot and Stevens. Your eyes
were yellow-gold of a bee's blur, arresting on my idea.
Your lip demurred: What interests me now is smashing the jar.

The fragments. Sunday, we drove to uplands of Autumn. You,
for the first time, in the driver's seat, cautiously
changing gear. The moors witnessing the L-plates.

I was so proud of your caution: the poet diffident
and responsible. A new man. New wings. Not crashing
from bed to floor with the sudden fit like rain on the moor,

the tell-tale temple bruise. The mark of self-murder.
Monday, the jar was too complete, moving in its stillness.
With intuitive discord you tested the harmony,

rang a warning. The hurled cup did not break, the tipped
over golden basted duck and gravy only spattered my coat.
Upstairs the once cracked clock had stopped, its window

of postcards ribboned and scored, augmented by your lover's
surge of words, waited for deliverance into fragments.
The wrenching apart of quotation marks. A better poetry.

The despoiler of balance still moves in his shaking.
The eternal jar is reassembling piece by piece.
The idea of order is presiding over the nature of fragments.

Unwritten Entries

Q. (Her) What's caused this?
A. (Anaesthetist) Ravages of alcohol.

Death waits, my mind compacted. He's chosen a lean pin
for my brain. No words left. Only chemical messages.

This could be a radio station. Space flight. Wired up, tubes in,
my heartbeat synthesized, every movement a jagged edge. Out
pours the black blood. Well rid of it. The turbulence of throwing
up. The music of machines soothes me, my drowsy words heavy
in oxygen under the mask. And here again comes the disjuncture,
inarticulation, memory violated, the jamming of all stations.

A night of blackwater rapids. The heart about to crack is lulled,
has been lulled by the heminevrin lullaby. Oh, so sweet,
the pipe is singing to me its shuttle pump. Easy, you can turn
it down. My eyes are searched with a torch. Every bell of the clock.
Where are you? I know. What day is it? I'll never know. And life
is sticking to me with its rods and tubes and wires. Plugged in.

It's hair shirt time. I see it clearly. And I cannot remove it.
Because it's my skin I'm trying to lift. I pluck and pluck.

We're all prisoners in this hut, manned by guards and barbed wire.
But here's John Prescott, fancy that. Where's the wine? I'll miss it.
Going out for fish and chips and a pint and a half of VODKA.
The last hallucination scuttles over the floor

and I crush it with my foot. An innocent rose petal.

Death behind me. Hospital pills jingle in my pocket. They turf us
out with broken bones, my thinning skin rivalling the ozone layer
scabs under sunshine. I limp to the car. She drives my life
like an ambulance. Destination she'll offer: more of this kind.

Punishment or treatment. It's hard to distinguish and tears,
sober tears tread my cheeks slowly, they're hard, not like
easy drunken weeping, lift my lashes against the bald light.

Songster

She was a small singing bird, a young wren
you caught in your hand and felt her heartbeat.
You chose two rings, one for her foot and then
one for your hand. She fluttered like green wheat
beginning to sense the wind, not ready
for ploughing. She flew into the bush and
when you came for me, I saw your greedy
eyes still alighting and smelt the ring band
on your finger. While we were arguing
the two rings fell from your pocket like crows
at a wedding, the giving and wearing
intentional as double knots, zeros,
the two rings plural and not singular,
irreducible in kind and number.

A Lily

for Rachel Ben Harry Nick

The last breath   not the last breath
her face white and worn   not shrivelled
thin ribbing of mouth we have lightly sponged

with tiny sponges on sticks   her breath
pumped and pumped in regular harshness
by her heart in charge   overseeing

the last race to the tape. And I see her
hands thrown up as she breasts it   the way
they do on TV. Except they stay at her side

thin under the sheet and single blanket.
She breasts it with a slowing breath.
And her eyes are opening. They are pearl

and silver unseeing. The lids slowly rise.
Rise as slowly as legs lowered in exercise
to flatten the stomach or flags lowered

for the dying. Rise slowly enough for me to say
Quick   get Harry who is outside watering flowers.
We hold her hand   or the sheet   the five of us

who have risen one by one from our beds
by the quickening rasping. The vigil keepers
in a row crouching close with their farewells

called like passengers on a liner seeing
the land move away. And now the breath
is light   so light I want to catch it on a mirror

like Lear for Cordelia. The nearly last breath.
And another fainter and longer and nearly the last
breath. We wait and here's another so soft

it barely stirs her lips. It is so important
to know when it is the last. And it must be
for the opal pearl eyes have opened   and there

isn't another. Her face utterly unchangeable
from the moment before without another breath.
And when the others have gone I hear the machine

 give a last whine. Maybe there was a silent other.
And the bedclothes maybe I can see them move.
I stare and they appear to move. They lift and sway

in their stillness. *She is like a lily*
says my daughter. Perfectly white and still.
The last I will ever see of my mother. The face

in the coffin   the waxen stern face is not my mother.
She is this tender skin   these unpressed
fading petals withering as death blows out

her breath. I close her weightless lids
on opalescent moons. We scatter into the garden
as the sun is rising. It must be slowly rising

strongly rising and turning the hands of time.

Intimacy IX

Red-orange daybreak growing in the North at black night
    under the hours' long raid, wives & husbands in the shelter
hiding deep fright,
    the knowing dread of bombers

on course, sky armada.
    In my green siren suit with matching pixie-hood I'm sleeping and waking,
bunk beds tiered like shelves in a larder,
    the women knitting, the men weaving stories like netting

to keep the sky from falling. The paraffin stove
    crocheting a jacket of steel over the soft light puckering,
smelling of safety, the light nesting like butterflies above
    on the cement ceiling.

Intimacy without windows,
    close as a heatwave's airless night,
open to the sound of bombers (not ours),
    a heavy locust cloud humming without number, unstoppable blight

horizon to horizon. *Someone's getting it.*
 The Scheherezades fearful of ending their stories, told on and on
until the All Clear brought us out,
 painted in sky, painted in sky-blood, firelight shone

on our faces, on my siren suit and hood,
 the North red, tips of flames like thorns,
our fear ashen as we all stood
 like a watcher who mourns

on the road back to Pompeii,
 returning to storm clouds of Vesuvius,
the red haze, black hail of boulders, eight miles away,
 – swift mouth stopping orange molten lava in a surprise rush –

as the crow would fly, but would not in that burnt air,
 and still burning levelling sea;
in such a whirlpool of fire
 sank Coventry.

Intimacy X

Tangee Natural,
 only the stain of a blush on my lips,
a stick of pure orange, I can recall,
 like plastic, but would paint the pink of rosehips

crushed to syrup, it was all the rage,
 that, and pressed powder
clouding my nose and cheeks in a stage
 mask of pale fright risking the attentions of my father.

Face chastened in the cloakroom of the flicks,
 I thought all traces of *Natural* and fake
despatched in a quick
 splash, for the sake

of the evening inspection,
    his eyes appraising my rubbed cheeks
and lips and reflection
    of my fear unwashed with the rest. Weeks

of life in a moment sweating, and in the heat,
    in my pores opening like flowers,
the scent of powder and paint;
    he sniffed close, like an aged bee that wavers,

on track of a close-by fragrance,
    his eyes magnified to scrutinise a trace
of colour, however *Natural,* unnatural by chance
    of lingering perfume, unknown to my face.

Not sure, he ordered a wrung flannel,
    just in case, and scrubbed my cheeks and lips,
in a vain trial,
    to crush the indelible *stamina* of secrecy,

my lips drubbed to red more like the rosehips
    flagrant on the hedgerows, tender as intimacy.

John Longden

Pass

An August Friday
       Dusk is late tonight
Lads are playin football
       on a patch a' turf
Wen aa go out to watch for
       our small bat they're gone

On the mat nex day
       a arf sheet a' paper
Off a spiral-bound
       notebook Aa unfold
A note that drifts in
       'n out a' capitals

Were a boy as needs sex
       lists is bill a' fare
Look over yer gate
       Aa'll be out on the wall -
Aa looks front 'n back
       'n there's noone sat there

There isn't even
       a police cadet
Did e tap not knowin
       as aa's ard a' earin
Ave aa urt is feelins
       snubbed is loneliness

Listenin to the news
        blamed the knock on puss
E couldn't reach me
        'N now aa carn reach im
But aa tuck is note
        in me pension book ::

Cage

Elegiacs

steel erects its tents
calls clamps a' navvies
calls priests nuns poliss
church infirmary schools

ony a church angs out
a century on but
cold rusts rent the shops
in gaps plugs the igh street

lost terraces bares
shards 'n bun pennies
brick flats fence this pub
wi' plywood winderpanes

drawin our idle 'ands
their bargain bitters ::

Teesside Twinned with the Universe
- A Sonnet for Wembley --

WOW as we breast the lip a' the long rise
      flanking the flatlands all along the Tees
      league upon league a' yellow crocuses
      embrace the dark flood-plain 'n fill our eyes
This swarm outshines our sister galaxies
      it fills the view the lungs the art the mind
      burstin f'm the black country a' the blind
      Here the entrenched osts a' Ironopolis
spread rape-gold vistas in the frozen night
      Gorse blooms invincible through all seasons
      blaze then a few sparks Come rhyme come reason
        frost or flood drought or blizzard calm or riot
Clevelands gold lamps light up their massed barrage
Our twinned night sky's the Boro written large ::

Marilyn Longstaff

Ice Change

When the Antarctic Winter set in
with its 6 months of perpetual dark
apart from the ghostly light of stars

planets   moon   on snow

And there was nothing to see
and nowhere to go
he began to sink/think/sink

descend   into his own head

And the language he had
had relied on all these years froze
couldn't begin to measure

never mind express what he was feeling

And as he searched to find the words
his face suffered an ice change
gave up its craggy stress

became smooth   bland

And his voice softened to the whisper
of the rasp of nylon gloves
grasping a synthetic rope

as heard through an anorak hood

Above and beyond

the rule of Durham Cathedral (Benedictine Line
roped-off Saint and Chapel of the Nine Altars

everything closed including the view)
to the back of beyond. We climbed concrete steps

through the woods from swollen Tees to High Force Hotel
me singing in full flood, *Climbing up the golden stairs to glory*

in honour of my newly dead Mum.
Sharp shower in the car park saw us briefly anoraked

but by the time we got to Dirt Pit and the old drovers' road
high beeches – copper, bronze, gold – crowned bright blue sky.

On the tops, we reminisced   'boot on grit', barricaded rights of way
how to find a route through. I've learned this thing about rules

and those who enforce them – it's true
they are both there to be broken.

No arguing with nature though. October sun and our path
start their descent   bringing us back down to earth

the call of duty.

Maybank Road, Plymouth

The woman shall not wear that which pertaineth unto a man, neither shall a man put on a woman's garment: for all that do so are abomination unto the Lord thy God (Deuteronomy 22:5)

Mum's bedroom breathes the doze of Californian Poppy
the damp of Izal lingers in the outside lav
kitchen exhales the scent of tinned tomatoes
and cheese on toast

flap of washing stretches across the silence
of carless, cobbled, rubbish-free back lane
and Mrs Pentecost is shrieking for Diane
I don't remember rain

in secret I'm wearing Marks and Spencer's trousers
conspiracy with Mum in seersucker blue
my first – three quarter length and banned by Dad
as anti-scriptural

our front door opens straight onto the long steep terrace
with Salisbury Road Juniors at the top, scholarship class
the chosen forty, my favourite hymn
(in minor) God is Love

Vest

If anything
started it for me,
it was that string vest, or the ghost
of its diamond pattern
through semi-transparent nylon shirt
in a shade which wasn't mustard, it was paler,
but it was that sort of colour.

You must remember,
this was in the days before sex
on the telly. Mini skirts were just coming in,
but apart from a few tentative Levis and Wranglers
and the odd parka, the boys I knew still wore
grey flannel trousers and sports jackets
(with leather elbow patches).

I'm talking
of course, about where I lived
in a northern backwater, not Southend
or Brighton, with their invading mods
in smart suits, slim ties and fashionable
short-on-top, long-at-the-sides haircuts,
out for a day at the seaside on scooters.

Nothing much,
the hint of that vest
pulled taut against his shirt
next to his skin – as he played
table tennis at Darlington
Salvation Army youth club.
But it was a beginning.

Seed Time

It is seed time and harvest. Sinking under a surfeit of apples.
Spoils from the Browns' garden, whilst they sun,
Sand and sangria themselves in Spain.
September holiday when schools have returned
And we are settling back into stressful routine.

It was similar in Saltburn. Sour cooking Bramleys,
Sweet Russets, Coxes and Braeburns. So – what to do with them?
A woman's life of picking, gathering, stewing, bottling;
Jelly, purée, cider, chutney, crumble and pie.
Comfort me with love, for I am sick of apples.

Salvation Army childhood. Singing, 'the seedtime and the harvest'.
I loved the sheaves of corn, dusty bouquets of beetroots,
And best, cellophaned boxes of pomegranates, apricots and pears.

Celebrating 'Harvest Home'. My mother given to add a touch of drama,
Had a string of dressed-up children reading verses from the Bible
On the theme of fruit and veg. And mine, the ten year old with tea towel
On my head, "Comfort me with apples, for I am sick of love".

The roaring laughter of the congregation.
This child's embarrassment. She doesn't see the joke.
And still the clergyman's naïve and trusting,
Bruised and battered daughter, green at the stem,
Unfit to deal with sexy serpents, whispering sweet nothings.

"Comfort me with apples for I am sick of love."

Porthmeor Beach, St Ives

Beach-combing along the low tide line in the shadow of the Tate
on a lovely late May morning

among the mussel shells and rope and nets
and other bits of jetsam and flotsam things

I came upon the upside down white-with-blue-stripes trainer.
It felt male (I think it was the right), about size 10.

It was Tom who spotted the tail in the heel.
He was going to leave it, but I pulled it out.

I'm not sure what kind of fish it was –
herring, mackerel, sea bream – I'm not good at Nature.

It was silver with a bright pink eye,
the eye of the not long dead.

It looked at me, bade me beware
swimming deep, fatal attraction, perfect fit,   tides.

Beyond Clichés on Saltburn Beach

a lonely sandwich and the black dog
and my dead Mum hanging round a lot

and the Saturday surfers   wet suit legs
torsos as hard and young as new winter weather

imagine this weather, the worst weather
for a picnic on the dunes

it was the kind of light that drained all colour
scenery grubby and nothing vivid

except my black dog mood
high tides had washed a lot of sand away

cliffs had slid   turf bunched up at the foot
like the scalded skin of Howard's arm that slipped

down the bone to gather around his wrist
in a soggy bracelet   sea, rough and grey

I had my eyes cast down, studying the shore
then I looked up   it was over the sea

a complete bow   all the colours and more
light so bright it silvered the breakers

inside the bow, sky like old varnish on an old master
outside the bow, the sky was darker

it was like a Gateway to a Golden World
the pier   wet black   a path through

anglers kept fishing, surfers surfed faster
gamblers in the amusements played on

as the light moved   Huntcliff's fields
were painted gold and the murky buildings

caravans, trees   of the seafront town
stood black against its ethereal glow

in all that wet, I was dry and warm
and the ocean rushed and roared with laughter

Barry MacSweeney

From 'Blackbird'

(Elegy for William Gordon Calvert)
polish felspar at Sparty Lea
burr the wind with Tyneside songs
skin mixie rabbit from ferret's jaws
melt & make no noise

bunch your hands & clap my head
invisibled by a thief at night
stolen from sleep you stole from your family
melt & make no noise

ruthless masters did not poison you
you opened doors saluting their children
proud to chauffeur rich men's sons
drugged by work you wouldn't rest
melt & make no noise

dominoes laugh in the sun at night
ash drifts down & coats the dogs
fired upwards in the art of flight
melt & make no noise

lapwing lapwing green or grey
singing the smell of earth
sand mingled with blood of lies
melt & make no noise

no requiem no hymn no journey song
stopping to drink from a broken stream

ghosts of miners on the fell
shadowy poachers armed with snares
melt & make no noise

stern with children who grew up wrong
crossing your path when I crossed the Tyne
independence is a wolf that slays
melt & make no noise

follow your eyes to the source of the Allen
follow your hands inside intricate car engines
follow your speech to a wheel that cracks
follow your body to the ash in my skull
melt & make no noise

suck in fire from four windows
blasted kitchen with flaming breath
bear silence which your leaving makes
melt & make no noise

From Hellhound Memos

Sunk at my crossroads, hellhounds baying
broken from chains, lips, jaws
slavering with death notice, rape
on my left and right, filthy money, yellow Jerusalem.
I'd walk in there, turn the tables, rinse
the crowd with phlegm, make their shoes walk.
Swag wings at the con machines, blister
fingers of the three lemon fools. Sing mad,
merle mad, trill a bone, door stance finally
with contre-jour, say what next ammonite, how
is oxygenation, where's your Elvis lipcurl now?

Pearl Says

Down from the rain-soaked law
and the rim of the world
where even on misty nights
I can see the little lights
of Penrith and Kendal and, yes,
Appleby, and hear the clatter of unshoed
horses which pound like my heart,
I also sense the moss greened underwater
stones of the Eden to the west. I trim
the wick for mam's asleep now, dad
long gone to Cumberland and work, and
read read my exercise books filled
with stories by Bar, my trout-catching
hero, dragons and space ships, sketches
in crayons you can't buy anymore.
When I stand on the top road and bow
in sleet, knuckle-bunching cold, or
slide over dead nettles on snow, do
not mistake my flung out silhouetted
limbs for distant arches and viaducts.
I am not bringing you legendary feats
of sophisticated engineering. I in
worry eat my fist, soak my sandwich
in saliva, chew my lip a thousand times
without any bought impediment. Please
believe me when my mind says and
my eyes send telegraphs: I am Pearl.
So low a nobody I am beneath the cowslip's
shadow, next to the heifers' hooves.
I have a roof over my head, but none
in my mouth. All my words are homeless.

Pearl At 4 a.m.

Moon afloat, drunken opal shuggy boat
in an ocean of planets and stars.
Fierce clouds gather over me
like a plaid shawl.

Gone, gone, click of quarter irons
to Nenthead, Alston and beyond.
I moved my mouth in the darkness of the kitchen,
spittle poured wrongfully into the pan fat.
Snow once more
in my broken face, reduced
to licking the swollen door post. Just a gargoyle.
Death upon us like a stalking foot-soldier, high
and mighty on the law, bayonet
fixed. A sudden glint there, and that's it.
Spluttering lard
and strange sparks
ignite my mind, for I am in love
with something I do not know.
It is the brusque wind,
the nearest falling tumblestones
dislodged by the spate, the finest
snowdrops under heaven.

Ode To Beauty Strength And Joy And In Memory Of The Demons

(for Jackie Litherland)

1

Forgive me for my almost unforgivable delay – I have been laying the world
                                                              to
waste
            beyond any faintest signal of former recognition. For a start, a very
                                                        brief
beginning
on my relentless destruction trail, I made the dole queues longer for they did
not
            circle the earth in the dire band of misery I had wished and hoped
                                                        before
my
            rise to power among the global demons.

241

All my demons, my demonic hordes, reborn Stasi KGB neck-twisters
and finger crushers, their overcoats the width of castles
        fashioned from the skins of Jews and poets, rustle with a fearful symphony
                within the plate-sized buttons, rustling pipistrelles
                        and other lampshade bats. Some carry zipper body bags,
                black and gleaming in the acid rain, from the mouths of others
                words in Cyrillic Venusian torture chamber argot
                        stream upwards red on banners backwards
                in a pullet neck-breaking snap in the final perversion
                        of the greatest revolutionary poster that
                                ever lived: the Suprematist Heart.
        And don't forget, he will not let you forget, the man with the final
                beckon, the forefinger locked in deadly
                        fearful invite. This demon, this gem-hard
                hearted agent of my worst nightmare, this MC with spuriously
                        disguised gesture, this orchestrator of ultimate hatred,
                                the man with no eyes, no cranium, no brow no hair.
        He will always be known as the Demon with the Mouth of Rustling
                Knives, and the meshing and unmeshing blades
                        are right in your face. The blades say: there are your
                        bags. Pack them and come with us. Bring your bottles
                        and leave her. The contract is: you drink, we don't. The
                rustling bats stay sober. When drunk enough they gather on your
face

        and you stand upon the parapet. You sway here and she is utterly

forgotten.
                All that matters are the sober bats and the lampshade overcoats,
which
                press towards the edge above the swollen tide. You jump, weighed with
                empty bottles in a number of bags – some hidden as it happens of
which
                        you were ashamed inside your stupid sobering torment. And of course
                        we jump, arms all linked, with you into the fatal tidal reach. We also
                        pay a price. But the demon who shall always be known as the
Mouth
                of Rustling and Restless Knives, he stands upon the parapet. Never
dies.
                And all that can be heard beyond the wind are the relentless blades.

2

And then there is the pure transmission of kissing you, when
solar winds seethe in amber wonder through the most invisible wisps
    and strands in a tender half-lit prairie sometimes, caught in
light which is not quite light, but as if the entire world was drenched slate,
    or reflected thereof, in the soon to be handsome dawn of a reckless
damp November, with the gunmetal heavens plated quite beautifully
    in goldleaf of fallen nature already so readily ready for the rising
sap of a dearest darling spring when we will start again and the curtains
    will not be drawn at dawn beneath the monumental viaduct of the
great engineer. The truly great span of the legs above the city, spread
    and wide, rodded north and south and electrified by power passing
through beneath the novas and planets and starres. Magnetised!

Free Pet With Every Cage

Get out the shotgun put it in the gunrack.
Here I am gargoyled and gargled out,
foam then blood,
Flatface to Nilsville. In the toe-tag toerag dark,
siege upon his paling, wires berserk like cyborg fingers
in the demon neon's placid acid rain.
All the faery cars are shattered, overparked.
This is the hell time of the final testament,
the ultimate booking, the whipped out ticket, little Hitler
with Spitfire pencil on permanent jack-up; when he's not red
carding
your fanned-out fucked-up Bournville chocolate cheekbones
he's planning an invasion down your throat.
Big Jack with the bad crack,
just so peak and gleaming visor, ferret eyes
glinty like fresh poured Tizer – the seepage of the coleslaw,
the duff mayonnaise.
This is the season of firestorm lightning, torment time
of hell is beautiful.
Wide-awake hell, hell with fingers in a tightened vice,

forget the armies of little white mice,
hell beribboned with garotted larks and lice.
Yes, hell is beautiful, the weirdest ABC ever spoken
here in the dead letter box
in Crap Future Lane.
Wind clicks the metal leaves tonight.
I speed alive in sequence deep,
beast field rain
throbbing to the lipless pulse of windwonder.
O tormented landscape, handscape,
deathbones hewed
at my pouldrons and gorgets. Down
in the tarred and feathered department
of gutted souls the cry is so wimp: What's in it for me
but the Labour Party and geometric raisin bread?
Chomp, chomp, go the pink bleat sheep,
down to Walworth Road.
I'm such a bad and drunken lad, a fiend fellow
in the useless art of swallowing and wallowing,
as to invite brazenly her puckerage, her mayoral
addresses of correction, her buzzing network
of helplines flashing down the gorge.

Just look, I snarled my lute
in waspish worsement, claggy gob
clipped claptight shut.
I sledged it fast off my funny bondage tongue
but no one believed me above the cellar: I died
every day since I gave up poetry
and swapped it for a lake from the chateaux of France
and all the saints – Bede, Bob, Sexton, Messrs Rotten, Johnson,
Presley and Cash – abandoned me.

Perhaps the purple plush pansies have an answer today.
Only my little yellow lanterns
spring vinelike
in their breezy Jerusalem
aiming for victory over the ordinary sunne.

Hell is the pavement against my shit face.
And the devil has seen Robert off on the bus.
The light of recovery is just a format.
The light of recovery is just a lost fairy tale
seeping with ferndamp
in the bluebell vales of your childhood.
The light of recovery is an ex-starre, furious with everlasting
darkness.

I am the addict, strapping on his monumental thirst.
The sky is livid like jigsawed lace
and there are no happy endings.

Tom In The Market Square Outside Boots

Tom you're walking up & down the pill hill again.
Tom you're taking your moustache
 to the Ayatollah doctor with his severe case
 of personality drought.
Tom I saw you in the Heart Foundation shop
 buying a cardigan five sizes too big.
Tom you're more bent over than when
 we sat together in the locked ward.
Tom your coat is frayed like the edges of your mind.
Tom they let you out to the chippy but you're not free.
 Tom we're falling in the wheat
 our feet betrayed by sticks and stones.
 Tom we're in the laundry and it's us spinning
 as they try to dry out our wet lettuce heads.
 Tom there's a cloud on the broken horizon
 and it's a doctor with a puncture kit.
 He's got a mind like a sewer and a heart like a chain.

 Tom, who put the rat in the hat box?
Who gave the snakes up the wall such scaly definition?
Who plastered the universe with shreds of attempting?
Who unleashed the foes to annex your head?

Who greased the wheels of the Assyrians' chariots?

Tom the shadows of men are out on the river tonight
                                   reeling and creeling.
  Invaders from Mars have arrived at last
   and they're working in the lock-up wards.
  They're dodgy Tom, strictly non-kosher – just raise your hangdog
blitzed out brain and look in the defenestrated alleyways
     which pass for their eyes.
  I suspected something in the fingerprint room
  & the sniggery way they dismissed our nightmares.
  Tom the door is opened
                       and you lurch down the path
   past the parterre and the bragging begonias
  but listen Tom
               on the cat's whisker CB
                          listen Tom listen and look
 you're still a dog on a lead a fish on a hook
  Tom you're a page in the book of life
   but you're not a book
    you're not the Collected Works of Tom – yet
  there's no preface but the one they give you
   there is no afterword because no one knows you
   there's a photo on the cover but it doesn't bear looking at
    there's a hole where your family used to be
    an everlasting gap in the visitors' index
    A SMILE FROM THE NURSES LIKE THE BLADE OF A KNIFE

    Tom – what happened to your wife?
    She used to visit – every Wednesday
    when buses were running before the cuts

    Now she's a lonely bell in a distant village
    sacked by the Government
    Mr and Mrs Statistics
                   and their gluey-faced children

    There's only one job on offer
    in the whole of Front Street
    delivering pizzas to the hard-up hungry

and a spanking new sign on the unused chapel
Carpenter Wants Joiners
Jesus Tom it isn't a joke
they crucified the miners
with Pharisees and cavalry
dressed up as friendly coppergrams
it wasn't Dixon of Dock Green Tom
it was the Duke of Cumberland and Lord Londonderry
rolled into one

Dark today Tom and the city roofs argent with rain
dark as a twisted heart Tom
dark as a government without soul
or responsible regard for its citizens

trains' rolling thunder north and south over the great redbrick viaduct
is the only sense of freedom I have today Tom
the high lonesome sound of the wheels on the track
like Hank Williams Tom we'll travel too far and never come back
which is why they drug us to a stop Tom
pillfingers over our fipples and flute holes
we're in a human zoo Tom and it's a cruel place

Tom you're away from a haunt but furled in a toil
Tom there's a spoil heap in every village without a colliery
there's a gorse bush on top you can hide in naked
but you can't escape the molten golden rays of the sky
bleaching the leukemia lonnens of ICI Bone Marrow City
Tom out here on the A19 the long September shadows of England
stretch from Wingate all the way to Station Town
long and strong and dark as the heart of the Jesus Christ Almighty
or the lash of the snakeskin whip he holds over us all
Tom are you mad by north-north-west
or do you know a hawk from a handsaw?
Are your breezes southerly?
All the fresh air is quite invalid Tom and all the peeping spirits
have ascended to your brain
like region kites
and the gall of the world is mixed in a cup

Tom there's a silent flywheel on every horizon sequestered by law
                               & severed from use

    O dear, Tom, our heels are kicking at the heavens
    sulphured eyebrows as we strike into the hazard universe of souls
    where angels on our shoulders stand tall to make assay
    for acid rain will fall and wash them white as snow
    the weather has turned Turk Tom and we are almost ruined
     all softly cooling bright Atlantic winds from Cork and Donegal
are cancelled now
and fever has us in its grippy flame
ill-fit saddles have galled our wincing jades
           all that is left is the mousetrap of the devil
    but only if you give up on humans

     Tom invisible limers are fingering twigs in the groves
     Tom the twin sears of my hammered heart are set to be tickled
              by leather-sleeved index fingers itchy and raw
    Tom there's a man in black with a lone silver star
    casting a shadow as long as his dreams

    Are your eyelids wagging Tom, so far from the burning zone?
    Have they fitted you out yet, did you have the bottle to object?
    Tom I can see you being folded like a linen tablecloth
    I can see the busy working hands working on you

We've been driven from the prairies Tom
             to an isthmus of disappointment
                whose pinched becks can never sustain us

Tom I frighted my friends
            by getting this way
              I sickled and scythed their garlands of wheat
tongue a runaway bogie with broken brakes
alone on the pavings written with rain I was a sacked village myself
palings downed and all fat fields returned to pitiful scrub
               Station Town Quebec Shincliffe to No Place

    a network of underground ghosts

                    bust at the seams

Tom will our dear decorated hangers be responsive to the hilts on the swords
                                                    of our days?
          Will a tigerish revival leap upon us
                              from a leaf-locked lair?
          Will we be allowed another trample through mud?
           Tom I doubt it as the sunne doubts the starres.
          But starrelight is our single fire Tom, single
          and silver in the bed of the sky.

Brown-bottled venom and its work
                         a past prescription be
and all folded warriors
                            to gentle station grow.

The glow-worm dims and the sea's pearled crashy phosphorescence
in matin mist.

          There's a lark aloft in the morning Tom
                         its breasty song our autograph
       embracing fortune
                     in this out of focus world

                         high and mighty

                                   and carried away on shields.

We Are Not Stones

Darkly-harnessed light will fall like a shawl
and be the hunky-dory
death of us all. A hawk-wing death,
a shrike strike death, a death in a lair.
This mossy path, frilled with feldspar
to prick your pearly toes, fresh from the marigolds,
the little stile not squeaking now, lubricated
hinges, hymns to the silence of adult interference,

new sunken screwheads glinty in sunlight,
the death of the white linen: our cot-death.
It was all, all of it, all for us, from the wonders
of our mysterious heaven
to the trout's opal seed-sac bubbling with jewels.
The water was anointment water,
a cool upland baptism. You, you
were Delilah and Mary-of-the-tears,
of the unspoiled lips lapping rushing whitewater.
Milton was a blind man and we knew nothing of him.
Paradise Lost to the ears of his daughter.
Where are they now, our camps of wild primrose?
Now we are adults too, all grown-up.
You're there, I'm here, miles from our happiness.
We are not stone, but we are in the grinder.
Everything is lost, and we are dust and done for.

\

Bill Martin

A19 Hymn

"Down in yon forrest
There stands a hall

The bells of Paradise
I heard them ring

It's covered all over
With purple and pall

And I love my Lord Jesus
Above any thing"

1

Gannet splash

A drowning

Ship marks
Squabbling gulls

Furrow-eyed ploughman
Tumbleweed words...

Leaping ditches
Who goes there after them?

Past sentinel winding heads
Along mourning beaches
Over black shingle...

Distant hills hail steeple rooster
Wind in his tail

No resting place for lost words
Driven across fields

To cliffs and bird-emptied shells
Their secret out

2

Depe dene wood
Beech tops reaching ploughed edge level

Dry limestone gorge
Word-water sink-hole...

Cliff-seep into stream again
Overgrown kiln

Perchers in crumbling church
Paradise bells hanging...

Kingdom keys and
Lovers ash and elm

Enchanter's nightshade.
Wood avens and water avens

Pall purple cover
There stands a bed

Purple orchid spotted orchid
Blackthorn burdock toadflax yew

3

Blood is west of his green day

Gibbet and tar his trundling cart

White rooks coming
Across field stubble

Crimson-berry sunset
A flaming tree

White birds flock to it
Silently roosting

Corpus inscription
Iron frames his heart

4

Seven keepers
Follow his morning star

Hollow oak bole
Remains of friendship

Carved wings and keys
Peter acorn's bitter cup

5

Three times denied to morning cock

Three times to thistle

Three times to cuckoo spit

Once for seashore
Sun up out of it
Twice for fish baked at the rising

Three times for egg
Stained polished and rolling

6

Worn hill grass
Friday's worn hill grass
I'll sing you four
For worn hill grass

Four for kestrel flesh-eyed the first word

Four for pandect-calf flying from pasture

Four for winged cat
Fierce fledgling bringer

Four for bright angel-man
Gathering in

7

Old Kingdom lonnen
Silk banner procession

Lift the gate
Brass blare from dene mouth

Join us says Tom the drummer
Follow say seven green officials

8

Crab-pot gift
Road near muffled surf

Shoals of mackerel
Moonshadow wrapping sea smells
Saithe-coley also
Companions seek sizzling

9

May now beside us
April over the cliff already

Mary's belfry
Bluebells ring grave stone

Lost wooden rood-screen
Slots and blackthorn north and south

Moth and rust sermon
Arch baring dog-tooth
Pack howling behind us

Sand rim paten
Broken sun reflections
Stained shattered window

May alongside us
April-coble morning
Herringbone heading east to chancel sea

Durham Beatitude

The Easington Colliery disaster in 1951
remembered at the Durham Miners' Gala

Gorse blazing on clifftop
I saw three ships
Thorns and May blossom
Explosion at pit

Saul's Dead March
Common grave and grief
Beatitude their banner
Weeping and drum beat
A gentleness flowered
In each drum silence
A Kingdom confronted
Each green thorn

They that mourn
Came here in July
Field blessed with banners
Thronged comforting hush

I saw three ships
Through the gorse sail in
They came to Death's harvest
They came to pulley-wheels

Song of the Cotia Lass

1

The keel took my heart
In full tide it was torn
The keel took my heart
Black blood to his flame

The waggonway fall
Was braked by the river
the horse on its tether
With nose-bag and corn

The keel took my heart
To whistle and wo-lad
Down in his brig of dust
Down to his hot ash breath

2

On lip of drift crying
I sang the raa up and down
Black the craa hinny
Ivvry day now

I sang over fell where
Grey pocked my
Green stitched hem
Smouldering sway there
Banners to brighten

The keel bought my heart
It was bonded and bound
The keel took my heart
In full tide it was torn

3

Who rose in the morning
To see the keels row then
Who'll rise in the morning
To see the keels go

It was down by the river
Ventricles pumping there
Shute and flat bottom
Leveller schull

Who rose and who'll rise
With banners and drum thump
The keel took my heart
Silk over it laid

4

The keel played at morning-tide
Bide and abide with me
Keel-brass. for my heart blown
Banner-water bidding

Rite blinds were drawn to
Down staithe banks drawn all the way
Hats doffed and held there
In the ebb-tide hush
Down in yon forest
The keel rang my heart away
Black bells of Paradise
Hutton and Harvey change

5

Foy-boatman blow the flame
Loosen his rope-fast sail
Scorch the wind southerly
Fill it with fire in flood

Blood rages over bar
Out in the molten toss
Fury and friend are lost days
Where you are

The keel sought my heart
In full tide it was tom
It beats every tree on fire
Wagga-pulse fossil dawn

Peter Mortimer

I Married the Angel of the North

I married the Angel of the North.
I led it down no church aisle
no church aisle could contain it.
There was no top hat or rice
no tin cans rattling after honeymoon cars
no cutting a three-tiered cake.
But I said to the Angel, "I do"
and the Angel said "I do" too.
I kissed it lightly though it has no lips
I put an arm round a small part
of its rusting legs. I ran my finger
down its ribbed feet.
I know the Angel can't embrace me
can't wrap those flattened wings around me
can't move its muscular legs to clasp me.
I know its sexual organs don't really exist
and I can't tell if it has breasts.
I know it can't spend all day with me
mooning and spooning and making daisy chains.
I know it can't stand on the cruise ship deck
under a hanging lantern moon, and whisper
this moment should last forever.
I know the Angel lives on its small hilltop.
I know I can never own the Angel
but I love the Angel of the North
and have married it.
Because this is a marriage that can last
and the Angel will never leave me.
Other people may marry the Angel as well.

This causes me no problems.
I stand by the Angel of the North
hear its wings sing the wind.
The Angel knows nothing of the old songs
its face turned away from memory.
Its metal head holds no images
of cloth caps, mufflers, dolly tubs,
the dark choking pit
or men welded to a tanker's hull.

I have married the Angel of the North
because it is bigger than me
because its roots are 100ft deep in northern soil
because it is always in when I call
because it is always in flight when I call
because it sees horizons the rest of us don't
because in my waking dreams
the imagined wush-wushing
of those great boat-paddle wings
pushes the slowing blood
through all our northern veins.

Advice to a Writer

Read everything you can
Remember it all
Forget it all
Avoid philosophers, politicians
and professors of English Literature
Prepare for poverty
Spend a lot of time alone
Spend a lot of time in noisy rabbles
Listen to criticism as much as praise
Remember critics would rather be writing a poem
Don't spend more than one year in a writers' circle
Invest in a large waste paper basket
Place your desk away from the window

Imagine everything
Never retire
Remember, the writing is more important than the writer
Don't advertise toothpaste or anything else
Go out in the worst kinds of weather
Live at least once on a small island
Lose yourself in a large city
Be nosey
Weep for the stupidity of humanity
Laugh loudly at the same stupidity
Only write true
Learn to know when you don't
(headache, sleeplessness, bad temper etc)
Learn to know when you do
(sleeplessness, headache etc)
Be absurd about the serious
treat seriously the absurd
Echo every writer that has ever lived
Write like nobody else
Occasionally sit at your desk in midnight's silence
and do nothing at all
Realise your writing changes nothing and is essential
Be at the centre of everything
Be at the edge and invisible
Never run out of teabags
Do one more draft
Remember, easy writing makes bad reading
Good writing outlives the writer
Bad writing doesn't live at all
Beware reactions from friends and family
Write more. Then write less
Avoid all literary theory
Dance and sing every day. Alone if necessary
Let one half of you be calm
Let the other half be restless
Feel naked without a notebook
Spend an inordinate amount of time
Observing a slug or some such
See what no-one else has seen
Even in a rusty nail, or a damp cloth.

Mrs Spratt

Eat lean? That's a joke.
Jack scoffs the lot
leaves me those gristly bits
like congealed snot. I mean,
who eats fat by choice?

I watch him sharpen the knife
snick-snack, crossed swords.
Beef, pork, lamb, all
carved as thin as stamp hinges.
The tender curves fall to the plate.
They're his. Mine's the fat.

"There now, my love! Fat
just how you like it!"

Maybe he believes it.
Who can remember when it started?
Swallowing is like some Sumo wrestler
forced down the throat.

People think we're wonderful
a balanced couple. Lean and fat
yin and yang. Jack smiles to hear them
it means as much to him
as his *TESSA* bonds, his electricity shares
his golf club committee.
"Teamwork!" he beams to his friends
and his arm clamps round me.
You could say it keeps us together.

One dinner party I rose slowly
smoothed down my little black number
and with a dab to the lips
whispered, "excuse me".
The mangled gristle heaved its way
up my throat, splashed down
into the toilet bowl's scented blue.
Two flushes, a squidge of toothpaste
some quick mascara, and no-one knew.

I should have spoken up years ago;
now the truth's too hard to swallow.
At night I trace fatty patterns
on the ceiling, feel Jack's pushy thing
inside me, and think of those chump chop lumps
that I chew and chew and chew.

If Love

(For Kitty)
If love was cloud
we would eat it from fairground sticks
if love was darkness
we would fill our black pots with its paint
 if love was the sun
we would pin it to our lapels
if love was the moon
we would pick our teeth with its crescent
if love was sand
we would build our dreams in its castles
if love was fire
we would flap its red silk at the dead
if love was a tree
we would know its reason for pointing
if love was water
we would frame it into mirrors
if love was rock
we would sink inside its clenched muscle
if love was colour
we would slide down its rainbow back
if love was death, was death
we would tilt its black hat, and kiss
its bone lips into singing

What Mother Told Me

Look before you leap
it's a long road that has no tulips
a stitch in time saves nine
every cloud has a silver fish
still waters run deep
a limping man has no accent
travel broadens the mind
practise what you eat
there's no smoke without fire
tall trees see the cavalry first
more hands make less work
a basted turkey knows the time of day
blood is thicker than water
the smaller the dog, the fiercer the wee-wee
it's always darkest before the dawn
love is blind drunk
an apple a day keeps the doctor away
a toothless woman can still dance with a bear
more haste, less speed
a crumpled hat holds many eggs
pride comes before a fall
let sleeping dogs, if they want to
it takes a worried man to sing a worried song
the longest journey starts with a cheeseburger
the devil makes work for idle hands
like father like chocolate
a fool and his mummy
live now pay later
he who laughs last is called Norman
never judge a book by its contents
too many Cooks, not enough Entwhistles.

Charlie Fook

Me name's Charlie Fook and me spelling's a laugh
I'd rather nick off and sit round in the caugh
School gives me a pain; I'm no good at study
Can't tell Mr Sims. Wouldn't understand wudy?
He pulls me up front, shouts 'Now spell Cologne!'
He's got to be joking – what me – all ologne?
Or sometimes it's phlegm, or caress, or lasagna
Can't hardly blame me for skiving off, cagna?
'Wake up at the back – and spell chipolatas!'
That some kind of sausage? Got me beat for statas
See, I'm bloody useless, I haven't a clue
Words don't make sense to me. What can I due?

This Poem is not Sponsored

This poem is not sponsored by:
Barclays Bank, Northern Electric, Budweiser Beer,
Trust House Forte, McDonalds, Reed International,
English Estates, Scottish & Newcastle or Snicker Bars

This poem does not acknowledge the assistance of:
Chase Manhattan, Carling Black Label, British Airways,
Natwest, BNFL, Kleinwort Benson, Texas Homecare,
Tonka Toys, McAlpine, British American Tobacco,
ICI, Scottish Widows, IBM, Balfour Beatty, Woolco,
Tate & Lyle or Nissan Cars

This poem's creation was not made possible by:
United Biscuits, Black & Decker, Currys Electric,
British Telecom, Heineken, Kwik-Fit Exhausts, Virgin
Atlantic, Coca Cola, Legal & General, Amstrad,
W.H.Smith, Storey Carpets, Cable & Wireless, Burger
King, Dulux Paint or Raleigh Bikes

Future poetry sponsorship is not actively sought from:
Pearl Assurance, Tetley Breweries, British Steel,
Nintendo, Gillette, Panasonic, Adidas, The Prudential,
Procter & Gamble, Barratt Homes, Safeway, Bradford
& Bingley, Tupperware or Spud-U-Like.

Sean O'Brien

In a Military Archive

The mirror on this corridor
Detains them in its waiting-room.
Sporadically the backward clock
Remembers its authentic boom
And flings the dead men to their knees.
They rise. They smoke. They watch their hands.
They mend the furniture and read.
The King's Own ----shire Ampersands,
Preserved as footnotes in the texts
Of Hockley, Blunden, Hart et al.,
At ease in the grave-geographies
Of Arras, Albert and Thiepval.
Now literature is sent, as once
Were razor-blades and letters,
That the dead may study suffering
In the language of their betters.

Cousin Coat

You are my secret coat. You're never dry.
You wear the weight and stink of black canals.
Malodorous companion, we know why
It's taken me so long to see we're pals,
To learn why my acquaintance never sniff
Or send me notes to say I stink of stiff.

But you don't talk, historical bespoke.
You must he worn, be intimate as skin,
And though I never lived what you invoke,
At birth I was already buttoned in.
Your clammy itch became my atmosphere,
An air made half of anger, half of fear.

And what you are is what I tried to shed
In libraries with Donne and Henry James.
You're here to bear a message from the dead
Whose history's dishonoured with their names.
You mean the North, the poor, and troopers sent
To shoot down those who showed their discontent.

No comfort there for comfy meliorists
Grown weepy over Jarrow photographs.
No comfort when the poor the state enlists
Parade before their fathers' cenotaphs.
No comfort when the strikers all go back
To see which twenty thousand get the sack.

Be with me when they cauterise the facts.
Be with me to the bottom of the page,
Insisting on what history exacts.
Be memory, be conscience, will and rage,
And keep me cold and honest, cousin coat,
So if I lie, I'll know you're at my throat.

Revenants

It's four o'clock, an autumn Sunday,
After a hailstorm and just before dark.
The dead are reassembling,
There beneath the dripping trees
Beside the pond, and more arrive
Continually by all the gates.
In the young middle-age of their times,

Demob suits and made-over dresses,
Men with their hands in their pockets
And women inspecting their patience
In compacts, they're waiting
As if there were something to add.
Friends, we are the unimagined
Facts of love and disappointment,
Walking among you with faces
You know you should recognize,
Haunting your deaths with the England
We speak for, which finds you
No home for the moment or ever.
You will know what we mean, as you meant
How you lived, your defeated majority
Handing us on to ourselves.
We are the masters now. The park's
A rainy country, ruining
The shoes you saved to wear to death,
In which we buried you.

The Park by the Railway

Where should we meet but in this shabby park
Where the railings are missing and the branches black?
Industrial pastoral, our circuit
Of grass under ash, long-standing water
And unimportant sunsets flaring up
Above the half-dismantled fair. Our place
Of in-betweens, abandoned viaducts
And modern flowers, dock and willowherb,
Lost mongrels, birdsong scratching at the soot
Of the last century. Where should we be
But here, my industrial girl? Where else
But this city beyond conservation?
I win you a ring at the rifle range
For the twentieth time, but you've chosen
A yellow, implausible fish in a bag

That you hold to one side when I kiss you.
Sitting in the waiting-room in darkness
Beside the empty cast-iron fireplace,
In the last of the heat the brick gives off,
Not quite convinced there will be no more trains,
At the end of a summer that never began
Till we lost it, we cannot believe
We are going. We speak, and we've gone.
You strike a match to show the china map
Of where the railways ran before us.
Coal and politics, invisible decades
Of rain, domestic love and failing mills
That ended in a war and then a war
Are fading into what we are: two young
Polite incapables, our tickets bought
Well in advance, who will not starve, or die
Of anything but choice. Who could not choose
To live this funeral, lost August left
To no one by the dead, the ghosts of us.

Reading Stevens in the Bath

It is Newcastle at evening. It is far
From the furnished banks of the coaly Tyne
But close beside the hidden and infernal banks

Of the unutterable Ouseburn. Howay. It cries
Its native cry, this poisoned soup of prawns.
Howay. The evil river sings. The mind,

In Forest Hall, the haunted disbelieving suburb
Like a field of snowmen, the mind in Forest Hall
Lays by its knitting and considers

Going to the Fusilier. Howay. But in the upper room,
The room upstairs, the upstairs room,
The blear of glass and heat wherein

Not much is visible, a large pink man
Is reading Stevens in the bath. Howay. It is bath-time,
The time of the bath, the green-watered, where the mind

Lies unencumbered by the body as by time.
It is the bath as absolute, admitting
No conditional of green, the bath in which the bather

Lies considering. And the mind takes out
Its lightness to inspect, and finding nothing there
Begins to sing, embodying, emboldening its note.

It is the singing body in the bath, the mind.
Bookless Fruiterers, tell me if you can
What he may find to sing about, that man

Half-audible, and howling, as it were, the moon
That rests its gravity on weary Forest Hall,
That sends its tidal song by Tyne,

By Ouseburn, by the purifying plant
And ultimately here, to this balneum absolute,
Steam-punkah'd bath at the end of the mind, whose singer

Sings beyond the scope of tongues and sanity
Of neighbours, howling like a wolf among the snowmen
To the moon which does not listen:

Say it's only a paper moon,
Sailing over a cardboard sea,
But it wouldn't be make-believe

If you believed in me.
Howay. Howay. Howay!

Railway Hotel

In Memory of Ken Smith
Why this hotel, and this town and this province of X
On this night in the Year of the Turnip? Why
This name and this face in the passport? Well?

Out there the foggy road still curves away
Across the railway tracks. Young birches in the sidings.
Sounds of shunting, off in the rusty damp.

The suitcase. Full of books? It could as easily
Be drill-bits, lenses, chocolate.
You must be travelling in something. *Time,*

You say, flicking the locks to inspect
The interior. Something that glows? You give
Nothing away. It goes under the bed again.

Down at the end of the hall is a wolf in a case,
Howling at the moon in 1910, illuminated
By the beer sign in the street. Perhaps

It went like this: you stopped for dinner here
To view the curiosities, and this
Was one of them. You never know.

At her high desk the red-haired proprietress
Sits in a draught with the radio doing a polka
To death, and once again she's gotten

Lipstick on her teeth. And nothing happens
For a hundred years but fog and shunting,
Lipstick and polkas, the half-lives

Of objects marooned by imagined
Utility. *So, are we going, or what?*

The River Road

Come for a walk down the river road,
For though you're all a long time dead
The waters part to let us pass

The way we'd go on summer nights
In the times we were children
And thought we were lovers.

The river road led to the end of it all -
Stones and pale water, the lightship's bell
And distance we never looked into.
A long time gone
And the river road with it.
No margin to keep us in mind.

For afterlife, only beginning, beginning,
Wide, dark waters that grow in the telling,
Where the river road carries us now.

Before

Make over the alleys and gardens to birdsong,
The hour of not-for-an-hour. Lie still.
Leave the socks you forgot on the clothesline.
Leave slugs to make free with the pansies.
The jets will give Gatwick a miss
And from here you could feel the springs
Wake by the doorstep and under the precinct
Where now there is nobody frozenly waiting.
This is free time, in the sense that a handbill
Goes cartwheeling over the crossroads
Past stoplights rehearsing in private
And has neither witness nor outcome.
This is before the first bus has been late
Or the knickers sought under the bed

Or the first cigarette undertaken,
Before the first flush and cross word.
Viaducts, tunnels and motorways: still.
The mines and the Japanese sunrise: still.
The high bridges lean out in the wind
On the curve of their pinkening lights,
And the coast is inert as a model.
The wavebands are empty, the mail unimagined
And bacon still wrapped in the freezer
Like evidence aimed to intrigue our successors.
The island is dreamless, its slack-jawed insomniacs
Stunned by the final long shot of the movie,
Its murderers innocent, elsewhere.
The policemen have slipped from their helmets
And money forgets how to count.
In the bowels of Wapping the telephones
Shamelessly rest in their cradles.
The bomb in the conference centre's
A harmless confection of elements
Strapped to a duct like an art installation.
The Première sleeps in her fashion,
Her Majesty, all the princesses, tucked up
With the Bishops, the glueys, the DHSS,
In the People's Republic of Zeds.
And you sleep at my shoulder, the cat at your feet,
And deserve to be spared the irruption
Of if, but and ought, which is why
I declare this an hour of general safety
When even the personal monster -
Example, the Kraken - is dead to the world
Like the deaf submarines with their crewmen
Spark out at their fathomless consoles.
No one has died. There need be no regret,
For we do not exist, and I promise
I shall not wake anyone yet.

Evangeline Patterson

History Teacher in the
Warsaw Ghetto Rising

after an engraving by Maurice Mendjisky

The schoolmaster once known as
Umbrella Feet
unfolds his six-foot length
of gangling bone

and, mild as usual,
blinks – his bi-focals
having gone the way of his pipe
and his tree-shaded study
and his wife Charlotte –
-
and, jacket flapping, as usual,
carpet slippers treading
rubble of smashed cellars,

advancing steadily into the
glare of the burning street

and holding his rifle uncertainly
as if he thought it irrelevant
– as indeed it is –

he leads his scattered handful
of scarecrow twelve-year-olds

towards the last twenty minutes
of their own brief history.

Jehanne

They say the men from the north are coming closer,
swallowing farms and villages as a hound
swallows gobbets. The monks are burying books
and gold vessels. The scholars and singers are gone
south. Only the holy anchorites,
whose piety is as savage as the northmen,
do not care what tide washes over them.

And I, Jehanne, in this orchard bury,
in many wrappings, as if it were a child, -
the coverlet that I worked for five years of winters.
My lady said, Jehanne, when it is done
you will be ready for marriage. And this spring
she said, Jehanne, it is nearly done. Who
will you take beneath your coverlet? But none
is left now to come walking in the orchard
while I sit pricking love-knots with my needle.

So here, with no one watching, I lay the violets
and the coloured birds and the tall branching lilies.
If it please the saints I shall live, and have a daughter,
and teach her to make violets with a needle.
But who can tell? The dark is coming closer.

Armaments Race

and Mrs. Stephanopoulos said oh yes I am happy
I am very happy and why not for I have
a fine husband and beautiful children

and we have our health and enough to eat and we all
love each other exceedingly and if I had just one wish
this is what it would be

that when we die we should all go to heaven together
in the same instant so that none might feel
pain or despair at the losing of any other
and I said oh Mrs. Stephanopoulos oh my dear
you should be truly a happy woman for never
have so many been toiling with such a blinkered devotion
in the deep-down mines and the shiny laboratories
to make your one wish come true.

Pauline Plummer

Travelling North from Middlesbrough

At seven am
in my rear-view mirror
a cobalt sky
a cloud of sandalwood behind a sinuous line of hills.

I pass
the night shift young
falling from the Rat Ride of thin dresses .and sharp trousers
into their stargazing bedrooms.   .

The bakery girls
roll up their floury arms, freckles like sultanas.
The Queen of Diamonds shakes up the sleeping school
with her mop. A tinker's horse
Crops the priest's garden.

Over Newport Bridge
riding its spine of blue steel
a heron unmoors and veers across the slurry
towards the oil rigs.

Past the prison's
fluorescent bulging walls, its pale sloping skylights,
its breeze block cloisters.

Beyond the dingy fields
the sea is an anklet of diamonds cut to forty facets.

Behind the husk of fire and phials of smoke
the light of houses squeezed into a saw's serrated edge,
phosphorescent with flocks of spotlights,
the steel pipes,
hissing steam,
a line of snake.

Whorlton Lido

Steam shimmers off walls
baked warm as loaves
The barley grows in slabs of ochre
burning the eye.

Panting dogs fight over discarded
junk food. River water, tawny as ale,
spews over rocks

Pale wiry bodies swing out on ropes
in daring curves under hexagonals
of branch and sky.

Men shriek, plunging into rockpools,
a blur of red faces, muscled tattoos
and obscenities.

Rows of children bob
along currents over rocks
worn smooth as backsides.

Behind a waterfall two lovers
form a triangle of flesh –
heads touching for a chaste kiss
sluiced by miles of stinging rainbows.

At night a crimson moon
floats in a dark sea,
The sheets stick to our skin like plasters.

Eldest Son

We joust in the kitchen,
Clash swords in the sitting room.
You're my son –
You challenge my tenderness
With your maleness.
Are you drumming your way
Out of a shell with fists?
My anger at your arrogance
Spills out like hot fat
Burning everything in its path.
Your face melts and
You are a small boy again
Fighting back tears.
My heart waves a white flag.

Uncles and Aunties

I was afraid of uncles,
with laughs like football crowds,
wearing bark coloured clothes,
taking up more space than allowed.

They smelt of cities and work.
Shirts could not contain
the bristles sprouting through collars
and cuffs, the fingers nicotine stained.

A man exposed himself
to me when I was just a kid.
Couldn't tell anyone of his revolting
pinkness, what his flapping trousers hid.

No wonder I preferred aunties –
in their flowery dresses, scrub rough hands,
faces dusted with icing sugar,
permanently permed, lips strawberry jammed.

Lovebite

Today
sat in a conference of teachers
your lovebite blushed
in the crook of my elbow

I folded it away
but every time I reached for a pen
it gave a bruised smile.

Buying a Blouse That Fits

Newspapers are flying
about the icy streets.
We drink warm beer
while ghosts in the juke box
serenade our broken faith.

The Thai waitress gives you
one of those are you pleased with my smile smiles
and after coffee
the manager asks you
do you want boys or girls?
Ah, the English are so cold, no?

You're going grey.
Have I aged?, I ask.
I lie about my size
but you buy me a blouse that fits anyway.

In the train the couple opposite
tear into each other
like a trapped bear biting off its paw.
Later in the hotel
you try my skin against yours for size.

What is the One Word Known to All?

One bright star
in a lilac sky – apricot light on water
a donkey brays the morning.

Mint tea, the first cup strong like life.
The second cup sweet like love.
The third bitter like death.

Guide us in the right path.
The first sura of the Koran.
What is the one word known to all?

It's written on the skin
of aborted calves, brushes from hair
taken from inside the ear.

Write it in verdigris.
write it in arsenic yellow.
The hawk over fields of rice.

Write it in black
so that it soars, a black kite
over a green silk river.

Ochre and mauve cliffs
marsh marigolds in a pool
a cloud of fire-finches.

A black and white kingfisher
over a grey green river.
The sun sucks up all colour.

A woman stands in a canoe
twins at her breasts.
Her husband holds up dazzling perch for sale.

Noon. A cow and a goat
at a trough. The cow cleans the other's
fur with the rasp of his tongue.

Let us find shelter
and breathe under the shadow
of a tamarind.

In riverside villages with mosque,
cool arches and charity.
Outside the sky combusts.

By a path melons stacked,
swollen green breasts
one cool red heart left open.

A boy in a man's suit jacket
cries with hunger
hits the dry air with his begging gourd.

Silver and bronze on red earth –
stacks of fire wood.
The desert strides south.

Children on the bank
hands outstretched, fingers curved
in the gesture for give me.

Mischievous eyes under an orange turban.
A dhow sails by
flute music and drumming.

A heron flaps out of its stupor
over lotus and reed bed.
Boys with slings hunt for their supper.

The sun going down glints
in the bowls on women's heads
the rhythm of their blossoming sarongs.
A cormorant dives
in a cloud of glitter.
Monkeys in riverside bush.

The fan at the charcoal
mutton simmering.
Put the sweetest piece in the mouth of one you like.

The Moon unveils her white face.
Cows scrape the earth with their hooves
horns like shining lyres.

Donkeys tethered to a post
a silver coin
in each liquid eye.

A love affair is sinuous stream
overflowing in the wet season.
A marriage is a slow flowing stately river
pressed between reeds and bank.

This may be all we know
of the one word known to all.

Katrina Porteous

Charlie Douglas

'We're gan' tyek hor off, th' morn,'
Said Charlie, squatting in his black-tarred hut;
And the other old fishermen muttered, spat, swore.
So after a thin night, cracked by storm,
I arrived by the harbour kilns at dawn,
Where the sour Jane Douglas smoked and heaved,
Rocking her burden of dans and creeves.
And Charlie, a tab in his toothless jaw,
Stared blindly out to Featherblaa',
Tiller in hand. And away she roared,
Her proud bows rising, blue and white,
The same cold colours as the changing light
Bowling over the wind-torn sea.
Now, all the creatures that creep below,
Lobster and nancy, crab and frone,
From many million years ago
Have secret places, and Charlie knows
The banks and hollows of every part.
He's learnt their lineaments by heart
And mapped the landscape beneath the sea.
O, I was the blind man then, not he.
Now Charlie's quiet. His words were few:
'Aah'll tell ye somethin'. Now this is true –
We're finished, hinny. The fishin's deed.
Them greet, muckle traa'lers – it's nowt but greed.
Whae, there's nae bloody chance for the fish t' breed...
An' the lobsters! Y' bugger! In wor day
W' hoyed aa' th' berried hens away!'
'And they don't do that now?' 'Darsay noo!'

285

As he spoke, I watched the steeple grow
Smaller, still smaller, marking where
His folk, for the last three-hundred years,
Were christened and married and laid to rest.
So I urged him to tell me of all the past,
That other, hidden, deep-sea floor;
And whatever I'd cherished in life before –
Home, friends – just then, I loved him more,
This crined old man of eighty-two;
I wanted to trawl him through and through
For all the mysteries he knew
About the sea, about the years.
 I wanted to haul his memories free
Like a string of creeves from the troubled sea,
Shining with swad and water-beads.
But turning his fierce, blind gaze on me,
His eyes said, 'Hinny, ye'll nivvor see –
Ye divvin't tell them aa' ye kna
Or aal your stories in a day.'

Glossary: dans: marker buoys; creeves: crab and lobster pots; nancy: squat lobster;
frone: starfish; berried hens: female lobsters carrying eggs; swad: the green, fringed
seaweed that clings to ropes.

The Sea Inside

Into a different element
We pull from the stony quay.
A chill wind breathes warm land away
And the uncertain sea,
Rippling light into darkness,
Dark into light, sets free
Rhythms that rock our boat and ropes
And shift us restlessly.

'There's nowt t' dae but wait, man.
There's nae fish.' Charlie scans
The empty miles. Why do I feel
Unsheltered, far from land?
Beyond, the Cheviot crouches,
Black Dunstanburgh withstands
The waves, the years; between them reach
The sea, the sky, the sand.

This is our forebears' country:
So the cold wind moans.
The stink of ware and salt on the fingers
And, in the bones,
The rush and heave of water,
Unknowable, unknown –
This is the sea inside us.
It rolls us round like stones.

Decommissioning

They are burning a boat on the beach.
Grim-backed, they watch
In a darkness that crackles with fear.

Their faces leap up through the flames,
Masks hacked out of wood,
Reeling, red as blood,
Round the funeral pyre on the sand.

The planks sunder and peel
Like the great black ribs of a whale.
Unclenched, they fall,

And the sparks stream away on the wind,
And they sting like spray, smart
Like the ice-driven spray of winter
That burns in the dark –

An ache they would understand
And suffer more easily
Than the small white scrap of paper

Whose vacancy
Tells what the landsman knows
Of a boat and its burden.
Charlie, Jack, Stephen:

They slip away through the smoke,
So many nails wrenched free,
Unfastened from the sea.

From The Wund an' the Wetter

Aah can mind the time when the men wad stand
On the top a the bank lookin' oot for' the land,
An' the soond a theer crack was as good as a sang
As th' reeled off the marks th' had lorned for sae lang:
For' Langoth an' Collith t' Comely Carr,
For' the Bus a' the Born t' the Shad an' the Bar,
Faggot, the Styenny Hyels, Fiddler's Fyace,
The Cock Craa' Stoene an' thon hob-hard place
At Herrod's Hoose Plantin on Aa'd Weir's hut;
The Chorch on the Black Rock, wheer ye shoot
Sooth for' the smooth at the Benty Gut:
T' the Cundy Rock an' the trink i' the sand
Reight ablow Featherblaa' – by, she was grand.
Ye could listen aa' neet. Th' wore spells, them words –
The map an' the key tae the treasure hoard.
Noo gi' us the marks for t' finnd 'em ageyn;
Howway doon t' the chorchyard an' ask the aa'd men,

For it's come wi' the wund an' gan wi' the wetter –
We'll noe be wantin' 'em noo...

But t' heor 'em gollerin' ower a boat

Wi' the soonds a the Norsemen still thick i' theer throat –
For' carlin t' fishroom, inwaver t' crook,
Ye'll nivvor finnd these i' the page on a beuk –
Ah, but they're bonny, the pairts on a cowble –
Dip a' the forefoot, lang i' the scorbel,
For' tack heuk an' gripe t' the horns a' hor scut,
For hor thofts t' hor thowelds – th' had nyems for the lot
That unlocked a hyel world...

                                   – Which is no t' forgit
The fagarrashin foond in a fisherman's hut –
(Ye'd say it could dae wi' a reight reed up!) –
Wi' pellets an' dookas an' pickets an' poys,
Swulls an' sweels an' bows for buoys,
Rowells an' bowelts an' barky sneyds,
The tyeble aa' claed wi' perrins a' threed,
Wi' hoppin's an' hingin's tha's toozled like tows,
An' pokes for the whullicks, an' bundles a skowbs,
An' cloots for' a dopper the caaldies ha' chowed.

But hey – look oot! – divvin't gan in theer:
Ye'll nivvor git lowsed, 'cos she's wizenbank fair!

It aa' tummels oot in a roosty shoower;
The nets unraffle wi' cloods a stoor.
Ye're varnigh scumfished afore ye can caal
For the becket, the brailor, the ripper an' aa'
The whuppin's an' leashin's aback a the waa' –
By, lad, she's a reight taggarine-man's haal!

An' it's nae bother – it's naen
T' shut the door on yon.
Put oot the light. Forgit the nyems,
We'll nivvor be wantin' them things ageyn –
It's come wi' the wund an' gan wi' the wetter –
We'll noe be needin' 'em noo...

Glossary: Crack: talk; bus: rock; shad: shallow place, bank; cundy: drainage ditch; trink: deep place in sand; gollerin': shouting; carlin: space forward in coble; fishroom: space amidships in coble; inwaver: inner supporting timber of coble; crook: forward timber inside coble; cowble: coble; forefoot: curved 'keel' forward in coble; scorbel: one of twin 'keels' aft in coble; tack heuk: place on coble's bow to attach sail; gripe: narrowing of coble at bow; scut: upper plank at stern of coble; thofts: thwarts, seats in coble; thowelds: thole pins for oars; fagarrashin: mess, upheaval; reed up: clear up; pellet: small float; dooka: large float; picket: boat hook; poy: boat stick; swull: basket for long line; sweel: swivel for attaching buoy to pot; rowells: rollers on side of coble; bowelts: graithing bolt, used to drag for lost gear; barky sneyds: snoods, attaching hooks to long lines, preserved with bark; perrin: bobbin; hoppin's: twine attaching net to tow; hingin's: same, south of Beadnell; tow: rope; poke: bag; whullicks: winkles; skowb: cut stick for pot rails; cloot: rag; dopper: oilskin; caaldies: rats; wizenbank fair: extremely messy; stoor: dust; scumfished: smothered; becket: loop of rope attached to pot; brailor: net on pole for scooping fish aboard; ripper: cross pole carrying double hand line; whuppin's: fastenings, bindings; leashin's: lashings; taggarine-man: tinker.

The Pigeon Men

Three men are leaning on the corrugated iron,
Staring out across the fields at the china blue
Stretch of sky beyond. They are waiting for something.
'Ye couldn't buy that view,'

Kit shakes his head. His son John reaches up on tiptoe,
A little apart, on the loft roof, watching. Their backs
Are turned to the hand-stitched patchwork of crees, sheds, fences,
The secret shacks

And small doors cobbled from sleepers and iron sheeting
Hauled up from underground. It was pit-work
That made them ache to be out here in the sunshine
Among the birds.

'See yon green fields? Yonder's where Horden pit was –
The biggest pit in Europe, that. Nowt there now. Gone.'
John bites his tab, says nothing; glares into the distance.
Then he throws up his white dove like a flag: 'Come on!'

And suddenly the sky is full of pigeons.
Over Blackhills Dene and Paradise they fly –
Places that are names on the map now only:
Warren House, Whiteside,

And Clifton, Coxon, Cuba Streets – the vanished
Homes of vanished men who never dreamed
How much of themselves they nailed in the crees and gardens.
Home the birds stream,

While John, on the stock-loft roof, waves the frantic fantail.
'Come on!' he yells to the open sky: 'Howway!'
And the white wings beat at the end of his outstretched fingers,
As if he too was ready to fly away.

From This Far and No Further

Who says
The world ends here?
Who brings
Peace and safety?
Who wields
The two-edged sword?
It's this far and no further now.

Who owns the past?
That spring,
The stream that bears
The money in.
It's a fine line,
It's a thin wall
That says: This far
And no further now.

It's a Tourist Trail,
It's a working farm,
It's a battleground,
It's a place to live,
Where each man kills
The thing he loves
And Leisure's
Where the money is.

And it's this far and no further.
It's a balancing act for the future.
It's the Park and the Trust and the farmer
Who keep things just the way they are.

And it's more sheep and fewer men,
And it's more paperwork to plough through;
And it's more moor and it's fewer farms,
And it's more authorities to bow to.

It's a wet night, it's a foul night,
When the wind cracks and the rain rattles
The stones of the Wall and the sores of the heart;
It's a night for the fire and the whisky-bottle...

In the Milecastle Inn they are talking prices:
'Fower poond-twenty a yowe, and a poond expenses!'
'When mine went to mart, Aah come away wi' a bill!
Ye can guess where the next lot ended up – In a hole
Wi' a bullet between the ears. D' ye think Aah'm daft?
Whae, Aah ha' t' be, t' be farmin' alang the Waal...'

It's a black-dark back-end night. There are lights on the hill.
Out there, young Willie's cutting silage still
Over the bones of a dead Roman, in the rain.
Snug in the firelight, Willie of Edge's Green,
Rowley, Davey, Graham, Nick – the same
Fire-red faces, gutturals and names
As when Haltwhistle burned, a sheet of flames.
The Romans came

Like a bunch of thieves,
Boned our land
Like a side of beef,
Built their camps
Where our steadings lay:
It's the Romans get the plenty and the farmer pays.

They split our shielings
As ye'd paunch a hare;
When ye cross at the wicket
They grab their share.
They hammer out rules
And we obey:
It's the Romans get the plenty and the farmer pays.

Now regulations
Grow thick as weeds
And nobody asked us
And nobody agrees;
But when in Rome
It's the Roman way –
It's the Romans get the plenty and the farmer pays.

And it's more paper and less sense,
And it's more bureaucracy to plough through;
And it's more moor and it's fewer farms,
And it's more authorities to bow to.

Seven Silences

Excerpt from: An Ill Wind
These are the seven silences of a black season:
First, all movement frozen. Shut down
The invisible machinery of the countryside – the hunt, the patter,
The auctioneer's song.

Next comes the silence you wait for the telephone to shatter.
You can't sleep. Can't eat. The silence of fear
Crackles like electricity down the wires; and the silence of paper
Drifts like snow through the door.

Such a queer thing to tell in sheep: a lamb a bit 'hangy'
Or a ewe that will not come to the trough.
Ice-sharp, the silence after the vet has given his verdict.
This is the silence of disbelief.

The next silence is the worst silence. This is the silence
Of the steaming kitchen at three a.m.
When half the cattle lie stiff in the yard and half are still waiting.
This is a silence with no name.

The sixth silence is the silence of grass growing,
Oceans of grass that hush, hush in the wind.
It is hard to get used to this silence: grass growing, and questions
Swelling like streams underground.

And what will you do with all the questions? When a whisper, a rush, a torrent
Bursts from the farmyard into Whitehall, what will you get?
Nothing but frozen faces, and the last silence:
A barred gate.

From Dunstanburgh

Oot a the neet
Wi'oot a soond,
Ower the heather
An' benty groond,
Ower the moors
An' ower the mosses,
Th' grab wor kye,
Th' steal wor hosses,
Th' raid wor hemmels
An' byres an' steeds

An' born wor hooses
Aboot wor heeds.

Th' come like the wund
Or the snaa' in June.
Th'll gollup the meat
For' off yee'r spoon.
Th'll tyek yee'r spindle,
Yee'r kist an' quern,
An' strip the blanket
For' off the bairn;
They'll whup the sark
For' off'n yee'r back,
Then trapple yee'r barley
An' fire yee'r stacks.

Th' bring nae baggage
An' when they've fled
Leave nowt but widders
An' empty beds;
Empty bellies
An' hairts as sair
As fields a stubble
And esh. Aah sweer,
Though this be the country
God forgot,
The divvil receive
The reivin' Scot.

Glossary: benty: rough grass; kye: cattle; hemmels: cow sheds; steeds: steadings, farm buildings; gollup: gobble; kist: chest in which belongings were kept; sark: shirt; esh: ash.

Fred Reed

The Teyd Has Ebbed

The teyd has ebbed, the livil sands are wet,
And Aa can waalk reflected hivvins yit
Amang the pale 'n' scintillatin' stars.

Aad Chep

Aad chep feelin' not se good;
Aad chep seekin' firewood,
Aall faculties the warse for wear;
The laangor chill is draain' neor.
Aad chep in the univorse
Hes knaan its blissins 'nd its corse.
B' pain he may smaall cumforts find;
Se seun t' be dust in the wind.
Ye wundor whaat it's aall aboot,
But let ne man his faith refute.

Pitmen

Time trails his neits 'n' days across the spheres
    Inta the last oblivion, yit the hope
Of freedum's triumph in each hoor appeors
    Nor is effaced hooe'er forlorn men grope
For grace.

Time is freedum's slave: t' hor he'll bend
His neit 'n' day endeavours t' the end.
An' whaat's time deun for us? – the human moles
        That craall belaa the orth's deep groanin' crust
T' howk frum nature's trissurehoose the coals
That for wor country's needs are still a must
T' mek the torbines hum, thear pooer laid
On aall the tools that implement wor trade.

Wey, we've won justice through wor unity.
        Wor common bond high pooer noo defies.
We've put an end t' profit-lustors' spree
        That gripped the throat of wor tormented cries
When wor sad plight wus nivvor undorstood,
An' dividends wor won wi' pitmen's blud.

Brazen Faces

We dandered roond bi Gallowget
When us went ti the toon
Nineteen hundred 'n' sivinty eight
On a Seterda efterneun.
Skinheads, yakkors, lud-brained louts,
The tousled haired disgraces,
Aall gannin' in ti St. James' Park
Ti show wor brazen faces.

Oh, me lads, ye shud hev hord us yellin',
Offensive blue 'n' blasphemous
An' crude abeun the tellin'.
A bunch of hooligans ti blare
Aall wi' brazen faces
Ti mek folks wundor whaat the future
O' the human race is.

Beech Tree

Yor leaves hev gyen wi' the wind
That chills the rumps o' the kine.
Aa wish it cud blaa memories
Frum this dull hairt o' mine.
Aye, coontless times yor gowlden leaves
Hev drifted doon t' rot,
An' mony a man 'n' mony a maid
Are gyen 'n' soon forgot.
Dumb pains, glad trysts, waarm ecstasies.
Aa had a slip of a lass,
But noo she sleeps belaa ye heor
And Aa weep in the grass.

Springan

Caa, caa, ye noisy craas!
Gobby a bard as ivvor waas.
Yon tree's se like a hoose o' lords.
Whaat's meant b' them donart words?
        Aa'm sure nebody knaas.

Abeun the hemmel, ower bye,
Wheelin' in the dappled sky,
Ye'll droon oot spuggies, lairks 'n' wrens,
An' set the laddies hoyin' styens
        Wi' yor feckless cry!

Like a kibble gyen amain,
Spring comes boondin' doon the lane,
An' buttercups 'n' pittlybeds
Lift thor bonny gowlden heids
        Aglistenin' wi' rain.

The lambs are lowpin' doon the neuk,
Or, dunchin' yows, they thrust 'n' suck.
Aa'll skelp yon tyke that's barkin' lood
An' chasin' coneys i' the wood
        Wi' neethor airt nor luck.

The born runs deep in yalla mud
And at the bend hes kirved a jud,
Then doon the swally lowps 'n' reels
An' blethors, froths, 'n' cowps hor creels
    Se rollickin' in flud.

Doon wheor the willas hev thor fling
Fornenst the footbridge, catkins hing,
An' heor the tits are aall agabbor,
The robin playin' hitchy-dabbor
    Afore he tyeks t' wing.

Belaa the knowe the slope's ablaze
Wi' saffron broom 'n' bluebell haze,
An' heor the stallion whustles oot
An' raises high his gyepin' snoot
    In statuesque amaze.

 The peewit's cry aches ower the field
Aall furrowed for a bagey yield,
An' stottin' doon the lonnen's ditch
The dronin' bummlor powks his snitch
    In dusty gowld concealed.

Wi' musky yarbs the air smells fine,
The low shines softly 'n' benign,
The arth wears resurrection's smock
For chthonian dreams the noo hev brock
    Amang the eglantine.

Diddle Diddle

Hey diddle diddle
Me Dad's on the fiddle
An' signin' on for the dole.
But they'll find him oot
An' he'll get the beut
For floggin' his cheap sea-coal.

299

Gareth Reeves

The Cockroach Sang in the Plane-tree

The heat of the moment,
the cold stare, the lovers' tiff,
shall cover the earth. All of you,
legs, lusts, nerves, good feelings, good looks,
genitals, hearts, hurts, shall ascend
and spread, shall keep on going round.
No one shall start again.

No torso shall get caught in the act.
Your last meal, petrified in the throat,
shall not be analysed.
You shall be a flicker on the scan,
a shadow punched in concrete.
Your DNA shall give its last twist.

"The end of civilization as we know it."
You won't know it.
There shall be no unthinkable.
All shall be thinkable,
atomized to a thought.
All shall be vapid.

Anything goes because everything shall go.
All shall be level, shall be up in the air.
No tone shall be suitable.
There shall be no tone

when the dust settles
forever and forever.

Touch Type

Fon'y mskr my houdr yout nsdr
sd you fif lsdy yimr
– jokes in jabberwocky, neo-Lilliputian,
a sort of pseudo-Urdu, I thought,
until I decoded it:
Don't make my house your base
as you did last time,
the left hand one key to the right
for the whole paternal letter.
On my next – flying – visit
I noticed his H and G were green:
he'd peer though thick lenses
to check the green keys
were between his index fingers,
then he'd cock his head and was off,
no second look, no proof-reading,
brain, to fingers, to postman, to reader.

When I was five and he was forty-three
for months a large chart of the key-board
hung over his desk. I thought that this
must be what it means to go freelance.
The chart was going more and more out of focus.
Other people's dads went out to work,
mine went upstairs
where for two years and £1000
he wrestled with a fat international
conspectus of World War Two writings,
his first commission. Home-front peace
was broken by orders from on high:
'Turn it down, I'm earning your living.'

The Home Guard was the nearest
they'd let him get to the action.
He was guarding a signal-box
(in case the enemy shunted along?)
when he woke to someone shouting

'Wake up, the war's over.'
He must have rubbed his eyes and blinked
at daylight on three sides.

After a morning's work
he'd sit back for his eye-drops.
The first one usually missed,
then a bull's eye.

The typewriter accelerated
from popping to a battery.

Gadgets

Write down in your own words what the poet means by...
'Means, my foot. It means what I bloody well wrote,'
barked Father when they set him for O Level prac. crit.

A student erupts in a seminar
'Why do we end up arguing what a poem's *about?*'
Touché; to fill the silence...

"And your suggestion?"
A poem should not mean but be etcetera?
A machine made of words, a sort of divine gadgetry?

Ambition was out, trust to inspiration:
over a bottle one evening, beneath his outdoor awning
Father set up a recitative:

'I shall go down for the odd limpid lyric.
Let's drink to that.'
As night closed in he opened up.

He was always making things –
stoppers for started bottles,
that bathroom contraption

whose rites I pondered, then gave up and asked:
it was to silence the tap-water if his bath
needed a top-up with hot while the Third was on

– Heath Robinson affairs. Inspired arcana.

The Entertainer

It's an octave short, no good for Chopin,
Schumann, Liszt – not that he liked them much
(my girl-friend went off at both ends) –
and Beethoven could be a squeeze;
but it fitted his eighteenth-century favourites,

though he played it less and less as the keys blurred.

It glints, a metallic green, promising
1930s cinema schmaltz.

Our piano-tuner twinkles 'Was your father
an entertainer?' Well, yes
and no… The man he might have been:

Velvet curtains glide
and he rises through the floor
in a black-and-red striped
smoking-jacket, white hair
edging the collar, a live cigar
perched on the piano-lid
in which his face appears
relaxing to improvisations
as his hands blindly
spread the effortless chords.

Deus ex Machina

When the train stopped
he jerked awake, panicked, stepped out
the wrong side onto the tracks
and found himself sprawled on a sleeper,
the electrified line inches away.

So he took to sleeping
to the end of the line.
If it was the last train,
the Drunk Special – not that he was –
he went back ten miles by taxi.

Is there a god of the blind? –
an inscrutable all-knowing
taxi-driver who ferries shaded men
in a limousine past irrelevant countryside,
with stereo background and a switch
to turn the world on/off.

Graeme Rigby

Motordreams

I
Give me oil in my lamp, keep me burning;
Give me oil in my lamp, I pray...

> *Oh, we've learnt our lessons.*
> *We won't go down that road again.*

The landscape fractured.
Voices.
There were voices in my head.
Driving in my car,
listening to the voices.

> *If we've learnt anything,*
> *anything at all from the Caterpillar.*

Listening at the cracks,
peering through the fissures,
the cracks between the dreams.

> *The future doesn't lie...*
> *Salvation doesn't lie*
> *in that direction.*

Give me oil in my lamp, keep me burning,
Keep me burning till the break of day...

II

Through the waste-hours of the night, I drove
through Leadgate, through New Kyo,
below Birtley, the grey shards of dawn
beyond Shiney Row.

First light on the long-backed hump of slag
above Herrington,
the toughened laminated windscreen silence
shattered in the cock crow.

> Climbing up Penshaw Hill,
> looking down:
> the North laid out
> panoramic.

Grey light folding the cranes of Pallion,
Austin & Pickersgill's,
the blue transits that wait by Murton
for the next shift.

First light lying across the scraped runways
of Sunderland Airport,
a broad MacAlpine earthwork morning
bulldozers have left.

> Black monument above me,
> I lie on Penshaw Hill,
> dreaming north above the Wear,
> dreaming the dawn.

III

Motordreams.

I saw it on Pontop Pike (one hill to another),
the beam of its headlights intercepting the signal.
It spoke through our sets and we listened,
a car that talked to the people.

My Sumitomo tyres are fat with the speeches of welcome. In my more
than capacious boot I carry untold wealth.

It spoke, predictably, from under the bonnet,
its gleaming paintwork, its chrome that shone;
we spoke in whispers and approached with care,
this car that reflected the sun.

I come from a miracle land. I have crossed the Pacific. I have crossed
America, shore to shining shore. Miracles are above nations.

It spoke of Wales, of Immingham, even Europe;
we placed a ban on dangerous questions.
It spoke of promise without making promises,
the car that ate Washington.

I am the dream of success on your television screens. I am a lottery prize.
Our ticket sellers are in your region today.

IV
Now is the time for all good men
to jump like performing fleas,
hoop after hoop after hoop after hoop,
they jump with a consummate ease:

Bob Clay as Jeremiah,
the rest as quiet as you please;
Tokyo Jim's got his business cards
printed in Japanese.

V
Motordreaming.

We stood on Sunderland Airport
in the soft wet sleet,
dreaming of the sun.

Watching their faces
pressed against the windows

of the Sunderland first team coach,

joking amongst ourselves,
we laughed at Humberside
who didn't even own their site

and at bloody Wales
with a bog on their site...
drove them round in a fleet of Ladas

and two of them broke down.

Only the weather.
Only the weather let us down,
a soft wet sleet on the airport...

It's raining Datsun cogs, we cracked,
careful not to be overheard.

VI
(From Penshaw Hill I saw it all: the car at the airport, the ceremonies of good
luck. On the green plains below me I saw men dance. Saw them dance and
heard the crack.)

Says Joe to Tom, *It's a glass*
of water in the desert sands.
We must drink it and we must pay.
What coins do you hold in your hand?

> They linked their arms and they danced,
> danced with the toe and the heel;
> and they raised their arms and they danced:
> The Dance of the One Union Deal.

Says Tom to Joe, *It's a game*
of cards. You're a gambling man.
I ask as a comrade and brother:
could I see what you hold in your hand?

The car had an open bonnet
(they danced with the toe and the heel)
and those pearly white teeth shined on it:
The Dance of the One Union Deal.

Says Joe and Tom to the rest,
*Let's dance to this very fine band
and we'll each of us trust this motorcar
with a free and an open hand.*

So Tom and Joe and the rest,
they danced with the toe and the heel;
danced as the jaws closed fast
on The Dance of the One Union Deal.

(From Penshaw Hill I saw it all. Saw it all and heard the crack...

*Did ye ivvor hear tell o' the Yatsoogi Sivvn, Joe?
Why aye, Tom. Ivvrybody's hord o' the Yatsoogi Seven. Is it not that
fillum ye mean, with Yul Brynner?
That'll be it, like...*)

VII
From a factory window I watched a flood,
four month strike-broken men,
headbands worn in protest,
streaming through the gates of Nissan.

This motorcar brings hope to the North.

Accountants told me: *Those who truly
love their union, love their company.*
In America we knelt. We prayed for partnership
between management and employee.

This motorcar brings hope to the North

At Longbridge, at component firms I talked
with men yet to be laid off.
The Midlands, I said to them,
have had the running long enough.

      This motorcar brings us hope in the North.

On a beach in Japan with a man from Tennessee,
we talked to each other.
They have a word for it, he said.
Neemo-shami. A coming together.

      Motordreams.

VIII
On Penshaw Hill I closed my eyes.
I saw it all coming together.
I saw them all coming together
on the plains below.

They stood before the open smile
of this car that ate Washington.
They looked into the jaws of a multinational
and saw a Little Tokyo.

IX
In the fractured landscape, climbing down,
head in neutral, clutch depressed;
out of sorts in a battered Cortina,
driving into the West.

Give me oil in my lamp, keep me burning;
Give me oil in my lamp, I pray.
Give me oil in my lamp, keep me burning;
Keep me burning till the break of day.

Mark Robinson

Poem (On Realising I am English)

*'The important thing is to adapt your dish of spaghetti
to circumstances and your state of mind.'*
Guiseppe Marotta

In the parallel universe where wizened Corsicans
rave over suet dumplings and rapturously murmur
improvised sonnets in praise of stotty,
barm cake, bloomer, cob, scone (to rhyme with gone)

no one would criticise me for never mentioning
the real grievance at the heart of this poem.
I'd be lauded for the tightness of my lip,
for the way you feel my teeth grit and grind,

for how I shrug off questions with a joke
about the endless spouting of emotion
I waded through to get here.

I think this as the glaze of a first pressing
spreads its lucent green over the frying pan,
ready to spit at the very suggestion of an onion.

From the Shadow of the Flats

beyond the bridge of the hills the flash of white water
        the arbor of steel the ridges of bark
beyond the nipples of chimneys the rake of the chutes
        the slush of the neon the chink of the till
beyond the tattoo of hunger the breath of a dream

beyond the forest of plumes the chase of the beach
        the gang of rough gardens the shelter of scrub land
beyond the gamble of hedges the fist of hydrangias
        the stain of wires fences the field of lost toddlers
beyond the slag of graffiti the breath of a dream

beyond the tic of late giros the whine of the pavements
        the smelting of scratch cards the gag of nappies
beyond the slave-song of mowers the coda of bad chests
        the pit of the weekend the cracking of locks
beyond the wheeze of sunday the breath of a dream

beyond the arc of the football the breath of a dream
beyond the clean sweep of river the breath of a dream
beyond the spray of red sun the breath of a dream
beyond the white noise of surf the breath of a dream
beyond the reach of our shadows the breath of a dream

lungs catching new air breath of a dream

Rio de Juninho

We could have had a gritty midfield battler,
cast from the bits British Steel had left over,
last welding done by a returner from Saudi,
dragged from Grangetown by a traveller's pony,
his forehead trailing on the dirty tarmac,
a matter of inches from his hairy knuckles,
his mam and dad proud and loud in the stand
when his prehensile studs rip carefully through

the arty-farty shins of a Dutch dazzler,

or a rough and tumble striker on the way up,
thick as a brick made of slag but big hearted,
with a forehead like a stoker's shovel
and sharpened elbows that have been known
to carve his names in defenders' backsides,
whose first words as a child were translated as
"I'll bite your bloody balls off you big arsewipe",
with a right foot as true as his tax returns,

but then we would not have seen,
walking by the still filthy river one day,
ten thousand yellow shirts dancing in the breeze,
a new look in people's eyes,
something not to be denied even by results,
that I know is ridiculous and still want,
a dreaming set off like a ticking bomb,
this chipped and battered town
twinned with a place so exotic
we did not know it was just like home.

Laying a Carpet With My Dad

We squeezed the settee out to the dining room
then rolled up the old carpet and flopped it on the stairs
to lie there till bin day like a subject we'd had to drop.

Feeding the shiny white banister through my hands
I ran up to my room or to the loo along its back.
The foam cracked and fell off, like scabs I picked at.

The Stanley knife was so sharp I was forbidden to touch.
Along the spikes of the Betagrip I ran my fingers
till I had scratched new patterns on the tips, the prints.

We rolled out the fragrant new carpet in strict rhythm,
counting, as if learning to dance, so that it didn't slant,
revealing more of the pattern with each movement.

Dad whipped round the edges trimming the excess and then
we set to pulling and pushing it to that taut perfection
my Mum expected. Nothing of a job, but satisfying.

The knee-kicker was an instrument of torture
you could fall in love with, for the give of the cushion
as you punched it forward, the grip of the pins, silver, not letting go.

Dad and I would sit in the middle of the empty room
and try to ignore the corner where the carpet did not quite reach.
That was where we would put the settee.

On the beach near Kinvarra our babies

play on the slate-grey sand.
The football rebounds from the surf
again and again. And again
the spite-sapping wind carries it back,
gently back to our son's excited arms.

I try to clamber out into the foam
along the ragged teeth of the rocks,
but the sand sucks at my unsuitable shoes,
like in Lou's favourite bedtime story
of my escape from building-site mud.

You can't stop laughing, keep repeating
'Typical, just exactly typical.'
The sun goes down and turns
the woman gathering Lucky Stones
into a shadow who waves goodbye.

The children chase each other up the slope
to where the seaweed meets the tarmac.
As we negotiate the tortuous roads
to this fortnight's home, they sleep.
We talk of your plans for the garden.

Something pretty. Something indestructible.
The sea returns the ball we left behind.
It rolls down through the weed, floats back.
Rolls down again, is pushed stubbornly back,
until it stays where it has been put.

Loose connections beneath the dashboard

From Yarm to Netherthong on an empty tank
without adding a mile to our history,
we have guessed our speed in the suburbs,
crossed our fingers in sweaty gridlock
and cruising on the M1 listened to rattles
accumulate like guilty verdicts,
first one sorry hand, then another,
then more until it's unanimous: off with his head.
According to the car we have not moved.
The landscape was having us on,
tugging hedgerows into the distant behind-us,
the wheels were turning in air, or mud,
and this holiday cannot yet have started,
the children are still screaming to leave.
But the momentum that carried us here
must register somewhere. The wheels
could draw a map or a house or a face
without turning the clock or taking a pound,
without scratching our part-exchange,
but something has shifted, has pushed us
99 miles towards older and wiser.
Repeating this trick is a difficult knack,
one that can get you from yesterday
to now to tomorrow and back.

My son, already disappearing into a man

(Caroline Forché)
- forgive me. Let the basket ball hoop
slip this caught breath through. Let
Grandad's silver model Jag chip
back to green in the Airfix drawer.
Let car boot aliens wait away 15p lives
in a broken tangle of headphones.
Let skateposters fade to black and red.
Let books tessellate, heroes rewind like tapes,
Disney on flu-ridden Wednesdays.
Let the Playstation beat us. Let Scalextric
click together to form a virtuous circle
to hum us into conversation.
Let broccoli yellow in the fridge.
Let your paintings grow away from you,
embarrassing in the bathroom.
Let the day get longer. Yes, let the days get longer.
Let small boys gaze at you in wonder as your bike
goes higher than their heads in The Dippers.
Let me and Mum walk past you in the street
and let you and your friends not see us.
Let the dusk go unmarked for the first time,
the treehouse fall in unnailed chunks
under leaves till Spring, your name sprayed
in primary school red, like a plaque on the lawn.
Let the homework rows be forgotten.
Let the twisted top E strings rust. Let
my broken guitars in the attic stay there,
superglued necks and impossible fingerings
silent but for the breeze-hum only the varnish
and dust can hear. Let how they got that way
go the way of all cries. Let this moment be our secret.
Let me teach you D and A and G.
Let them be enough for now. Let
this basic language have its uses. Let me be foreign
in this strange land. Let me just about get by.

Jon Silkin

For David Emanuel

      I shall pass you the tall moment.
It was on the still day I saw my son
        Lying in his sleep. The birds,
        Clamoring, they

        Poked their shining faces
In the child's window. That was a shy day,
        The sun walking through the mist,
        The pale hours

        Following his first
Day when we ran into the solid, brass
        Light, alive to this life.
        And to-day, I stole

        Into the small sleeping
Room of his dreaming and saw him, half
        Of my sure flesh, strong
        To be surer yet

        Of his unabiding flesh.
It wasn't the ripe glory of the sun
        Nor the dogs grinning below
        At a mouldy joy bone

        It was my son. Half Jew
And wholly human sleeping in the curved eye
        Of his future. And I
        Alone with the sun in

Its morning, I with
Two large eyes staring into his god's eyes:
He was half mine, half
That woman buried
In the hot raiments of her sleep.
I could not wholly wake him. But I turned to the
Intruding sun that
Stole so

Fearfully in his room. I
Thanked it that this morning it touched my eyes that
They flung wide to
The joy of my son,

That he entered and shook my love,
And took my heart into his small heart. May love like this
Remain with him, as the innocence
Of the sky remains crowned with the sun.

Epilogue

All the people in my poems walk into the dark
All the animals walk up to the ark.
The people are deaf and limping like flies;
Cunning shining soft sad they walk,
And they do not know but they walk into the dark.

All the animals in my poems walk in the sun
Blinking their eyes and licking their paws; they go
On and on up the proud procession of stairs
Up the proud straight stairs like a holy circus
And they do not know but they walk in the light.

If all the people and all the animals

Joined dark with light; if all the proud people
And soft-stepping circus climbed their way in the dark
Walked with the black seals and walked with the spidery flies
They would all go into the great light, and they would know.

Leaving The Free Trade

Ah, that's the heart of it; if we
could have free trade. A bar. . . yet what
bar is it? . . . one that
was a house. You stand close
to your lager, lightly warm. You smile.
Politeness is all the rage.

A tree that's grass, serrate leaves prick
off a stem – within the top
thick dots of deft, light
green pollen. The smells
of our class:
beer smoke and envy sift
between the strong lax fangs of leaves.

'Shall you leave early?' 'Please.'Wan smiling
in a white demeanour. Your heavy
animal grace. 'Do you prefer
this one?' – my grin stared at. 'What
is it?' as you turn
thirst to lager. As if a thing
in a painting, I'm
a trap, and rat smiling behind slats,
its head, that had
chewed its tucker, lowered
between the two scapulae, fur thinned
at where ears stiffen. We are
docile, becalmed. You: your moist
mindful, animal tenderness
is smiling.

This house, its ceiling
in lozenge tracery, a rose, is slicked
with murky pink, the bar
a furniture one must step
round. 'Love, throw the darts.' The board
chuckles within its rings, zinc
competitions – 'I will,' you
tell me – bull, zero,
thud of points entering rings. You put
your hand with mine. It's The Free Trade;

 the eyed male minimum changes
to amenable companion, of a double nought
paired sequins, the two
nude bodies – us – heaving
that has scraped thin, paint
chipped off wood
in a pub with ship-builders
in a front room
of a seventy-year house built
to be modest –
humbling pain, the sweet
hot alteration, tenderness,
amour. I touch you. You are good
to me. 'You shall not,' you say, 'escape
as easily this time.'

The ships, all
shift from their moorings – in
a big swelling flight, fill with
departure, sail-ships
stirred with the wind – move down-hill
into the sea, through the arms
of their double pier. We are on the sea,
we are ships, from The Free Trade
the great chill amours of the north,
with lamps winking, gone.
The waves are furrowing themselves,
a sloshing aftermath.

A man from the shipyards

In the process of becoming a Quaker, Penn, still in the navy, asked whether or not, or for how long, he should continue to wear his sword. 'Wear it for as long as thou canst,' Fox replied. (The Quakers by A. Neave Brayshaw)

'In the destructive element immerse' Joseph Conrad - *Lord Jim*

Penn, from the shipyards, bears a sword – 'natural
to a man of war' . . . 'what must I do with it?'
'wear it as thou canst,' Fox answers. Thou is
thou yet, although that natural, aching
psyche in its wet plasm of snowy
righteousness requires, 'your life for my child's'.
That some women
are not made more compassionate than all men.

As if for arbitration, with his sword
Penn leads the beasts – a forest clearing, by leaves
melted to twilight, the sword
like a bird biting
the leaves to line its children's nest; and not
much different, she, a human animal,
pulling his senses to her breasts, annuls
jealousy. Penn would change us,

the soul's light standing to its flesh,
its sleek shape, as charge;
he would merge the natural with the common flesh
as leaves with light merge,
where a community of stealth, of mild and fierce creatures
and dangling hair touching the breasts, gathers. . .

'not that we can't see,' Penn says, 'but the pain
because we do,' his sinewy mind
all-eyed, spotting like
a candle in snow. Penn and Fox
smudge with earth, lying between
friends, digesting the consequences

of hunger. They speak their minds, each day –
-the leafy day, the branching night
in harmonious succession
-- natural, again, most natural,
as when at length the living God
like living water
lifted his creatures up. Natural.

Penn took a fork from his pocket
as if he had meant to swallow meat. At which
the creatures shuddered in their forms, yet did
not creep away to weep. And tears,
which are the edge of grief, started, like blood,
the animals whining in upstart pain,
abandoned now, to be love's careless victims,
in that compact never to kill. Of love
they thought but little after that, as if
love, a watery human element – *in that*
destructive element immerse – were fit
for breaking, the lesser magnitude than care.
Then Fox's tears dropped,
the land held in his thinking
of rocks, sand, tears.

Watersmeet

In Northumberland, by Hexham, where the North and South Tyne rivers meet on their way east.

1

The railway arch views a trinity of water
one stream, and a second, then, each in the other.
Here a walker hoists his pack, a tree
hanging a troubled burden of fruit, off one
to the other shoulder.

Precious this water is to my tiredness.

The tracks are taken up, the tracks endure
the pitiful life   .
of objects omitted from the future.
In the absent railway, the catkin spills her pollen
where a man with roots walks. She is the first
to entice life to hers, after
the short-day's solstice.
Christmas light spills glad-shouldering hymns,
the carols' large glib cheer
we stoop to, that omits irony, foe to men,
that is men,
which stars the ginger shape of biscuit, nips the tongue with all-spice.
You must not spend all the candle until the year dies.
And was it kind,
God's child entering an ancient world?

2

Waterboatmen dent one river. A spiky-bone trout
flickers by, slim, insouciant.
A second stream, simmering volcanic water,
sways on journals in the turning globe.
And when the magma bursts
over which this pointed water runs,
its gushing mineral scrapes life off, a toss
of sulphur, men's little forks turning
blebs of soil.
And who am I stubby suburban grafting
behind a white-scented privet,
its leaf catspiss,
but a moss, in dried
wavering fingers of summer?

3

Two rivers join, and how
decipher in whose character the other bathes?
Is character tested by the ego's smoky lamp,
the paranoid, blocking out steady generous feeling,

that, riding in each other's flow, is the only certitude? This, of marriage.
As if in marriage, its papery certificate,
its papery water wrinkling calm and simmering water,
which is the ghost of all that is marriage,
water that is marriage, each ego modifies
to the other. This water and that flow. Both flesh.

And they are all that other, which is,
in all its character and boisterous ego,
what nature is. Each emboldened in its form
in exuberance. Creation sprays of itself,
a stubby plant that creeps close to earth,
how should it grow? or the buried tarot,
fluted rough potato, the alpine sea-waves
of bitter grass, the spiked straw-hue marigold
its triangular space meticulously hoed
and pressed up to the house, a diadem of wood,
the tiled ceramic shaped in quaking movement.
The liminal and aching fields rule out
bamboo whose root system grips earth as if
a man in a woman, with frail sheds
of black pine, and red pines, the mecan trees
lamping small loose-skin orange fruits,
their sweet fleshy segments loose, in a tremor
of spiked leaf.

So it spreads over all volcanic earth,
seismic fertility, bitter smelling narcissus
and twisted matsu, all
water's exuberance, all character
and the ego of plants, unlike the human,
that does not vaunt, brag, or shoot.
It is as if only cemeteries are fertile
if to be human is fertile.

If you speak so much, God, can I hear myself?
Only in loneliness, that privilege,
I burn and share myself. But like water, I mingle
and exalt another.

4

Two rivers meet, union, unpromiscuous, by chance,
and sport in each other. The saint kneels with one vision
and offers by this water
with unpresuming ego his thread of gratitude
towards his spangled God.

Are rivers sprung only that we may receive them?
Is fertility our only garb? (Some dress in Chryslers.)

The air is smelling of our thankfulness.

5

If you had churned water and earth to mud
but withheld the flash-flood, torn with stony jags

    it would have been enough

if you had flaked tarry plutonium
in which a modicum of moisture

    it would have sufficed

if you'd withheld tectonic mud
its diffident treacherous plain

    it would have been enough

if you had melted the sun
like a cube of sugar
if you had pressed the lake like a stud, into earth
if it were virid, if virid from harsh pine
crammed to its scummy rims

    it would have been enough

if clean water from a tap
and the glacier had retreated into hiding

it would have been enough

  If it had been milk on a teat;
an unfailing tap,
the snow-melt unforeclosed by profit
the flash-flood out of the ring of mountain
with sulphur, the swan-reflexing glib
sleek-feathered lake,
the salt on the teat
in thirst, that had once not been thirst, love,
the mountain, its celestial drip
plutonium, again, warped in tarry flakes,
the tectonic mud, and the water-drop
of the republic of ants

    it would have been enough

It was enough. For there is water
sinking through a rotted gravel, short
of the sea's rims.

It keeps an ancient freshness.

But the sea, *Into me with you.*

Water sinks through stones, and discloses
rose, umber, and jade, quartz, picked from our fields
chipped from mines, or scooping a cave
where a defeated huntsman barks like his red fox.
Or there are stones of no colour. There are always these.

But if waters flow in each other
without consciousness, from Watersmeet,
yet are themselves, as we cannot be
only ourselves,
we, without the single, watery, blessed state,
are yet like water mixed

the sigh into gravel, I make, touching your breast.

And if your breast knows that water lingers
in its milk, let me touch you
and postpone the sea, and defer the sea's licking
my feet, for as you know, all of this
meeting is where we have been, and when stopped
cannot be taken from itself.

The Soul Never Has Enough

Sitting by you in the yard as if
you were my child, mountain ash, I see
He has chosen to have silence in your mouth.

Wordless beatitude. As the snow dominantly
smells, of snow, and you lose leafage,
the wind's noise hones to notes on your physique.

Soul, soul, grief's slippage
is your silence. I must not speak.
No end, and no more. With the wind, darling, you engage.

Colin Simms

Jill Merlin of a calm, clear morning

flights the Ladygill pastures
almost at ground-level at first

at first noticing, a sight-burst
hard to focus on.
From a blur greyer than their
colours, and the colour
the grey-in-tone
(to do with) as the earth

and the light is (all) angle and strength
the flight, at any length
stretches the sense (of it) its air
single and sudden, single and swifter
than any flicking right-and- length--
'spar' - because further and bolder

left-and-right and across
line of road, sight, horizon
is display for you, I say:
she is accustomed to me
(is) generous of that energy
– and she's not hunted yet today

personal as tracer focuses in on us
little grey-brown long wing shows-off
all over the hill within our vision
but beyond it. Learn if we will
she'll whiffle down as if onto prey
look back at us, and go into the grey   *(Feb 21, 2004)*

Basil - Birthday Poem

for March 1st 2003

One of the shortest rivers, Rawthey
runs sixteen or eighteen miles – shortly
off Baugh Fell's indefinite summit
to its joining the Dee near Brigflatts.
Out of Bowderdale it collects the Cautley
beck from Cautley Spout off Cautley
Crag where, Baz, we felt the spirit
of peregrine sit, and before we saw it!

Raven's idle wingflaps, sharps and flats
bass-baritone cawing and haughty
heard even above our drinking there in
the 'Cross Keys' – yet a Temperance Inn!
A683 Rawthey Bridge to by-Brigflatts
three boys' separated emotions
recalled in Backside Beck's rumbling plaits
experience echoed for each; first visits
there with Ed Flintoff, and Margaret
Hartley: Raven, peregrine, merlin!

Still as the Meeting-House, as thought-filled,
that "High Cwm", spout solid wall – water.
Rawthey Bridge to the chapel at Cautley:
the old packhorse track is still shorter
along the pasture-sides of Blae Caster,
trespass or right-of-way our laughter
raised jack-merlin, silent over his pipit,
to shout defiance over Thwaite of Cautley.
Raise whisky-flask and sup it, *"sip it"*,
wishing our spirits more wick, less portly...

[First stanza incident 1980, second stanza 1970, 1974 and 2000)

Feb 28th, Garrigill

Afternoon in Redesdale

Mattie Biggs, getting the last round in,
"Why are there no Roman words at all in
our dialects, Cumbrian or Northumbrian
or eether O' the North-Riding yans"?
She: "there are words on the maps alright
me: 'look who made the maps'- all: "Quite"!

From the 'First and Last' pub for us
in England, uphill to old Bremenium
("at the sound of the unruly torrents")
we compared Cataractonium
its Swale in flood there, when we went,
no louder than this Sill in its gill
-both rise and fall forever, never still.

Will it have been outpost for Brigantes first
or Votadini; surely once a hill-fort?
Rome improved upon such redoubt indeed
that Bremenium, High Rochester, needs
be featured on the Ptolemy Mappa Mundi
(learned at school) the Empire's far sallyport
for scouts, barracks for several centuries.

At the camp below, at the Rede crossing,
'Lisha', we celebrate three or four 'firsts':
Mattie the first-born in Rochester after the War;
the Pearl-bordered Fritillary, Northumbrian;
then a first marten specimen into a collection
Basil's first witnessed Otter hunt, 1911.
All four our first picnic at Habitancum.

for B.B., M. Biggs, M. Wilkinson;
visits 1979-84

We Couldn't Pass

We couldn't pass a graveyard sprinkled with Border names without a word.
The word that rose on its own insistence, like we couldn't come to Chollerford
and the watters high again that they dared not follow across the wor(1)d.
(He one of the few with me who'd agree with me
it was too easy, wrong, to only come there by car)
until it didn't need to be heard, this extra word and for
how can so few names so increase our own word-hoard?

Lychened on every grey, red, blue stone and brown along every burn and road
fresheted at every wind's turn there's a place for little children and in the air
and squall and hail and rain and snow loaded stain on every moonchange/
goad.

He'd agree with me on the modesty of the phrasing
(rightness is in the phrasing, fox gazing or yowes grazing
have their own rhythm only if they feel secure)
poor though the analogy be, and though ignorant stare...

In the shimmer on every sike and burn and beck, bogburst and curtain flow
down every hill and fellside and in every summer's dry burn trickle and stir
in however little light, every last breath, every drop of blood chose that way
their world over, and their world now so wide
rose and ran in these winds and springs
(day after day, what Kipling called the English way)
we knew to be those self-same shades of grey.

Every last drop of blood and every last sigh and cry of that spirit
runs today in the springs of that country, which is this underfoot
overhead. We bring our poor yellow, purple ribbons for your hair, and put
motherland is in it for us, merit; and through our mothers inherit.

with BB at Dallowgill and Garrigill; 1984 (2002 revision)

At the Morden Tower

A mere ex-Objectivist regrets there are less about –
-the men who found and the men who named them
Gila monsters and He-men; replaced by hedonists

With the best of our poets, another rare tradition
I like to think of them, pioneers, men of distinction.
Those stony deserts shelter frisky risks, an attraction
These stones drew to Newcastle the best from all the world
of its time which cannot last; men themselves last less
"Good if there's five in a century in any one country"*
the best of forms, fauna (like buffler), can, maybe, come again.

Tower as bastle, Basil's bastle at that; castle of unrest.
This is the place that Tom and Connie made, for the best;
and became, thus, best place in the world, for the kingdom –
-and never mind conveniences, central-heating, even Mammon.

Less than the best is arrayed here now; played-at, lest
tradition be lost; but I'm for letting them 'wait on'
for excellence - they'll be having Andrew Motion next!
Poetry won't be lost, the soar and stoop of things not gone
though recognition of it rusts for want of patience, discretion,
presence of the falcons who bring the heart to the mouth
who have to be rare or solitary yet neither tarry nor scare.

Listening's gone out of favour in noise and social whirls;
surprise and engagements run away with the jolly-girls:
while miles away in place or time something yet unfurls
which was in the promise of the earlier days of the Earls...

*B.B.
CS 1985-86

Michael Standen

The Land

The land up here in winter shows its age,
Many millennia appear;
From fields, houses, industries,
The moors spring clear.

On cold and cheerless days like this
Our hold upon the earth is slight:
Colourless grass and comfortless
Lie of the land put right

Our fondest wishes which we graze
In pastures of human scale,
And something in us bleak as it
Makes word and wonder, wish, fail.

The Outcome

Voices come back to me on tape,
Our children, little, coaxed to sing.
How harmless now their countering
Resistances to what we wanted at the time!
The time announced and date and place
By voices, mine and hers, which sound
Now strangely young and almost strange.
But it's hard to know how sounds come out,
Or times transposed come out,
Or what to make of such a cheat,
Or why completely unexpected love
Should be the reeling outcome.

333

Along the Purley Way

I took my son on my dead father's behalf
To see the remains of Croydon Aerodrome
Still spreading amazingly along the Purley Way.
Associated buildings shine in sunsets of day or mind
Like a last convincing idea of the future.
Now it's just fast-food warehouses, it's all junk.
The security guards in unbuttoned coats
Know it's not where anything's at, even in Croydon.
There's where my unapprenticed chippie son has been
Helping Leisureworld plc put in
Millions, put in lights to blow your mind
Around half an acre of former office basement.
Two-quid lager needs the help of strobes
To jackpot back into your reeling head;
Quality's an old obsession doesn't pay.
Thus Croydon swings and knocks things down
But has left enough along the Purley Way
Of what no one would know unless they knew
How from there a streamlined future flew
When my father, turning thirty, cast weather runes,
Careful in his new civvies, buttoned up.
The sun for me rubs these buildings new,
Glints imagined grass. Two sons, we almost
Hear the whir of time's fly-past.

'Consett R.I.P.'

(Newcastle Evening Chronicle, 1980)

Slaughtered more like it, a serpent on a hill,
A monster brinking the day with black crests
For miles visible and for more miles by the stain of its breath;
Round here all the epics are posthumous.
It was until now a 'company town'
And we only half saw it for what it was truly -
A beast to put down with a kingly sword -
Kings and knights were never pleasant or thoughtful.
From now on the sunsets must redden themselves
And the snow may fall in July, but of ordinary no-colour;
Such industries are all going . . . East.
But let me not prink in the reach-me-down miseries
Of the people of Consett - that is their own affair
And the rubbish of welfare, tidying up,
Litters of forms, appropriate spaces,
Rooms awkward for prams and needing repainting. . .
That they have seen before.
                                    But not before,
Not for one and a half hundred years,
The weight of the corpse on its hill
Bleached out of breath.

For Norman Nicholson

I see Yvonne and you in nineteen sixty-six
With both of us, both boths standing in Beckermet
Discussing mosses and, I think, liverwort
When a lively wind slammed more quickly down the street
Than anything but the occasional Norton,
Some young lad up, pursuing hell for leather –

And time had come for your eleven hundred
To head off south from that small terraced house we had
And lived in three quick years. The Sixties: a decade
Which is meant to mean in general retrospect
Great seismic shifts of taste and values, word for which
Was placed in verse by dry stonewalling Larkin,
As well as all the ready-mix journalists.
It was never my feeling then and is not now.
Yes, fells have fashions and the hemlines rise or fall
But only through Man's pastoral activities:
Their skylines are drawn by sky and rock, not Man,
As Wordsworth saw it; as Wordsworth saw also
That the spirit which is in Man shapes up to them
And what he does truest must stand against the fell;
I see that as a test your work has stood; and shall.

Under the Road

Just a tremor now on the road might remind you
how underneath this shiny morning county
the workings groan and shift and how
men came as needed to win the coal
for several generations, a thick seam
to slowly be compressed by our much lighter lives
as we scurry over the earth to hilly recreation –
-a vibration in the hands from the road,
and from under the road.

County Durham

Anne Stevenson

Enough of Green

Enough of green,
though to remember childhood
is to stand in uneasy radiance
under those trees.

Enough yellow.
We are looking back
over our shoulders, telling our children
to be happy.

Try to forget about red.
Leave it to the professionals.
But perceive heaven as a density
blue enough to abolish the stars.

As long as the rainbow lasts
the company stays.

Of black there is never enough.

One by one the lights in the house go out.
Step over the threshold. Forget
to take my hand.

In the Tunnel of Summers

Moving from day into day,
I don't know how,
eating these plums now
this morning for breakfast,
tasting of childhood's
mouth-pucker tartness,
watching the broad light
seed in the fences,
honey of barley,
gold ocean, grasses,
as the tunnel of summers,
of nothing but summers,
opens again
in my travelling senses.

I am eight and eighteen and eighty
all the Augusts of my day.

Why should I be, I be
more than another?
Brown foot in sandal,
burnt palm on flaked clay,
flesh under waterfall
baubled in strong spray,
blood on the stubble
of fly-sweet hay.
Why not my mother's, my
Grandmother's ankle
hurting as harvest hurts
thistle and animal?
A needle of burning,
why this way or that way?

They are already building the long straw cemetery
where my granddaughter's daughter has been born and buried.

Demolition

(Langley Park, Durham)
They have blown up the old brick bridge
connecting the coal works with the coke works.
Useful and unimposing,
it was ever a chapel of small waters,
a graceful arch toothworked with
yellow bricks notched into red bricks,
reflecting there sudden bright winks
from the Browney – an oval asymmetrical image
that must have delighted, as fisher-children,
these solid shiftless, grey men
who follow so closely the toil of its demolition.

The digger's head drops and grates, now swings up–
yellow fangs slavering rubble and purple brickdust.
Its watchers wear the same grave, equivocal expression.
They might be grieving;
(their fathers built it, or their father's fathers).
Or they might be meaning
Boys won't be going to the mine no more.
Best do away with what's not needed.
That's Jock Munsey's lad in the cab there, surely.
Good job it's at home, not away on the telly.

When the camel is dust it goes through the needle's eye

(North Wales)
This hot summer wind
is tiring my mother.
It tires her to watch it
buffeting the poppies.
Down they bow
in their fluttering kimonos,
a suppressed populace,
an unpredictable dictator.

The silver-haired reeds
are also supplicants.
Stripped of its petals,
clematis looks grey
on the wall, My mother,
who never came here,
suggests it's too hot
to cook supper.

Her tiredness gets everywhere
like blown topsoil,
teasing my eyes and tongue,
wrinkling my skin.
Summer after summer, silt
becomes landfill between us,
level and walkable,
level, eventually, and simple.

Innocence and Experience

(1942)
I laid myself down as a woman
And woke as a child.
Sleep buried me up to my chin,
But my brain cut wild.

Sudden summer lay sticky as tar
Under bare white feet.
Stale, soot-spotted heapings of winter
Shrank in the street.

Black headlines, infolded like napkins,
Crashed like grenades
As war beat its way porch by porch
Up New Haven's facades.

Europe: a brown hive of noises,
Hitler inside.
On the too sunny shelf by the stairs
My tadpoles died.

Big boys had already decided
Who'd lose and who'd score,
Singing one potato, two potato,
Three potato, four.

Singing sticks and stones
May break my bones
(but names hurt more).

Singing step on a crack
Break your mother's back
(her platinum-ringed finger).

Singing who got up your mother
When your daddy wasn't there?
Singing allee allee in free! You're
Dead, you're dead, wherever you are!

Moonrise

While my anxiety stood phoning you last evening,
My simpler self lay marvelling through glass
At the full moon marbling the clouds, climbing
In shafts, a headlamp through an underpass,
Until it swung free, cratered, deadly clear,
Earth's stillborn twin unsoiled by life or air.

And while our voices huddled mouth to ear,
I watched tenacity of long imagination
Cast her again in a film of the old goddess,
Chaste of the chase, more virgin than the Virgin,
Lifting herself from that rucked, unfeeling waste
As from the desert of her own ruined face.

Such an unhinging light. To see her. To see that.
As no one else had seen her. Or might see that.

Leaving

Habits the hands have, reaching for this and that,
      (tea kettle, orange squeezer, milk jug,
         frying pan, sugar jar, coffee mug)
manipulate, or make, a habitat,
become its *genii loci*, working on
quietly in the kitchen when you've gone.

Objects a house keeps safe on hooks and shelves
        (climbing boots, garden tools, backpacks
          bird feeders, tennis balls, anoraks)
the day you leave them bleakly to themselves,
do they decide how long, behind the door,
to keep your personality in store?

Good Bishop Berkeley made the objects stay
just where we leave them when we go away
by lending them to God. If so, God's mind
is crammed with things abandoned by mankind
        (featherbeds, chamber pots, flint lighters,
         quill pens, sealing wax, typewriters),

an archive of the infinitely there.
But there for whom? For what museum? And where?
I like to think of spiders, moths, white worms
leading their natural lives in empty rooms
        (egg-sacks, mouse-litter, dead flies,
         cobwebs, silverfish, small eyes)

while my possessions cease to study me
        (*Emma, The Signet Shakespeare, Saving Whales.*
         Living with Mushrooms, Leviathan, Wild Wales).
Habit by habit, they sink through time to be
one with the mind or instinct of the place,
home in its shadowy silence and stone space.

On Going Deaf

I've lost a sense. Why should I care?
Searching myself I find a spare.
I keep that sixth sense in repair
And set it deftly, like a snare.

Granny Scarecrow

Tears flowed at the chapel funeral,
more beside the grave on the hill. Nevertheless,
after the last autumn ploughing,
they crucified her old flowered print housedress
live, on a pole.

Marjorie and Emily, shortcutting to school,
used to pass and wave; mostly Gran would wave back.
Two white Sunday gloves
flapped good luck from the crossbar; her head's plastic sack
would nod, as a rule.

But when winter arrived, her ghost thinned.
The dress began to look starved in its field of snowcorn.
One glove blew off and was lost.
The other hung blotchy with mould from the hedgerow, torn
by the wind.

Emily and Marjorie noticed this.
Without saying why, they started to avoid the country way
through the cornfield. Instead they walked
from the farm up the road to the stop where they
caught the bus.

And it caught them. So in time they married.
Marjorie, divorced, rose high in the catering profession.
Emily had children and grandchildren, though,
with the farm sold, none found a cross to fit their clothes when
Emily and Marjorie died.

Subhadassi

Fishing

I tackle-up. My mind's all carp: slick slow-movers
mottled with leather, or mirror. We're armed to the teeth
with par-boiled potatoes and honey, a killer
combination, but this morning nothing's biting.

An aeon later, frozen, walking legs like someone else's
up the steps, I look back to find the pond haloed
by spindles of silver birch; catch one big spare
rib of a ripple sounding its length. I'm spell-bound. Something's stirring.

Blue Lies

I knew better than to call the sea *irreducible*
or claim it was *endlessly delighting in its own simplicity.*
I was happy not to catch it at all
knowing it was in league with the moon,

that sunbleached goat's horn riding the clouds
as the heat gave the last of itself to the waves
that told the same old story, putting on their silver nets
behind the tamarisks. It was enough to swim in it.

Now I'm the one that's blue,
acting like the tide's gone out forever,
shrunk inside the postcard by my kettle.
Water deeper than a thousand sinks. That nakedness.

peeled

an time when a said a could take all me clothes off
cos I felt so open even though it were october
an you lot took piss for a decade –
that night when a put too many mushrooms in pan
second a heard me dad reversin out o drive
an you lot came out o woodwork

an wi loads o sugar'n'milk'n'nescaf
wi downed it in a oner an got right outa there,
away from semis; through intake an golcar flats
over scar lane an onto edge
where weavers cottages windows were searin red
an a took a piss in british legion car park
an knew it were comin on cos pissin
were like growin a stalk o wheat

 an across valley slawit were meltin
into marsden an pike were screechin
wi laughter an lal were goin bendy
an scad were lost as per usual an wilf cun't talk
as per usual an all shamanic gridsndots like in cave paintins
nmiros neverythinbloodyelse it seems just now
were soarin through us fields o vision

an we stopped at old sandstone steps by canal
to weigh stone that were left
an stone thatd been worn bi millions o millworkers feet
leavin a curve o empty space an wi concluded
thi were exactly equal down to a milligram

an it came on really strong as we fumbled
down t appleyards – we were talkin g force six –
an the wer police sirens hung in trees
an when we got there us lager guzzled itself in corner
so we sat on bench except scad who sat on is arse
starin down canal an saying *but where are we really*

an even though us pupils still teemed us faces
you cruelly took piss an all innocence left yer
when a said a could take all me clothes off.
Its outlived us crimped hair us docks us schoolin;
us smiths albums us girlfriends us drug habits –
in most cases us friendships.

Well, I meant it.

Cygnus

Here may be seen how being blessed
Has its foundations in the act of sight,
And not in love, which comes afterwards.
DANTE Paradiso XXVIII 109-11

If I were half-blind, which I am –
my eye-world dropping-off to shapes
no more than vague suggestions,
the all-that-is-in-the-detail lost

so that my fingers must become
precision instruments to skim surfaces,
assist in weighings to confirm hunches –
then in these days that blur to nights

and nights that linger, my skin would come
in search of you: follow your scent,
lock-on to your body heat sensed in my palms
like a prickle or an ache, that would not fade

till it lighted on, say, a braid, or nap:
the down at the back of your neck,
perhaps. Corroborating evidence,
I'd map that rare constellation

mazed in the freckles in your back
– sole vantage offered from your bed –
knowing full-well that this would turn
all the lights back on again.

Treason

Down on the cutting at the edge of the park
we laid new two pence pieces on the tracks,
hid behind rosebay willowherb till the 125 flew past,
found shiny, melted metal scattered in the grass –
their second minting, in the North;

the train by then in the longest tunnel on earth.
Twenty years later it came out, in reverse,
with me in second class. By the same sandstone bridge
I glimpsed two kids on the parallel lines;
felt the weight of loose change in my pocket.

Annealed

He plugged the window's hole with honeycomb
against the wind and sleet from Uzbekistan;
pumped the leather bellows with his feet and hands,
eager for the iron to find pomegranate red:
the colour that was good for the plunge into honey.

The sweet steam took him back to the harvest fair
and the girl – he'd thought of her as Liesl –
who sold him enough for the winter;
told him that bees made love and that made honey.

Honey that made a metal fit to shoe the Meister's horses;
fit for the horses to spark the black volcanic stones of Slovakia
as they cantered through his forests with an ooze
of hounds around them, welded to a scent of fox.

He licked honey from the edge of his knife:
a blade that would never go blunt; her sting he would never pull out.

My Idea of Hell

The strip-light flickers on mock-wood panelling.
There is a fish tank. Fish – some Angels –
coast its length. A man leans against the counter
having his way with the last of a tab.
With his heel he turns it into the lino:
one more dark star in the floor's constellation.
Are you having it now or will you take it away?
I am having it now. I will also take it away.

Multi Story

It's no heaven, but when concrete streams
were calmed to slabs, sculpting a cube visible
for miles, our minds grew full under its promise.

Even Caine, as *Carter*, was drawn North on a train
to drink from a thin glass, corkscrew up nine flights
in a sporty white number to put things straight.

Now rust bleeds from the elephant's skin.
Its lifts are tired. A stone's throw from the seventh floor
a slick new bridge articulates the Tyne.

Paul Summers

north

(home thoughts from abroad)

we are more than sharply contrasting photographs
of massive ships and staithes for coal, more than
crackling films where grimey faced workers are
dwarfed by shadows or omitted by chimneys, more
than foul mouthed men in smokey clubs or well-built
women in a wash-day chorus. we are more than
lessons in post-industrial sociology, more than
just case-studies of dysfunctional community.
we are more than non-speaking extras in
fashionable new gangster movies, more than
sad lyrics in exiles songs. we are more than
the backbone of inglorious empire, or the
stubborn old heart of a dying beast. we are
more than the ghosts of a million histories,
more than legends inscribed in blood, more
than exhibits in some vast museum, or the
unbought remnants of a year long sale,
we are more than this, but not much more.

if keir hardie was the man on the moon

what would he make of it? we wondered;
looking down, night after serious night,
on the ancient tiles of our street:
just hanging there in the indigo
like a stringless conker,
distant & ownerless &
fingering the cello curve
of his immaculate tash.
he'd be stunned by our quiet world,
perplexed at our lack of shift patterns,
our weekend hangovers, our luxurious carpets,
& he'd notice the chimneys no longer smoked.
he'd see our fitted wardrobes bulge
with fake armani, in tasteful
soft pastels & unbleached linen.
he'd study our satellite dishes,
watch open university programmes
in the dead of night, learn envy
from the billboard ads,
grow hungry for the horsepower
of our nippy five-door peugeots.
just before morning, he'd shift his gaze,
browse the horizons in search of old haunts;
he'd wake up the tramp on the library steps,
inquire on the whereabouts of some lost friend,
& then he'd remember he's the man on the moon
& not know whether to laugh or cry.

the hundred years war

even now when winter comes
they huddle in a clique of pints
recalling between bingo lines
bleak paragraphs of angry times.
old archie's in his element
& licking scotch from ancient lips
lists every strike since twenty-six
& every blackleg dead or not
proud testament, he'd not forgot:
& by the time the whisky comes
each horses charge, each copper's fist
each treachery on archie's list
is credited to micky holmes
for scabbing back in eighty four f
or shitting at his brother's door
for always being *a sly faced cunt*
now that they'd come to think of it.
the barmaid clinked the tables clear
came close enough to overhear
& in some youthful liberal fit
began to find defence for it:
so mixed into their slurred goodnights
more anger still & threats of fights
how micky holmes had made his bed
& curses that would see him dead
then home to pristine pebble-dash
they'd purchased with their hand-shake cash
to sleep, to sleep perchance to dream
of a hundred years war & a flooded seam

wash-day

(for my mother)
four pristine sheets flap their white surrender
& her, humming the chorus of shirley bassey's latest
with three gypsy pegs between her vinyl teeth.

behind her on the cobbles, an orange plastic basket
filled, then filled some more, with schoolboys shirts
& shapeless gas-board overalls, coiled like cables
& steaming like entrails in an open wound.

i watched her at the sink, teasing out dirt,
pounding a gravy stain into submission,
wrestling a bedspread made heavier with water;

& then, the wringing out, her face contorted,
a salt-burnt trawlerman hauling in his catch,
as if in that second her mottled veins would burst.

each towel, each blanket, each pair of socks,
like snapping the necks of hapless birds
or twining a rope to use in her escape,

her red knuckles, red bones,
made more arthritic with every load,
& set these days like a budgies claw,
her own silent monument to then, before.

hand me downs

i was not born with a silver spoon
but did once lick yoghurt from one
in the room of a russian emigre
on the eve of my brother's wedding
& i have known too well
that there is such a thing

as a free lunch despite granda's
limp proverbs suggesting the contrary
& i have grown to value words
& visited art galleries
as if they were zoos
& seen more movement in the lowrys
than the other boys at school
& more truth in most things
than many boys at any school
& i did not mind the hand me downs
though the shoes gave me bunions
& those brown high-waisters
cost me dearly with the girls
& i should never have spied
on sharon thompson taking a bath
in the exciting days of her puberty
but will never regret it
& oranges are not the only fruit
& processed cheddar not the only cheese
but had it not been for the co-op
going upmarket in 1978
i'd never have known
& i have learnt to see beauty
& feel no guilt for its lack of utility
& i have grown to value words
& visited art galleries
as if they were zoos.

the comrades

every season brings change:
more empty seats for overcoats
& greasy caps, to prop up sticks.
their collars grow more loose,
their feet rattle in pristine shoes.

the incredible shrinking men
meet sundays for dominoes:
their fingers grip the ebony,
like brambles on unkempt graves;
they eye the kitty like preying cats,

faces receding to sharpened bone,
the skin of one-time double-chins
hangs paper-thin in breathless flags
& when they laugh, their straining necks
like pelicans remembering storms.

rant

okay, so hijacking that armoured car at the TA open day was a bit extreme; and proclaiming from the gun turret that the beginning of the end of the bourgeois capitalist state machine was nigh, naive in retrospect, but i was only fourteen, and i get embarrassed too when everybody mentions it at those cosy family get togethers that we seem to have less and less because you think they always end up being a shouting match. perhaps those awkward blushes were the nearest thing to red tinged solidarity we'll ever have and i appreciate that, you're not the first members of the labour aristocracy to be duped by the hegemonic forces of the dominant ideology and i'm sure you'll not be the last. and even now i appreciate your reasons for only regarding me as a sane mature adult when i partake in those pleasant conversations about patio tubs and hardy perrenials in which i make absolutely no reference to the unending class struggle, that's your perogative. but don't go treating me like some stupid teenage dreamer who's still wearing combat pants in an effort to reincarnate che guevara just because i happen to care about a few things now and again. i'm really beginning to think that passion is an alien concept to this family, not the type of passion you loudly display for placido domingo singing nessun dorma or for 'reasonably' priced australian chardonnay, or sunday shopping trips to asda or ikea, i mean a passion for bigger things, for dreams, ideas, for things that don't have a bar-code. to you, ignorance is bliss when really it is slavery; to you, protest is taboo when really it's essential; to you, apathy is a way of life when really it's disease; to you, change is a threat when really it is promise; to you, these lines are rhetoric when really they're confession; to you, i am a stranger when really i am your son.

on quarry moor

as frail light crumbles like dried leaves, like stale bread
the bell-pit crater is patient, a shallow bowl of quiet moss
hoarding its cache of rabbit shite muggies like inca gold

a manic cloud-crowd flirts as it flits, dirtied & distempered,
a mob of hungry rooks circling harehope's empty barrows
& sheep tracks underscore the shivering lapwing's cat-call,

an ancient shepherd's secret bleats ducking the wind-blast
shell-shocked, tired, the lime-kiln slumps & ruffled lichen
cocks a curious ear to thirsty heather's crackling foot-fall.

as frail light crumbles like dead mortar, like poisoned soil
my father & his children, us, breathe deeply in the saccharin
air of home, of dusk, & build a cairn for ghosts with dirty nails.

Andrew Waterhouse

Climbing My Grandfather

I decide to do it free, without a rope or net.
First, the old brogues, dusty and cracked;
an easy scramble onto his trousers,
pushing into the weave, trying to get a grip.
By the overhanging shirt I change
direction, traverse along his belt
to an earth stained hand. The nails
are splintered and give good purchase,
the skin of his finger is smooth and thick
like warm ice. On his arm I discover
the glassy ridge of a scar, place my feet
gently in the old stitches and move on.
At his still firm shoulder, I rest for a while
in the.shade, not looking down,
for climbing has its dangers, then pull
myself up the loose skin of his neck
to a smiling mouth to drink among teeth.
Refreshed, I cross the screed cheek,
to stare into his brown eyes, watch a pupil
slowly open and close. Then up over
the forehead, the wrinkles well-spaced
and easy, to his thick hair (soft and white
at this altitude), reaching for the summit,
where gasping for breath I can only lie
watching clouds and birds circle,
feeling his heat, knowing
the slow pulse of his good heart.

Not An Ending

He never lived in that valley
or anywhere else. On the night in question
he did not stand by the river or ignore
the new rain or drop stones into the water.
There were no tree songs around him,
no unidentified birds, no flowing to the sea.

Her eyes were not blue. Those were not her boots.
She walked more quickly. He did not hear
her last word or want to. He may
have shrugged, but never shook.
He had no regrets and would not think
of her again. He would not think of her again.

Burning your Brother's Guitar

You may have a brother; if not imagine one who gave you
his guitar, at a forgotten time, for an unknown reason.
Suppose that this guitar has travelled with you from house
to safe house, always left in darkness under a bed
in the sparest room. Recall that your brother's guitar
which became yours, was well beyond tuning, the action too high
for comfort, the varnish dull, scratched, pitted. All chords
were lost.

       Suppose that you could not discard your brother's
guitar until after midnight January 1st 1989, when drunk,
needing warmth, with no party in sight, you pulled your brother's
guitar from the darkness under the bed in your sparest room.
Remember, that you stamped down hard, snapping the neck,
crushing the body, then threw the pieces of your brother's guitar
on the fire. Assume that the strings curled in the flames,
as if touched, touched privately and that you slept
on the floor in the heat until morning, then prodded
the ashes; grateful for the honest, precious metal
that remained after you had burnt your brother's guitar.

One Day in Late Adolescence

It being suggested that I get out of myself more,
I get out of the family home and into low cloud.
A door bangs behind me and here lies North Marsh Road
and December, where the lamps have been on all day.
Adjacent, there may be a town, tidal river, power station;
but this view is cut to pavement and a Maestro browning nicely.
Also, the aged appear, trolleys pulling them home.
They breathe heavily, making their own winter.

At the crossroads I wait for a lorry dribbling sand.,
then straight over past The House of Close Relations,
but I will not call being sick of myself and all others.
To the right are allotments where my father buries
something most days. Note the freshly turned earth,
hear the pigeons mumbling about the sun and spilt grain.

And now a sharp rise, up the embankment and I look down
upon the weighty Trent, brown, see the whirlpools eating
themselves and a barge grows from the fog, slips around the bend,
bearing coal to Hull and even beyond. It disappears,
making a wake I must follow, which is where I will leave myself,
hunched and walking by a river in December,
hoping that one day I will return in human form.

Butterfly on Stained Glass

(Church of St. Mary the Virgin, Holy Island)
is undecided, at the dead saint's feet;
having rested well since October;
but now, needing more light and heat,
stumbles from brown sandals, to grey cowl,
to pink hand, then finds that clear glass
with blue sky behind, settles, and the sun
illuminates her outstretched wings:
each uncounted scale laid out between veins,

the red-orange sheen, black and yellow patches,
blue lunules on the margins
                              and I reach up,
cup her in my hands, walk through old incense
from transept to porch, to the open door,
release her into this day, her unsteady wings
catching the light again over celandines
and gravestones and on towards the sea.

Northerly

Starved hedges just hold the fields in place,
plantations sit heavy on the fall and rise
to rough ground where the storm scatters gorse
and buildings among the first hills
and this sky without clouds is losing the sun,
but making planets, satellites, a moon;
identified objects, below which you drive home
through the light and half-light and less,
as my reflection grows in the window
and something wants stirring behind me
and again this house needs your weight.

Alternative Endings

he gets the girl or some other mammal
or the mysterious stranger in the first scene
turns out to be his father, which explains everything
or it's the iceberg's turn to sink this time
or they give up looking for the leg
or the six pairs of twins in tights are reunited,
recognised, loved; also there is a final couplet
or the sheep dog forgets his trapped master,
tries to find a better flock
or a small brown dot appears on her face,

expands, collapses and the film burns .
or the baby is sung awake by the monster
or a. naked surfer paddles into the sunset
or she says Ha and leaves quickly
or the cavalry dismount, grow their hair,
help around the teepees
or the alien decides to talk to the chimps instead
or clouds part, that stumpy celestial finger points,
a choir begins and all our sins are forgiven
or the wooden boy stays wooden,
or the sub-titles fall from the screen
or the last tree is carefully wrapped
or it is not in fact not a dream he is not dreaming
or the doctor runs out of heart stakes in the crypt
or there is accordion musique
and rain runs down a window pane
or the camera pulls back slowly: two people,
beach, the eastern coast, full outline of our island,
our continent, our mainly blue planet, stars, the rest.

Bath-Time

For Hala

The ceiling is blue and the walls are yellow;
hanging, is a shoal of red and green fish,
turning so slowly, turning so slowly;
among your soaps and creams rest oyster shells,
also limpets and a line of seahorses
ride up towards the true mirror as we float
together in your large bath, steam rising
around us and I sink between your legs,
lean back against your breasts and smiling
you pour water over my face, my hair,
again and again as if I had just emerged,
needing to be woken up and well cleaned
before you could help me onto dry land.

Modern Grammar: Use of the Personal Pronoun (Nominative)

I am a good person,
as are you.

She has just arrived here,
cannot speak English
and is probably a whore.

He looks at children.

It is obvious:
we must stick together.

They need to be dealt with.

Annie Wright

The Night Is Holding Its Breath

I gaze into the pond, wander over the grass
to the apple tree, before I realise I've not breathed.
I let it out, a telltale trail on chill air,
afraid it might be discovered, bagged,
assigned a code and used in evidence.
Trying to be normal, not to arouse suspicion,
I am eaten up with fear. I lean against
the firm back of the apple tree. It upholds me,
lightly, easily, unjudgingly. It does not harm
or bully me, blackmail or provoke. It does not
resent me, hate me or condemn.
It demands nothing from me, although it could,
as I stand here looking for stars, taking its support.
Through its upthrust arms I saw the comet,
heard the urgent message to flee.
I have climbed, hugged and harvested this tree.
Now your new leaves tremble as I say goodbye;
tomorrow, when I've run, it's you I'm going to miss.

Ascending The Bell Tower

When we stop in niches, fumble for mouths,
no-one sees our stolen kisses. I follow,
up, up, charged to remember the precise feel
of good blue cotton, your dark
mouth-cave, cold rancour of recent pasts.

Slit, hooded eyes frown down on prison insects
trudging perimeter, clockwise circles.
Not one crosses pristine, geometric grass
or notices the emerald scent of spring.
Not one casts a glance at the huge bird
hovering

Cars dance in bee formation
at the hive's entrance.
Shrive me, shrive me!
How can you, when I will not repent?
We spiral back on ourselves.
From the gizzard we are vomited out,
pellets of skin, bone, hair,
onto a square roof, unbearable lightness.

 My stomach lurches. Breathe, you say,
don't look, breathe.
On the narrow ledge I'm reassembled,
my bones spun sugar,
the grey shell cracked.

I unhook from the parapet,
test the four corners of the known world,
temple, tower block, prison, angel.
Angel, angel, truly I am
in the company of angels, o love, love, extend
hubristic wings,
watch me stream in the firmament, follow me
flying, winging, sinning, jubilant, home!

After The Fire

When she asks me to pick up the shopping bag
containing the maroon plastic screw-topped jar,
I am expecting, perhaps, the weight of liquorice
allsorts, pear drops or the Pontefract cakes
that were a favourite, so even when she tells me
to be careful, how she got a shock it was so heavy,
even then I'm totally unprepared for the weight
of what is left of you – approximately that half stone
of potatoes you used to joke I could fetch home
in my school hat. Suddenly I'm seeing you years ago,
riddling the boiler coke, flakes falling like flour
while greyish lumps rattled round the sieve
before you tipped them back into the fire to render
down to ash. Once you would have dug the mound
into your vegetable beds, wasting nothing. I rattle
the jar discreetly; it sounds like the finest rain.
It's all ashes, nothing sinister. I took the lid off earlier.
Nevertheless, my stalwart mum is on edge. Feeling
the indignity of trundling you in the shopping trolley,
she has brought you home by taxi, but now the question
of what to do next weighs heavily. I can see she'll not
rest easy dad, until we've laid your ashen ghost.

The Poets

GILLIAN ALLNUTT was born in London in 1949. She spent half of her childhood in Newcastle and in 1988 she returned to the North East. With Fred D'Aguiar, Ken Edwards and Eric Mottram she edited *The New British Poetry* (Paladin, 1988). She has published six collections of poetry, *Spitting the Pips Out* (Sheba, 1981), *Beginning the Avocado* (Virago, 1987), *Blackthorn* (Bloodaxe, 1994), *Nantucket and the Angel* (Bloodaxe, 1997), *Lintel* (Bloodaxe, 2001) and Sojourner (Bloodaxe, 2004). *Lintel* was a PBS Choice and *Nantucket and the Angel* and *Lintel* were both short-listed for the T.S. Eliot Prize. In 2005 she was awarded the Northern Rock Foundation Writer's award. She lives in County Durham.

MAUREEN ALMOND was born in Ferryhill, County Durham in 1945. She grew up in Thornaby and worked as a personnel manager before becoming a full-time writer and teacher. Writing-residencies include BBC Radio Cleveland, Stockton on-line, St. Luke's Hospital and North Lodge Park, Darlington. Her publications include *Hot* (Mudfog, 1997), *Tailor Tacks* (Mudfog, 1999), *Oyster Baby* (Biscuit, 2002) and *The Works* (Biscuit, 2002). She lives in Yarm.

KEITH ARMSTRONG was born in Newcastle in 1946. He has worked as a community-arts worker, librarian and publisher. Writing-residencies include Durham, Easington, Sedgefield, Derwentside, Teesdale, Wear Valley, Chester-le-Street, Sunderland and Hexham Races. He has edited a history of the Durham Miners' Gala. Several of his lyrics have been recorded by Durham indie-folk-punk band The Whisky Priests as *Bleeding Sketches*. His publications include *Pains Of Class* (Artery, 1982), *Dreaming North* (with Graeme Rigby, Portcullis, 1986), *The Jinglin' Geordie* (Rookbook, 1990) and *Imagined Corners* (Smokestack, 2004). He lives in Whitley Bay.

PETER ARMSTRONG was born in Blaydon-on-Tyne in 1957. After training as a psychiatric nurse he specialised as a cognitive therapist and currently works in the Newcastle CBT Centre. He is a member of the Northern Poets' Workshop and is an editor of *Other Poetry*. His publications include *Risings* (Enitharmon, 1988); *The Red Funnelled Boat* (Picador, 1998) and *The Capital of Nowhere* (Picador, 2003). He lives in Tynedale.

NEIL ASTLEY was born in Hampshire in 1953. In 1978 he founded Bloodaxe Books, where he has edited over 800 poetry books for Bloodaxe and several anthologies, including *Poetry with an Edge* (1988), *New Blood* (1999), *Pleased to See Me* (2002), *Staying Alive* (2002), *Do Not Go Gentle* (2003), *Being Alive* (2004) and *Passionfood* (2005). He has published two collections of his own poetry, *Darwin Survivor* (Peterloo, 1988), *Biting My Tongue* (Bloodaxe, 1995), and two novels, *The End of My Tether* (short-listed for the Whitbread First Novel Award) and *The Sheep Who Changed the World* (Both Flambard). He lives in the Tarset Valley in Northumberland.

LIZ ATKIN was born in Lincolnshire in 1951. An artist, she has exhibited in London, Edinburgh and Europe. She has published three books of poetry, *Glee with a Blue Background* (Diamond Twig, 1998) and *The Biscuit Tins of England* (IRON, 2003) and *Still* (Flarestack, 2005). She lives in Newcastle.

BOB BEAGRIE was born in Middlesbrough in 1967. Writing-residencies include the Hartlepool Headland and the University of Teesside. He has produced text for public artwork at various sites on Teesside. A former editor of Mudfog Books. His publications include *Gothic Horror* (Mudfog, 1996), *Masque: The Art of the Vampyre* (Mudfog, 2000), *Huginn & Munnin* (Biscuit, 2002), *Endeavour: Newfound Notes* (Biscuit, 2004) and *The Flesh of the Bear* (edited, Ek Zuban, 2004) a bilingual anthology of poets from Teesside and Turku in Finland. He lives in Middlesbrough.

PETER BENNET was born in Staffordshire in 1942. He moved to the North East in 1971. He taught at five schools then worked in adult education in the North East, including sixteen years as Tutor Organiser for Northumberland University with the Workers' Educational Association. He was Associate Editor of *Stand* 1995 - 1998 and is a co-editor of *Other Poetry*. Publications include *The Long Pack* (Flambard, 2002), *Ha-Ha* (Smith/Doorstop Books, 2003), *Noctua* (Shoestring, 2004) and *Goblin Lawn: New and Selected Poems* (Flambard, 2002). He lives near the Wild Hills o' Wanney, Northumberland.

DAVID BURNETT was born in Edinburgh in 1937. In 1964 he moved to Durham. Now retired, he worked for many years as a university librarian specialising in older printed books and manuscripts. With others he was responsible for establishing Colpitts Poetry and the Bunting Archive. He has published nearly a thousand poems in small presses and in some forty books, pamphlets and keepsakes, including *Something of Myself* (Black Cygnet, 1994), *Evergreens* (Black Cygnet, 2002) and *Quoins for the Chase* (New Century, 2003) a collection of aphorisms on poetry. He lives in Durham.

RIC CADDEL was born in Bedford in 1949. Brought up in Kent, he studied at Newcastle University and worked for twenty-eight years in Durham University Library. He founded Pig Press, initiated Colpitts poetry readings in Durham and co-founded the Basil Bunting Poetry Centre and Archive at Durham University. His editing work includes *OTHER : British and Irish Poetry Since 1970* (with Peter Quartermain, Wesleyan, University Press 1999) and *Basil Bunting : Complete Poems* (Bloodaxe, 2000). He published twenty-three books of his own poetry, including *Sweet Cicely* (Taxus, 1983), *Larksong Signal* (Shearsman, 1997), *Magpie Words : Selected Poems 1970-2000* (West House, 2002) and *Writing in the Dark* (West House, 2003). He died in 2003.

KEVIN CADWALLENDER was born in Hartlepool in 1958. He has worked as a policeman, a roadie and a clown. Writing-residencies include the Co-op and the *Sunderland Echo*. His publications include *The Last Great Northern Whale* (Rookbook, 1992), *Public* (IRON, 2000), *Voyages* (Cleveland Arts/Mudfog 2002), *Smelter* (with Cynthia Fuller, Mudfog, 2004) and *Baz Uber Alles* (Dogeater, 2004). He lives in Sunderland.

GEORGE CHARLTON was born in Gateshead in 1950. He was educated at Gateshead Grammar School, Newcastle Polytechnic and Newcastle University and taught at Newcastle College. He retired from from poetry in 1994and from teaching in 2002. He has published two books of poetry, *Nightshift Workers* (Bloodaxe, 1989) and *City of Dog* (Bloodaxe, 1994). He lives in Gateshead.

BRENDAN CLEARY was born in 1958 in Co Antrim. In 1982 he moved to the North East, where he edited *Stand* and *The Echo Room* and organised readings at the Morden Tower. As well as many pamphlets he has published four books of poetry, *White Bread and ITV* (Wide Skirt, 1990), *The Irish Card* (Bloodaxe, 1993), *Sacrilege* (Bloodaxe, 1998) and *Stranger in the House* (Wrecking Ball, 2001). He currently lives in Brighton.

BOB COOPER was born on Teesside in 1950. He is a Methodist minister who currently works as a creative-writing tutor. His publications include *Bruised Echoes* (Outposts, 1977), *Light From The Upper Left* (Smith Doorstop, 1994), *Beyond Liathach* (Tears in the Fence, 1995), *Drinking Up Time* (Redbeck, 1998), *Pinocchio's Long Neb* (Smith Doorstop, 2001) and *All We Know is All We See* (Arrowhead, 2002). He lives in Middlesbrough.

ANDY CROFT was born in Cheshire in 1956. He moved to the North East in 1983 to teach in adult education. Writing-residencies include HMP Holme House and the Great North Run. Among his books are *Red Letter Days, Out of the Old Earth* (with Graeme Rigby), *A Weapon in the Struggle, Selected Poems of Randall Swingler, Comrade Heart, Holme and Away, Red Sky at Night* (with Adrian Mitchell) and thirty-seven books for teenagers, mostly about football. His books of poetry include *Nowhere Special* (Flambard, 1996), *Gaps Between Hills* (with Dermot Blackburn and Mark Robinson, Scratch, 1996), *Headland* (Scratch, 2001), *Just as Blue* (Flambard, 2001), *Great North* (IRON, 2001) and *Comrade Laughter* (Flambard, 2004). He lives in Middlesbrough.

JULIA DARLING was born in Winchester in 1956. After training as a Cordon Bleu chef, she moved to the North East in 1980 to work in community arts. She was a founder member of poetry performance group the Poetry Virgins, and with Ellen Phethean founded Diamond Twig Press. She was writer in residence at Live Theatre 2002-3. In 2003 she received the Northern Rock Award, and was a Royal Literary

Fund fellow at Newcastle University. She became Fellow in Creative Writing and Health at the university and was involved in many projects linking writing and health, including Operating Theatre and schemes to introduce poetry into hospitals and GP waiting rooms. With the artist Emma Holliday she produced the First Aid Kit for the Mind, and with Cynthia Fuller, edited *The Poetry Cure*. She wrote many plays for stage and radio, collected as *Eating the Elephant*. She wrote a book of short stories, *Bloodlines*; two novels, *Crocodile Soup* and *The Taxi-driver's Daughter*; and two collections of poetry, *Sudden Collapses In Public Places* (Arc, 2003) and *Apology For Absence* (Arc, 2004). She died 2005.

ALISTAIR ELLIOT was born in Liverpool in 1932. After several years living in the United States, Scotland and Iran, he moved in 1967 to the North East where he worked as a librarian. He took early retirement in 1982. He has translated Verlaine, Euripides, Sophocles, Heine and Valéry and put together anthologies of *French Love Poems* and *Italian Landscape Poems* (both Bloodaxe). His many books of poetry include *Talking Back* (Secker and Warburg, 1984), *My Country* (Carcanet, 1989), *Turning the Stones* (Carcanet, 1993), *Facing Things* (Carcanet, 1997) and *Roman Food Poems* (Prospect, 2003). He lives in Newcastle.

LINDA FRANCE was born in 1958 in Newcastle. She grew up in Dorset and moved back to the North East in 1981. She has written for the stage and worked on many Public Art collaborations in the region. She has published six books with Bloodaxe, *Red* (1992), *Sixty Women Poets* (edited, 1993), *The Gentleness of the Very Tall* (1994), *Storyville* (1997), *The Simultaneous Dress* (2002) and a verse-biography of Lady Mary Wortley Montagu, *The Toast of the Kit Cat Club* (2005). She lives near Hexham.

CYNTHIA FULLER was born in Kent in 1948. She moved to the North East in 1979 and teaches literature and creative writing in adult and higher education. She worked as a poetry editor for *Writing Women* for many years, and recently edited *Smelter* with Kevin Cadwallender, and *The Poetry Cure* with Julia Darling. Flambard have published three books of her poetry, *Moving Towards Light* (1992), *Instructions for the Desert* (1996) and *Only a Small Boat* (2001). She lives in County Durham.

DESMOND GRAHAM was born in Surrey in 1940. He taught in universities in Africa and Germany before moving to Newcastle in 1971. He is currently Professor of Poetry at Newcastle University. His books on other writers include *The Truth of War, Poetry of the Second World War: An International Anthology* and a biography of Keith Douglas. Recent books of poetry include *Not Falling* (Seren, 1999), *After Shakespeare* (Flambard, 2001) and *Milena Poems* (Flambard, 2004). He lives in Newcastle.

JACKIE HARDY was born in Luton in 1946. She lived in the Tyne Valley for twenty years, where she worked in adult education. For many years she was the editor of the British Haiku Society journal, *Blithe Spirit* ; she recently edited an anthology, *Haiku : Ancient and Modern*. Her books of poetry include *Counting the Waves* (Bloodaxe, 1998) and *The Dust is Golden* (IRON, 1999). She now lives in Sheffield.

TONY HARRISON was born in Leeds in 1937. He moved to Newcastle in 1967 when he was appointed Northern Arts Literary Fellow. He has translated written, and directed many plays for the National Theatre and the RSC, including *The Misanthrope, Phaedra Britanica, The Oresteia* and *Hecuba*. He has written several award-winning poems for the screen, including *The Blasphemer's Banquet, The Gaze of the Gorgon, Black Daisies for the Bride* (awarded the Prix Italia 1994) *A Maybe Day in Kazakhstan, The Shadow of Hiroshima*, and the feature film *Prometheus*. His most recent film-poem is *Crossings*. His many collections of poems include *Earthworks* (Northern House, 1964), *The Loiners* (London Magazine, 1970) awarded the Geoffrey Faber Memorial Prize, from *The School of Eloquence* (Rex Collings, 1981); *Continuous* (Rex Collings, 1981); *Selected Poems* (Penguin, 1984), *v.* (Bloodaxe, 1985), *The Gaze of the Gorgon* (Bloodaxe, 1992) awarded the Whitbread Prize for Poetry, *The Shadow of Hiroshima and other film poems* (Faber, 1995) awarded the William Heinemann Prize 1996, *Laureate's Block* (Penguin, 2000) and *Under the Clock* (Penguin, 2005). He lives in Newcastle.

BILL HERBERT was born in Dundee in 1961.He moved to Newcastle in 1994 to take up the Northern Arts Literary Fellowship. He has taught in the Department of Creative Writing at Lancaster University and currently teaches Creative Writing and Modern Scottish Poetry at the University of Newcastle. Writing-residencies include Cumbria Arts in Education and the Wordsworth Trust. He has written a study of Hugh MacDiarmid, *To Circumjack MacDiarmid* and edited (with Matthew Hollis) *Strong Words : modern poets on modern poetry*. He also edited the interactive CD-ROM *Book of the North*. His books of poetry include four books with Bloodaxe, *Forked Tongue* (1994) short-listed for the T.S.Eliot Prize, *Cabaret McGonagall* (1996) short-listed for the Forward Prize, *The Laurelude* (1998), *The Big Bumper Book of Troy* (2002) which was short-listed for the Saltire Prize, and *Bad Shaman Blues* (2006). He lives in North Shields.

NORAH HILL was born Middlesbrough in 1945. She has worked as a librarian, for the DHSS and currently works as a volunteer at a centre for recovering drug-addicts. In 2002 she was elected Middlesbrough's poet-laureate. She has published a book of short-stories, *Of Many-Coloured Glass* (Paranoia, 1992) and two books of poetry, *Over the Border* (Mudfog, 1998) and *Like* (Mudfog, 2003). She lives in Stockton.

GORDON HODGEON was born in Lancashire in 1941. He moved to the North East in 1972 to work for Teesside LEA. He retired when Cleveland County was abolished in 1996. He is an editor of Mudfog Books. His publications include *November Photographs* (Platform Poets, 1981) and *A Cold Spell* (Mudfog, 1996). He lives in Yarm.

RICHARD KELL was born in Co. Cork, Ireland in 1927. He grew up in India and Ireland He has worked as a teacher and a librarian and was a senior lecturer at Newcastle Polytechnic until his retirement. He was an editor of *Other Poetry*. His books include *Control Tower* (Chatto and Windus, 1962), *Differences* (Chatto and Windus, 1969), *The Broken Circle* (Ceolfrith Press, 1981), *In Praise of Warmth* (Dedalus, 1987), *Rock and Water* (Dedalus, 1993), *Collected Poems* (Lagan, 2001), *Under the Rainbow* (Lagan, 2003) and *Letters to Enid* (Shoestring, 2004). He lives near Stockton.

VALERIE LAWS was born on Tyneside in 1954. She has written several stage plays and French and German text-books for schools. Her books of poetry include *For Crying Out Loud* (with Kitty Fitzgerald, Iron, 1994), *Star Trek: the Poems* (edited, IRON, 2000), *Moonbathing* (Peterloo, 2003) and *Quantum Sheep* (Peterloo, 2006). She lives in Whitley Bay.

S.J. LITHERLAND has lived in Durham since 1965. She worked as a journalist for twenty years and currently teaches Creative Writing. She is a founding member of Vane Women writers' collective in Darlington. With Peter Mortimer she edited *The Poetry of Perestroika* (IRON, 1991). Her poetry collections include *The Long Interval* (Bloodaxe, 1986), *Flowers of Fever* (IRON, 1992), *The Apple Exchange* (Flambard, 1999), *The Work of the Wind* (Flambard, 2006) and *The Homage* (IRON, 2006).

JOHN MILES LONGDEN was born in London in 1921 and grew up in Middlesbrough. During the war he served in the Signals and afterwards worked as a statistician in the Ministry of Fuel and Power, then in the colonial service in Nigeria. He later held academic posts in Addis Ababa, Ethiopia and Australia. After a series of breakdowns he returned to Middlesbrough, where he founded Teesside Writers' Workshop and Middlesbrough's long-running the Writearound Festival. He published several pamphlets and one full-length collection, *LPs and Singles* (Mudfog, 1995). He died in 1993.

MARILYN LONGSTAFF was born in 1950 in Liverpool and grew up on Salvation Army premises all over England and Wales. She has lived in the North East since 1964 and is a member of Vane Women. She has published two books of poetry, *Puritan Games* (Vane Women, 2001) and *Sitting Among the Hoppers* (Arrowhead, 2004). She lives in Darlington.

BARRY MACSWEENEY was born in Newcastle in 1948. He left school at sixteen and worked all his life as a journalist, in Newcastle, Kent, Darlington, Bradford and South Shields. He published over thirty books and pamphlets of poetry, including *The Boy from the Green Cabaret Tells of His Mother* (Hutchinson, 1968), *Odes* (Trigram, 1978), *Ranter* (Slow Dancer, 1985), *Hellhound Memos* (Many Press, 1993), *Pearl* (Equipage, 1995), *The Book of Demons* (Bloodaxe 1997), a Paul Hamlyn Award winner, *Wolf Tongue; Selected Poems 1965-2000* (Bloodaxe 2003) and *Horses in Boiling Blood* (Equipage, 2004). He died in 2000.

BILL MARTIN was born 1925 in County Durham. He left school at fourteen ; during the War he served the RAF as a wireless operator and mechanic. From 1953-1983 he worked as an audio-technician. His many poetry publications include *Easthope* (Ceofrith, 1970), *Cracknrigg* (Taxus, 1983), *Hinny Beata* (Taxis, 1987), *Marra Familia* (Bloodaxe, 1993) and *Lammas Alanna* (Bloodaxe, 2000). He lives in Sunderland.

PETER MORTIMER was born in Nottingham in 1943. He moved to the North East in 1970, and founded IRON Press in 1973. His plays have been produced by most of the region's leading companies, including Cloud Nine, which he founded in 1997. His many books include *The Last of the Hunters*, *The Poetry of Perestroika* (edited with Jackie Litherland), *100 Days on Holy Island*, *Cool for Qat* and the best-selling *Broke Through Britain*. Poetry collections include *Utter Nonsense* (IRON, 1979), *A Rainbow in Its Throat* (Flambard, 1993) and *I Married the Angel of the North* (Five Leaves, 2002). He lives in Cullercoats.

SEAN O'BRIEN was born in London in 1952. He grew up in Hull and moved to the North East in 1990. In 1992 he was appointed Northern Arts Literary Fellow. He is currently Professor of Poetry at Sheffield Hallam University. He has held residencies at the Universities of Dundee and Leeds, in Denmark and Japan. In 1992 he founded the Northern Poetry Workshop. His plays have been staged by Live Theatre, the National Theatre, the RSC, BBC Radio 3 and 4. He is poetry critic of the *Sunday Times*. His books include *The Deregulated Muse: Essays on Contemporary Poetry in Britain and Ireland* and *The Firebox: Poetry in Britain and Ireland after 1945* and seven books of poetry - *The Indoor Park* (Bloodaxe, 1983), *The Frighteners* (Bloodaxe, 1987), *HMS Glasshouse* (OUP, 1991), *Ghost Train* (OUP, 1995), *Downriver* (Picador, 2001), *Cousin Coat: Selected Poems* 1976-2001 (Picador, 2002) and *The Inferno* (Picador, 2006). His work has received the Gregory, Somerset Maugham, Cholmondeley and E.M. Forster Awards. He has twice won the Forward Prize. He lives in Newcastle.

EVANGELINE PATERSON was born in 1928 in Limavady, Northern Ireland, and grew up in Dublin. She moved to Newcastle in 1991. She was a founding editor of *Other Poetry* and published several books of poetry, including *Bringing the Water Hyacinth to Africa* (Taxvs/Stride, 1983), *Lucifer at the Fair* (Taxvs/Stride, 1991), *Lucifer with Angels* (Dedalus, 1994) and *A Game of Soldiers* (Stride, 1997). She died in 2000.

PAULINE PLUMMER was born in Liverpool in 1947. She moved to the North East in 1981. She currently teaches creative writing on MA Creative Writing at Northumbria University and is an editor of Mudfog Books. She has published four collections of poetry, *Romeo's Café* (Paranoia, 1992), *Palaver* (Scratch, 1998), *Demon Straightening* (IRON, 2000) and *Bamako to Timbuktu* (Mudfog, 2003). She lives in Cllercoats.

KATRINA PORTEOUS was born in Aberdeen in 1960. She grew up in Co. Durham and has lived on the Northumbrian coastsince 1987. Writing-residencies include the Shetland Isles and the Aldeburgh Poetry Festival. Her books include *The Lost Music* (Bloodaxe 1996), *The Wund an' the Wetter* (IRON, 1999), *Turning the Tide* (Easington District Council, 2001), *The Bonny Fisher Lad* (People's History, 2003), *Dunstanburgh* (Smokestack, 2004) and *Longshore Drift* (Jardine Press, 2005).

FRED REED was born in Ashington, Northumberland in 1901. He started work as a miner at the age of fourteen. He was co-founder of the magazine Northumbriana, and elected vice-president of the Northumbrian language Society. His books include *The Sense On't* (Northern House, 1973), *Cumen 'n'Ganen* (Erdesdun, 1977), *Northumbrian Miscellany* (Northumbriana, 1978) and *The Northumborman* (IRON, 1999). He died in 1985.

GARETH REEVES was born in Slough in 1947. He is Reader in English at Durham University. His books include *T. S. Eliot: A Virgilian Poet*, *T. S. Eliot's 'The Waste Land'*, and, with Michael O'Neill, *Auden, MacNeice, Spender: The Thirties Poetry*. He has published two books of poems, *Real Stories* and *Listening In* (both Carcanet). He lives in Durham.

GRAEME RIGBY was born in Sussex in 1952. He grew up there and in Bahrain and moved to the North East in 1977 to teach. He is a playwright and librettist, a founder-member of Big Boys Don't Rhyme, organiser of BigFest, and a member of the film and photography collective Amber. His novel *The Black Cook's Historian* won the Constable Trophy in 1992. He edited, with Andy Croft, Harold Heslop's *Out of the Old Earth*. Poetry publications include the poetry and jazz collaboration with Keith Armstrong, Rick Taylor and Paul Flush, *Dreaming North* (Portcullis, 1986) and *50 Botanical Travellers* (Portcullis, 1990). He lives in rural Gateshead.

MARK ROBINSON was in born in Preston in 1964. He worked as a vegetarian chef before moving to the North East in 1993 to work in literature and arts development. He currently works for Arts Council England, North East. He founded and edited *Scratch* magazine and press from 1989 to 1998. His books include *The Horse Burning Park* (Stride, 1994), *Gaps Between Hills* (with Dermot Blackburn and Andy Croft, Scratch, 1996), *Half A Mind* (Flambard, 1998) and a study of poetry readings, *Words Out Loud* (edited, Stride 2002). He lives in Eaglescliffe.

JON SILKIN was born in London in 1930. He founded the literary magazine *Stand* in 1952 and was appointed Gregory Fellow in Poetry Leeds University. In 1965 he moved to Newcastle. He wrote and edited many critical books, including *Poetry of the Committed Individual*, *The Penguin Book of First World War Poetry*, *The War Poetry of Wilfred Owen* and *Out of Battle: Poetry of the Great War*. He published nearly a dozen books of poetry, including *The Peaceable Kingdom* (Chatto and Windus, 1954), *Nature with Man* (Chatto, 1965), *Little Time Keeper* (Carcanet, 1976), *The Ship's Pasture* (Routledge, 1986) and *Making a Republic* (Carcanet, 2002). He died in 1997.

COLIN SIMMS was born in Swaledale in 1939 and grew up in Cleveland. He has published many books on natural history and ornithology and over forty books of poetry, including *Poems and Other Fruit* (Headland, 1972), *Flat Earth* (Aloes, 1976), *Time Over Tyne* (Many Press, 1980), *Eyes Own Ideas* (Pig, 1987), *Poems to Basil Bunting* (Writers Forum, 1994), *Otters and Martens* (Shearsman, 2004), *The American Poems* (Shearsman, 2005) and *Selected Poems* (Salt, 2005). He once read his poems non-stop for twenty-two hours to raise money for charity. He lives in Alston.

MICHAEL STANDEN was born in 1937 in Surrey. He moved to the North East in 1967 to work in adult education, retiring as WEA District Secretary in 1995. He co-edits *Other Poetry* and is one of the organisers of Colpitts Poetry, Durham. He has published five novels, *Start Somewhere, A Sane and Able Man, Stick-Man, Dreamland Tree* and *Over the Wet Lawn*, a short-story collection *Months*, and two books of poetry, *Time's Fly Past* (Flambard, 1991) and *Gifts of Egypt* (Shoestring, 2002). He lives in Durham.

ANNE STEVENSON was born in Cambridge of American parents in 1933, and was brought up and educated in the United States. A life of teaching and book-selling took her to Dundee, Edinburgh, Oxford and Hay on Wye before she was appointed Northern Arts Fellow in 1981 and she moved to Langley Park in Durham. She has written many books, including *Bitter Fame : A Life of Sylvia Plath*, two studies of Elizabeth Bishop and *Between the Iceberg and the Shop : Selected Essays*. Her books of poetry include *Reversals* (Wesleyan, 1969), *Correspondences* (OUP, 1974), *Four and a Half Dancing Men* (OUP, 1993), *Granny Scarecrow* (Bloodaxe, 2000), *A Report from the Border* (Bloodaxe, 2003) and *Poems 1955-2005* (Bloodaxe, 2005). In 2002 she was chosen to receive the first Northern Rock Foundation Literary Award. She received an Honorary D Litt from Durham University in 2005. She lives in Durham.

SUBHADASSI was born in Huddersfield in 1967. He was ordained into the Western Buddhist Order in 1992. The following year he moved to the North East where he taught chemistry and established Newcastle Buddhist Centre. His publications include *FWBO New Poetry* (edited, Rising Fire, 1997), *Sublunary Voodoo* (Mudfog, 1998) and *peeled* (Arc, 2004) which received a special commendation in the 2005 Forward Prize. His home is in Northumberland.

PAUL SUMMERS was born in Blyth, Northumberland in 1967. He is one of the founding editors of the magazines *Billy Liar* and *Liar Republic* and a co-director of Liar Inc Ltd. He has written for TV, film and theatre and mixed-media collaborations. His poetry publications include *140195* (Echo Room/Blue Cowboys, 1995), *Vermeer's Dark Parlour* (Echo Room, 1996), *Beer & Skittles* (Echo Room, 1997), *The Last Bus* (IRON, 1998), *The Rat's Mirror* (Lapwing, 1999), *Cunawabi* (Cunawabi, 2003) and *Big Bella's Dirty Cafe* (Dogeater 2005). He lives in North Shields.

ANDREW WATERHOUSE was born in Lincolnshire in 1958. He moved to the North East in 1975 to study agriculture at Newcastle University. He taught environmental studies at Kirkley Hall, Morpeth, Northumberland and bought a ten acre site at Longframlington in order to plant a wood of native trees. He wrote three books of poetry, *In* (Rialto, 2000), which won the Forward First Collection Prize, *Good News from a Small Island* (MidNAg, 2001) and *Second* (Rialto, 2002). He died in 2001.

ANNIE WRIGHT was born in Malton, North Yorkshire in 1953. She grew up in Surrey and moved back briefly to the North East in 1969, before returning in 1988. She has published two collections of poetry, *Including Sex* (Bay, 1995) and *Redemption Songs* (Arrowhead, 2003). She is a member of Vane Women and works as an English Adviser for North Yorkshire primary schools. She lives in Darlington.

Acknowledgements

Gillian Allnutt: heartnote, About Benwell in *Blackthorn* (Bloodaxe Books, 1994) The Garden in Esh Winning in *Nantucket and the Angel* (Bloodaxe Books, 1997) Village in County Durham, Arvo Part in Concert, Durham Cathedral, November 1988, Barclays bank and Lake Baikal in *Lintel* (Bloodaxe Books, 2001) 'The Old Town Hall and St Hilda's Church, Middlesbrough' by L.S.Lowry, Convent Girl in *Sojourner* (Bloodaxe Books, 2004).

Maureen Almond: Beret, Booter, I Know Exactly, Trinkets in *Tailor Tacks* (Mudfog, 1999) Friday Nights in Magma, 2001. Brian, New Year in *Oyster Baby* (Biscuit Publishing, 2002).

Keith Armstrong: The Jingling Geordie in *Dreaming North* (Portcullis Press, Gateshead Libraries 1986) Folk Song for Thomas Spence in *Bless'd Millennium (*Northern Voices, 2000) Cuba, Crocodiles, Rain in Pains of Class (Artery, 1982) My Father Worked on Ships, Pigs Might Fly, An Oubliette for Kitty, in *Imagined Corners* (Smokestack, 2005).

Peter Armstrong: A Metamorphosis, Her Rosary in *Risings* (Enitharmon, 1988) The Red Funnelled Boat, An Englishman in Glasgow, From an Imaginary Republic, Among the Villages in *The Red Funnelled Boat* (Picador, 1998) Bellingham, The Club Organist at Enon in *The Capital of Nowhere*(Picador, 2003)

Neil Astley: A Month in the Country in *Darwin Survivor* (Peterloo Poets, 1988)East of Easter, The Dressing Station, The Road, For Want of a Nail, Blackened Blues in *Biting My Tongue* (Bloodaxe Books, 1995) The Green Knight's Lament.

Liz Atkin: It didn't belong to Peter Pan in *Glee With a Blue Background* (Diamond Twig, 1998); Evacuees in Smiths Knoll Instructions in Magma, The Biscuit Tins of England, in *The Biscuit Tins of England* (IRON Press, 2003).

Bob Beagrie: Cook, the Bridge and the Big Man in *Route*,Tourist, Never Enough, Reincarnation, Bruise, The Were-Tongue in *Huggin & Munnin* (Biscuit, 2002).

Peter Bennet: Genealogy, Content, Filming the Life in *Ha-Ha* (Smith/Doorstop Books 2003). XXI and XXII in *The Long Pack* (Flambard Press 2002) Fairytale in *Noctua* (Shoestring Press 2004)

David Burnett: Alexandria 31BC, The Olive Grove, Late Autumn in *Evergreens* (Black Cygnet Press, 2002) An Orkney Calendar, Summer Snow in *Something Of Myself* (Black Cygnet Press, 1994).

Richard Caddel: For Tom, Larksong Signal in *Larksong Signal* (Shearsman Books, 1997) From Wreay Churchyard, Ramsons in *Uncertain Time* (Galloping Dog Press, 1990) Going Home in *For John Riley* (Grosseteste, 1979) Nightstory in *West House Anthology* (Gutcult Magazine), Nocturne in Black and White, Shiner: Moves Towards Winter in *Writing in the Dark* (West House Books, 2003) Stars on a partly cloudy night in *Ground* (Form Books, 1994) All poems are copyright to The Estate of Richard Caddel.

Kevin Cadwallender: Baz Nativity, Baz Inherits a Dad, The French Connection, Tracy's True Colours in Baz Uber Alles (Dogeater, 2004) The Building Trade, Marooned in *Public* (IRON Press 2000) Baz and the Freedom of the Press in *Heterosexual Honkies* (Wysiwyg Chapbooks: The Collective 1996) Baz Lex Talio Nis first appeared in *Baz Poems* (Rebel Inc, 1990).

George Charlton: Nightshift Workers, Sea Coal, Gateshead Grammar, The Lost Boys in *Nightshift Workers* (Bloodaxe Books, 1989) Benton Static, The Girlhood of Iseult in *City of Dog* (Bloodaxe Books, 1994).

Brendan Cleary: The Exchange Visit, Newcastle is Benidorm, Are You Lonesome Tonight? in *The Irish Card* (Bloodaxe Books, 1993) Unhappy Hour, The Death of Maria in *Sacrilege* (Bloodaxe Books, 1998) The Wedding in *The Slab Magazine*, (2004)

Bob Cooper: In Wrynose Bottom in *All We Know Is All We See* (Arrowhead Press, 2002) On The Newcastle Metro in *Drinking Up Time* (Redbeck Press, 1998) The Day Frankie Nearly Died in *Pinocchio's Long Neb* (Smith Doorstop, 2001)

Andy Croft: Great North Mile 1-2 in *Great North (*IRON Press, 2001) Methuselah's Losers, Just as Blue in *Just As Blue* (Flambard Press, 2001) Dives and Lazarus, Outfaced, The Neon Thrush in *Comrade Laughter* (Flambard Press, 2004) Edge in *Headland* (Scratch, 2001)

Julia Darling: Be Kind in Sauce (Diamond Twig, Bloodaxe Books, 1993) Too Heavy, Waiting Room In August, Chemotherapy, Things That Should Never Have Happened, Satsumas in *Sudden Collapses in Public Places* (Arc Press, 2003), Probably Sunday in *Apologies for Absence* (Arc Press, 2004)

Alistair Elliot: Old Bewick, At Appleby Horse Fair, MCMVI, The Love of Horses, in *Turning the Stones* (Carcanet, 1993) Facing South in *Facing Things* (Carcanet, 1997)

Linda France: North and South, If Love Was Jazz in *Red* (Bloodaxe Books, 1992) Caracole in *The Gentleness of the Very Tall* (Bloodaxe Books, 1994) The Meat Factory, Mess With it in *Storyville* (Bloodaxe Books, 1997) The Lady's Mantle Letter, The End of August, Stagshaw Dhamma, The Simultaneous Dress in *The Simultaneous Dress* (Bloodaxe Books, 2002).

Cynthia Fuller: Her Story in *Moving Towards Light* (Flambard Press, 1992) Adult Education, Easy Rider in *Instructions for the Desert* (Flambard Press, 1996) Radicals, Carter's Garden, Buried, Sleep in *Only a Small Boat* (Flambard Press, 2001).

Desmond Graham: The Accompanist, She is learning her hands in *The Marching Bands* (Seren, 1996) Prospero, The Pound of Flesh in Not Falling (Seren, 1999) Rosalind in *After Shakespeare* (Flambard Press, 2001)

Jackie Hardy: Whale-watching in *Canuting the Waves* (Bloodaxe Books, 1998) Through my Window in *Presence*.

Tony Harrison: Newcastle is Peru, Durham, Facing North in *Selected Poems* (Penguin 1987) Passer & Fig on The Tyne in *Laureate's Block* (Penguin, 2000) Initial Illumination in *The Gaze of the Gorgon* (Bloodaxe Books, 1992)

W. N. Herbert: Touching Lot's Wife, Garibaldi's Head, Bede's World in *Cabaret McGonagall* (Bloodaxe Books, 1996) The Manuscript of Feathers, A Breakfast Wreath in *The Laurelude* (Bloodaxe Books, 1998) The Entry of Don Quixote, Firth of Tyne, The Chronicle of Ronny Gill, Song of the Longboat Boys in *The Big Bumper Book of Troy* (Bloodaxe Books, 2002).

Norah Hill: Sometimes I Stand in *A Hole Like That* (ed Mark Robinson, Scratch 1994) Ormesby Hall, Autumn, Town Hall Concert in Like (Mudfog, 2003) Doggy Market in *Over the Border* (Mudfog 1998)

Gordon Hodgeon: For November in *November Photographs* (Platform Poets, 1981) Potato Sellers, Cleveland in *New Writing From The North* (MidNAG 1988) *A Cold Spell in A Hole Like That* (ed Mark Robinson, Scratch, 1994) in Conference in *A Cold Spell* (Mudfog Press, 1996) The Strap in *The Penniless Press* (1999) *Waiting in Smelter* (ed. Kevin Cadwallender and Cynthia Fuller, Mudfog, 2003).

Richard Kell: The Balance in *Control Tower* (Chatto, 1962) Walking with Matron, Sabbath Triptych in *The Broken Circle* (Ceolfrith, 1981) The Chain of Being, Currents in *Rock and Water* (Dedalus, 1993).

Valerie Laws: Your Great Grandma... and Bones from a Medic's Dustbin in For Crying Out Loud, (Iron Press, with Kitty Fitzgerald, 1994) The Heart does not break, Nantucket, 1810 in Moonbathing (Peterloo Poets, 2003) Quantum Sheep in *Quantum Sheep*, (Peterloo Poets, Spring 2006).

S.J.Litherland: A Story about Cricket in *The Apple Exchange* (Flambard Press, 1999) Poetry as a Chinese Jar, Moving in its Stillness, Sonnet 34, A Lily in *The Work of the Wind* (Flambard Press 2006):

John Longden: Pass, Cage, and Teesside Twinned With The Universe in *LPs and Singles* (Mudfog Press, 1995) .Copyright the Literary Estate of John Longden.

Marilyn Longstaff: Seed Time in *Puritan Games* (Vane Women Press, 2001) Above and beyond in *Rewriting the Map* (Vane Women Press, 2003) Beyond Clichés on Saltburn Beach in *Smelter* (ed Kevin Cadwallender and Cynthia Fuller, Mudfog Press, 2003) Ice Change,Maybank Road, Plymouth, Porthmeor Beach, St Ives in *Sitting Among the Hoppers* (Arrowhead Press, 2004)

Barry MacSweeney: Pearl Says; Pearl at 4a.m. in *Pearl* (Equipage, 1995) Blackbird in *Black Torch* (Pig Press, 1980); Hellhound Memos in *Hellhound Memos* (Many Press, 1993); Ode to Beauty, Strength and Joy; Free Pet with Every Cage; Tom in the Market Square in *The Book of Demons* (Bloodaxe Books, 1997);We Are Not Stones in Pearl in *The Silver Morning* (Poetical Histories no.49, 1999) All published in *Wolf Tongue* (Bloodaxe Books, 2003). Copyright The Literary Estate of Barry MacSweeney.

Bill Martin: A19 Hymn in *Cracknrigg* (Taxus 1983) Durham Beatitude in *Hinny Beata* (Taxis 1987) Song of the Cotia Lass in *Lammas Alanna* (Bloodaxe Books, 2000)

Peter Mortimer: I Married the Angel of the North, Advice to a Writer, Mrs Spratt, If Love, This Poem is not Sponsored in *I Married the Angel of the North* (Five Leaves, 2002) Charlie Fook, What Mother Told Me in *A Rainbow in its Throat, New and Selected Poems* (Flambard Press, 1993)

Sean O'Brien: In a Military Archive, Cousin Coat in *The Frighteners* (Bloodaxe Books, 1987) Revenants, Reading Stevens in the Bath in *Ghost Train* (Oxford University Press, 1995) The Park by the Railway in *The Indoor Park* (Bloodaxe Books, 1983) Railway Hotel first published in the *TLS*, 2003.The River Road in *Rivers, poems by John Kinsella, Sean O'Brien and Peter Porter,* (Fremantle Arts Centre Press, Western Australia, 2002) Before in *HMS Glasshouse* (Oxford University Press, 1991).

Evangeline Paterson: History Teacher in *The Warsaw Ghetto*, Jehanne, Armaments Race in *Bringing the Water Hyacinth to Africa* (Taxvs Press, 1983) Copyright The Literary Estate of Evangeline Paterson.

Pauline Plummer: Travelling North, Buying a Blouse in *Demon Straightening* (IRON Press, 2000) Eldest son, Whorlton Lido, Uncles and Aunties, Lovebite in *Romeo's Cafe* (Paranoia Press, 1992) What is the One Word Known To All in *Bamako to Timbuktu*, (Mudfog Press, 2003).

Katrina Porteous: Charlie Douglas, The Sea Inside, Decommissioning in *The Lost Music* (Bloodaxe Books 1996) Excerpt from *The Wund 'n' the Wetter*,Book and CD with piper Chris Ormston, (IRON Press, 1999) The Pigeon Men in *Turning the Tide*, collaboration with photographer Keith Pattison and artist Robert Soden (District of Easington, 2001). Excerpt from This Far and No Further, BBC Radio 4, 2001. Seven Silences, excerpt from *An Ill Wind*, BBC Radio 3, 2001. Excerpt from Dunstanburgh, first broadcast on BBC Radio 4, 2004. Published as *Dunstanburgh* (Smokestack Books, 2004).

Gareth Reeves: The Cockroach Sang in *The Plane-tree*, Touch Type, Gadgets, The Entertainer,Deus ex Machina in *Listening In* (Carcanet Press, 1993).

Fred Reed: Aad Chep, *Northumbrian Miscellany* 38 Beech Tree, *Northumbriana*. Brazen Faces, *Northumbrian Voice* (1978) Diddle Diddle, *Northumbriana*, Pitmen, *Cumen and Ganin* (1977) Springan , *The Sense On't* (Northern House Imprint, 1973) The Teyd Has Ebbed - *Northumbriana*. All poems published in *The Northumborman* (IRON Press, 1999). Copyright the Literary Estate of Fred Reed.

Graeme Rigby: Motordreams, published in *Dreaming North* (Portcullis, 1986).

Mark Robinson: Poem (On Realising I Am English) in *The North* (2001) From the Shadow of the Flats, Rio de Juninho in *Gaps Between Hills* (Scratch, 1996) Laying a Carpet with My Dad, On the Beach Near Kinvarra Our Babies in *Half A Mind* (Flambard Press, 1998) Loose Connections Beneath the Dashboard in *Smelter* (ed Kevin Cadwallender and Cynthia Fuller, Mudfog Press, 2003).

Jon Silkin: For David Emmanuel, Epilogue in *The Peaceable Kingdom* (Chatto & Windus, 1954) Leaving The Free Trade, A Man from the Shipyards in *The Ship's Pasture* (RKP, 1986) Watersmeet, The Soul Never Has Enough in *Making a Republic* (Carcanet/Northern House, 2002) Copyright The Literary Estate of Jon Silkin.

Michael Standen: The Land, The Outcome, Along the Purley Way, Consett RIP, For Norman Nicholson in *Time's Fly Past* (Flambard Press, 1991) Under the Road in *Gifts of Egypt* (Shoestring Press, 2002)

Anne Stevenson: Enough of Green in Enough of Green (OUP, 1977) In the Tunnel of Summers, Demolition in *The Fiction Makers* (OUP, 1985) When the Camel is Dust in Four and a Half Dancing Men (OUP, 1993) Innocence and Experience, Moonrise, Leaving, On Going Deaf, Granny Scarecrow in *Granny Scarecrow* (Bloodaxe Books, 2000)

Subhadassi: Fishing, Blue Lies, peeled, Cygnus, Treason, Annealed, My Idea of Hell in *peeled* (Arc, 2004) Multi Story was published on posters on the Newcastle Metro in 2000.

Paul Summers: If Keir Hardie was.. Hand-me-downs, The Hundred Years War, Rant, Wash-day and North in *The Last Bus* (IRON Press, 1998) The Comrades in *The Rat's Mirror* (Lapwing Press, 1999) On Quarry Moor appears in *Home*, a spoken word/music collaboration with Dave Hull-Denholm.

Andrew Waterhouse: One Day in Late Adolescence, Burning Your Brother's Guitar, Climbing My Grandfather, Not an Ending in *in* (The Rialto, 2000) Butterfly on Stained Glass in *Good News From A Small Island* (MidNag, 2001) Northerly, Alternative Endings, Bath-time, Modern Grammar in *2nd* (The Rialto, 2002.), Copyright The Literary Estate of Andrew Waterhouse.

Annie Wright: The Night Is Holding Its Breath, Ascending The Bell Tower in *Redemption Songs* (Arrowhead Press, 2003) .